böhlau

Ulrike Babusiaux · Mariko Igimi (eds.)

"Messages from Antiquity"

Roman Law and Current Legal Debates

BÖHLAU VERLAG WIEN KÖLN WEIMAR

Jointly supported by the Office of the Judiciary, Thailand, under the framework of the project "The Diploma in Contemporary Legal Studies" at Kyushu University.

Deutsche Nationalbibliothek Cataloguing-in-publication data:
http://dnb.d-nb.de

Cover: Hadrian's Temple, Rome. © Mariko Igimi

Proofreading: Dore Wilken, Freiburg
Cover design: Michael Haderer, Vienna
Typesetting: Michael Rauscher, Vienna
Printing and binding: Hubert & Co., Göttingen
Printed on acid-free and chlorine-free bleached paper
Printed in the EU

Vandenhoeck & Ruprecht Verlage | www.vandenhoeck-ruprecht-verlage.com

ISBN 978-3-412-50803-6

Table of Contents

PART THREE:
MODERN DEBATES IN THE LIGHT OF ANCIENT LAW

Preface

This book is a compilation of papers presented at the conference held in February 2016 at Kyushu University (Fukuoka, Japan) under the title "Messages from the Antiquity: How can Roman law contribute to current debates in law?" For the occasion, Prof. Mariko Igimi invited Roman law researchers from around the world to discuss the importance of Roman law with the students of the LL.M. in International Economic and Business Law. The aim was to identify and build links between Roman and modern law through such interaction. We came to understand that Roman law is significant on the one hand because it provides the historical basis of civil law in continental Europe and other civil law jurisdictions, including Japan. On the other hand, the texts of Roman law also provide us with a space to reflect on "new" issues of legal politics. Therefore, they help to analyse legal problems and might provide support for the development of solutions.

The unique experience of having such a diverse group of students from all over the world, including common law jurisdictions such as UK and New Zealand participating in the discussion, served as the main inspiration to open a gateway for a larger group of readers to different ideas and questions on the persisting relevance of Roman law, in the hope that they will discover "new" elements in "ancient" law. Hence, this book is for students, legal practitioners and academics who wish to widen their horizons with a different perspective on Roman law. To the European reader, it might be interesting to find the ongoing importance of the Roman legacy in Japanese law, whereas the almost unbroken continuity of the European legal tradition might be of special interest to Asian readers. By any account, the diversity and scope of the different articles in this book will show once again that the study of Roman law from very different perspectives can be rewarding, valuable and informative.

The approach we have chosen (also to be seen in the introduction) was an "experiment" that required courage and openness on the part of all who were involved. We would, therefore, like to thank all of the contributors, who were ready to partake in this unusual dialogue between modern legal problems and legal culture from the antiquity.

Special thanks are given to the students and the staff of the International Programs in Law at Kyushu University, 2015–2016, who made the conference a great success as well as to all those who were instrumental in the editorial work for the articles gathered here, namely the assistants of the chair of Roman law, private and comparative law at the University of Zurich: Franca Eckstein,

Adrian Häusler, Yvonne Kastner, Una Paunovic, Elisa Stauffer, Martina Steiner and Thamar Xandry.

Finally, we would like to thank you – the reader – for your intellectual curiosity and we wish you both inspiring and thought-provoking reading.

Ulrike Babusiaux (Zurich) Mariko Igimi (Fukuoka)

Ulrike Babusiaux, Zurich, and Mariko Igimi, Fukuoka

Messages from Antiquity

Roman Law and Current Legal Debates. Introduction

When we speak about Roman law, we refer mainly to the collection of Roman legal writings (*Digesta*) and imperial constitutions (*Codex*) assembled by the Byzantine emperor Justinian in the 6th century AD. Together with Justinian's introduction to the study of Roman law (*Institutiones* Justiniani) and his new legislation (*Novellae*) these two collections form the so-called *Corpus iuris civilis*[1]. Despite the extensive editing and deleting as well as some interpolations, the Justinian sources still pass down the law of the late Roman republic, and of the imperial period, which lasted roughly from the 1st century BC to the 3rd century AD[2]. Roman law, however, is not just a historical topic but must be considered to be the origin of many modern legal systems, which is why it is continuously taught at the law faculties in many countries around the world.

This book is not a manual of Roman legal sources nor a traditional textbook on Roman private law but aims to approach Roman law from an unprecedented perspective. As the title of the book indicates, this is an attempt to use ancient law, i.e. Roman law, in order to engage with current legal debates by analysing it from a modern perspective. The underlying assumption is that Roman law is not only a tradition simply maintained from the past but also a window to another legal experience from a different time setting that might prove beneficial to solve contemporary issues.

Although it is a general question of whether lessons can be learnt from history, it is commonly accepted that our perception of history changes according to our current needs and contexts.[3] Hence, every generation has been obliged to reconsider the historical sources, in order to identify new aspects of the issues from the past. Even the renowned texts are not free from innovative interpretations and unanticipated questions. Contrariwise, dealing with the past simulta-

1 The name *Corpus iuris civilis* has only been given in the Middle Ages.

2 On Justinian and his collection see the survey (in English language) written by *Wolfgang Kaiser*, Justinian and the Corpus iuris Civilis, in: David Johnston (ed.), The Cambridge Companion to Roman Law, Cambridge 2015, 119–148.

3 *Karl Popper*, The Open Society and Its Enemies, Vol 2, The High Tide of Prophecy: Hegel, Marx and the Aftermath, London 1945, Ch. 25: Has History a Meaning?, 246–267, especially the "searchlight theory of science" (247).

neously mirrors current issues and challenges of our time and possibly opens a dialogue between the past and today.

Dialogues can be carried out from various points of view. Firstly, we should stress the role of Roman law as the evolutionary basis of modern private law in numerous jurisdictions. Indeed, the civil law systems not only in continental Europe but also in other parts of the world, such as Japan, derive from Roman law. In some respect, even the common law systems are influenced by it. Going back to the sources of our own laws and considering solutions and arguments developed there, can lead us to better applications of the law today.

Roman law, however, is not limited to the retrospective approach to trace back to the origin of our legal rules and concepts. Roman law sources are the testimony that the jurists in ancient Rome, just like the lawyers of today, had to tackle with new and unsolved questions of their times. The Justinian legislation, therefore, offers excellent materials for legal reasoning that has been in use for centuries and still is, to deal with the contemporary issues of the time. Very common methodological instruments of the legal studies today, such as analogies and fictions, can be found in the Roman legal sources. More importantly, the casuistic approach of Roman law also provides modern jurists with experiential knowledge.

This significance of Roman law further offers a space for reflection to the modern jurists by presenting legal interpretations from the past, that can be used for comparison. Roman law scholars are constantly reflecting on their own modern legal systems through their research on Roman law. They often realise the similarities of legal conflicts and interests in human life between antiquity and today. Material for the comparative law can be found, therefore, not only in other contemporary jurisdictions but also in history. The geographical as well as the historical search for solutions and applicable rules might even disclose what is essential in law.

All three approaches are to be seen in this book. The first part of the book reassembles the contributions dealing with the Roman law as the historical foundation of modern law and thus attempts to find applicable reasoning in the ancient sources for modern debates and current legal problems. In the second part, modern debates and open questions are examined from the point of view of a Roman jurist with contemplation to provoke dialogue on legal reasoning in specific contexts. The third part, finally, is a collection of reflections on challenges for modern jurists. It draws a contrast between problems of Roman legal history and current debates in order to raise awareness and to promote the analysis of legal developments today and in the past.

The dialogues presented here are embedded in an international polyphonic choir. In fact, the very diverse backgrounds of the contributors lead to the multi-layered discussion reaching from the modern to ancient world as well as from the Orient to the Occident. The variety of topics, the range of methodology, and the richness of arguments presented here prove the importance of such dialogues in the globalised world, which would foster a mutual understanding by providing better knowledge of similarities and differences. This, finally, is the reason for choosing the English language; it allows us to share our views to more people than could ever be reached if we applied the predominant languages used in the study of Roman law today.[4] The present work is an experiment that shares the spirit of any historical discovery: nothing ventured, nothing gained.

4 For a brief historical background and the state of Roman law today, see *Ulrike Babusiaux*, The Future of Legal History: Roman Law, in: American Journal of Legal History (AJLH) Nr. 56, Oxford 2016, 6–11.

PART ONE: ROMAN LAW AS THE HISTORICAL FOUNDATION OF MODERN PRIVATE LAW

Johannes Platschek, Munich

Strict Liability for Defects as to Quality of an Object Sold

Application and Exclusion in Roman and Contemporary German Law

I. Vendor's Liability for Defects as to Quality of an Object Sold in German Law: Statutory Warranty, its Exclusion and Consumer Protection

An object has been sold. It turns out it is deficient as to quality and that it already had been deficient at the time of its delivery to the purchaser. According to the German Civil Code (*Bürgerliches Gesetzbuch*, BGB), the vendor is liable to the purchaser regardless of his fault for the defects as to quality of the purchased good, which already existed at the time of the transfer of risk, i.e. generally at the time of delivery (§§ 437, 434 BGB). First, the purchaser is entitled to demand supplementary performance ("*Nacherfüllung*", § 437 n. 1 BGB). Thereafter, if the supplementary performance fails, he can withdraw from the contract or reduce the purchase price ("*Rücktritt*" or "*Minderung*", § 437 n. 2 BGB). This strict liability, a statutory warranty, can be excluded by the parties by mutual agreement in advance (so-called "*Gewährleistungsausschluss*"):

> **§ 444 Exclusion of liability.** … [A]n agreement that excludes or restricts the rights of the buyer with regard to a defect … (transl. Langenscheidt Übersetzungsservice)

That means that the vendor's strict liability is non-mandatory ("*dispositives Recht*"), with the sole exception of the case where an entrepreneur sells to a consumer ("B2C", "Verbrauchsgüterkauf"). In that case the vendor's statutory warranty cannot be excluded in advance (§ 476[1] BGB):

> **§ 476 Deviating agreements.** (1) [1] If an agreement is entered into before a defect is notified to the entrepreneur and deviates, to the disadvantage of the consumer, from sections 433 to 435, 437, 439 to 443 (= sections on seller's liability for defects) …, the entrepreneur may not invoke it. … (transl. Langenscheidt Übersetzungsservice)

In the field of the so-called "*Verbrauchsgüterkauf*", the vendor's strict liability is therefore *compulsory*. This is applicable since the major reform of the German law of obligations in 2002, implementing European law on consumer protection.[5]

It has been harshly criticised: the law not only restricted the entrepreneur in the name of consumer protection; it also restricted and infantilised the consumer. There could be a valid interest of the consumer (and purchaser) to agree with the entrepreneur (and vendor) on an exclusion of the statutory warranty, since in case of exclusion, the consumer could achieve a more favourable price by negotiating with the entrepreneur. It had been emphasised that it was a kind of state paternalism to take away the consumer's possibility to reach a better price by renouncing his own statutory rights and to save money. According to this view, § 476(1) BGB is unconstitutional ("*verfassungswidrig*"), violating the principle of private autonomy.[6]

This, in turn, was countered by a sobering but realistic insight: There was no effective consumer protection without compulsory law. An exclusion of statutory warranty brought an aleatory character to the sale. The consumer would buy a pig in a poke (German: "*die Katze im Sack*" – "the cat in the bag"). Therefore, any non-business-minded, inexperienced consumer needed protection, even against his own adventurousness (that can be heavily supported by the vendor). The fact that any business-minded, skilled consumer is incapacitated along with the others ("*mitentmündigt*") was due to "the essence of typified consumer protection".[7]

Furthermore, in many areas of trade it is not realistic to describe exclusion of warranty by agreement as a result of individual price negotiations. Frequently, the exclusion of warranty by agreement is customary in a particular trade; before the enacting of § 476(1) BGB it was simply impossible, for example, to buy a used car without the exclusion of warranty. No used car dealer would ever have been disposed to sell a car at a *higher* price, against *not* excluding statutory warranty. The car dealer did not want to bear the risk of a defect, even if his risk would have been rewarded by a higher purchase price. He had to avoid intricate,

5 Article 7(1) of the Directive 1999/44/EC of the European Parliament and of the Council of 25 May 1999 on certain aspects of the sale of consumer goods and associated guarantees.

6 *Claus-Wilhelm Canaris*, Wandlungen des Schuldvertragsrechts – Tendenzen zu seiner "Materialisierung", AcP 200 (2000) 273–364, 362; *Klaus Adomeit*, Das Günstigkeitsprinzip – jetzt auch im Kaufvertrag oder: der Kfz-Mechaniker von Canaris, JZ (2003) 1053–1054; *Stephan Lorenz*, in: Münchener Kommentar zum Bürgerlichen Gesetzbuch, Munich 2016[7], BGB § 475 n. 1 fn. 1.

7 *Boris Schinkels*, Zur Abgrenzung von zulässiger Beschaffenheitsvereinbarung und Umgehung der Gewährleistung beim Verbrauchsgüterkauf, ZGS (2003) 310–316, 314: "*liegt im Wesen des typisierten Verbraucherschutzes*"; similiar *Johannes Wertenbruch*, in: *Hans-Theodor Soergel* (Begr.), Bürgerliches Gesetzbuch mit Einführungsgesetz und Nebengesetzen, Stuttgart 2009[13], BGB § 475 n. 49.

time-consuming calculations about risk and price. There simply was no such dealing. To talk about § 476(1) BGB as "infantilising" and "incapacitating" the purchaser in these cases is nearly absurd, given that in former times the purchaser had no room for negotiations.

Others see congruence of the goals of private autonomy and consumer protection under § 476(1) BGB. If the entrepreneur (and vendor) wants to avoid liability despite § 476(1) BGB, he has to test the object for defects and has to inform the purchaser about any found defects. Since if the purchaser is aware of a defect at the time of conclusion of the sales contract, he loses the right of warranty in respect of this defect (§ 442(1) BGB). Therefore, they claim, § 476(1) BGB supports the purchaser's information and optimises the basis of his decision to buy, i. e. the basis of private autonomy.[8]

II. Vendor's Liability for Defects of an Object Sold in Roman Law: The Aedilitian Edict on Sale of Slaves on the Market

1. "Message from Modern Times"?

In the most important textbook of Roman law in German language one reads that "[i]n modern terms, the edict serves **consumer protection**".[9] "The edict" means the edict of the *aediles curules*, concerning the sale of slaves (and cattle) on the market.

The *aediles curules* are Roman magistrates, controlling the slave market in the city of Rome. Trials between vendors and purchasers can be brought before them. They are promulgating the principles of their jurisdiction in their edict that has been – partially – transmitted to us in its wording:

> D. 21,1,1,1 Ulp. 1 ed. aed. cur.
> Aiunt aediles: 'QVI MANCIPIA VENDVNT CERTIORES FACIANT EMPTORES, QVID MORBI VITIIVE CVIQVE SIT, QVIS FVGITIVVS ERROVE SIT NOXAVE SOLVTVS NON SIT: EADEMQVE OMNIA, CVM EA MANCIPIA VENIBVNT, PALAM RECTE PRONVNTIANTO. QVODSI MANCIPIVM ADVERSVS EA VENISSET, SIVE ADVERSVS QVOD DICTVM PROMISSVMVE FVERIT CVM VENIRET, FVISSET, QVOD EIVS PRAESTARI OPORTERE DICETVR: EMPTORI OMNIBVSQVE AD QVOS EA RES PERTINET IVDICIVM DABIMVS, VT ID MANCIPIVM REDHIBEATVR.' ...

8 *Tilman Repgen*, Kein Abschied von der Privatautonomie. Die Funktion zwingenden Rechts in der Verbrauchsgüterkaufrichtlinie, Paderborn et al. 2001, 98.

9 *Max Kaser/Rolf Knütel/Sebastian Lohsse*, Römisches Privatrecht, Munich 2017[21], 266: "Modern gesprochen dient das Edikt dem **Verbraucherschutz** [emphasis in the original]".

(transl. J. A. C. Thomas:) "The aediles say: 'Those who sell slaves are to apprise purchasers of any disease or defect in their wares and whether a given slave is a runaway, a loiterer on errands, or still subject to noxal liability; all these matters they must proclaim in due manner when the slaves are sold. If a slave be sold without compliance with this regulation or contrary to what has been said or promised in respect of him at the time of his sale, it is for us to declare what is due in respect of him [better: and if it will be said that there has to be responsibility for that (not: quid eius praestari oporteat dicetur), J. P.]; we will grant to the purchaser and to all other interested parties an action for rescission in respect of the slave. '"

2. Edictal Duty to Inform

The vendor is compelled by the edict to inform the purchaser about certain features of the slave: his possible illness, physical handicaps, a predisposition to escape from his master or rove about, or his being charged with tort actions. If any of these defects is later found without previous information by the vendor, he is liable regardless of his knowledge, i. e. regardless of his fault. The purchaser can bring an action for rescission, i. e. to return the slave within six months after the conclusion of the sale, receiving back the paid price (so-called *actio redhibitoria*), or he can claim back a part of the paid price (so-called *actio quanti minoris*).

3. Edictal Duty to Give Contractual Warranty (*stipulatio duplae*)

Furthermore, the *aediles* oblige the vendor to give the purchaser a contractual warranty on the absence of edictal defects in form of an oral promise (*stipulatio*). A model of this contractual warranty is included in the aedilitian edict, being formulated as *stipulatio duplae* ("stipulation for double the price"), as we learn from:

D. 21,2,37,1 Ulp. 32 ed.
Per edictum autem curulium etiam de servo cavere venditor iubetur.
(transl. *Thomas*:) "The vendor of a slave is also required to give the undertaking [*cautio = stipulatio*, J. P.] in respect of a slave under the edict of the curule aediles."

D. 45,1,5 pr. Pomp. 26 Sab.
Item duplae stipulatio venit ab iudice aut ab aedilis edicto.
(transl. *S. Hart*:) "Also a stipulation for double the price comes from a judge or from the aedile's edict."

D. 21,2,31 Ulp. 42 Sab.
... stipulatio quae ab aedilibus proponitur ...

(transl. *Thomas*:) "… the stipulation required [better: promulgated, J. P.] by the aediles …"

The contractual warranty by *stipulatio duplae* stands beside the sales contract. If the warranty is given, it creates an obligation of the vendor to pay compensation in case any deficiencies that were already there at the time of conclusion of the sale appear. The action deriving from *stipulatio duplae* is the civilian *actio ex stipulatu*. It can be brought before every Roman jurisdiction magistrate (particularly the *praetor*) for an indefinite period of time. The *aediles* are treating the vendor's *stipulatio duplae* as a kind of accessory to the slave sold. If the vendor does not grant this contractual warranty, the purchaser is *therefore* entitled to return the slave within two months using the *actio redhibitoria* in the *aediles*' court receiving the paid price. Otherwise, he can claim compensation for the missing *stipulatio duplae* within six months:[10]

---

10 *Nunzia Donadio*, La tutela del compratore tra *actiones aediliciae* e *actio empti*, Milan 2004, 85. Differently, *Berthold Kupisch*, Römische Sachmängelhaftung: Ein Beispiel für die 'Ökonomische Analyse des Rechts'?, TRG 70 (2002) 21–54, 40 invokes scholion "ἐὰν" to B. 18,6,2 (*Scheltema* 1148): If the sale was accompanied by a *stipulatio*, the mentioned time limit of six, respectively twelve, months is applied to the *actio redhibitoria*, respectively *quanti minoris*, because of a defect of the slave sold. However, if there was no *stipulatio*, there were reduced time limits applying to the same actions – *because of a defect of the slave sold*. According to *Kupisch*, it is the extended time limit for actions caused by defects in cases of sale with *stipulatio* that "justified the surcharge on the purchase price because of giving a warranty stipulation in the first" ("*die den Aufschlag auf den Kaufpreis wegen Erteilung einer Garantiestipulation überhaupt erst rechtfertigte*", supra 41). By giving his warranty promise and thereby extending his liability in time, the vendor signaled a higher quality ("*mit dem Garantieversprechen und der damit einhergehenden längeren Gewährleistungsfrist signalisiert der Verkäufer eine höhere Qualität*", supra 41 fn. 74). Does that mean that everything else – court's competence, cause of action, type of action, amount of liability for defects as to quality – would be the very same in slave sales with and without *stipulatio*, the *only* difference being the time limit of the actions? Concerning the "economic analysis of law": Is the difference of four, respectively six, months between the time limits really of such an importance that "the purchase price as regulating element" ("*der Kaufpreis als regulatives Element*") becomes relevant? Can we expect a Roman purchaser to pay a higher price only to reach a time limit of six months instead of two for *actio redhibitoria*? *Kupisch* does not consider *actio ex stipulatu*. As mentioned above, the *stipulatio* makes the vendor liable to compensation by *actio ex stipulatu* (*Kaser/Knütel/Lohsse* [fn. 5] 268, who – *nota bene* – agree with *Kupisch*) – certainly with no time limit. Furthermore, D. 21,1,58,1 Paul. 6 resp. shows that the liability from the *stipulatio* can be realised by the rescission of the sale. That means that the *actio ex stipulatu* can have the very same content as the *actio redhibitoria*. Why then should the time limits of the aedilitian actions depend on the fact whether the vendor is liable (without time limit) by *actio ex stipulatu* or not? The mentioned Byzantine scholion is – as it proves by citing D. 21,1,28 – not an independent witness. It rather tries to combine the information from the Digest. In doing so, the scholion has no more authority than any modern attempt to explain D. 21,1,28, see *Éva Jakab*, *Cavere* und Haftung für Sachmängel. Zehn Argumente gegen Berthold Kupisch, in: Kaufen nach Römischem Recht. Antikes

D. 21,1,28 Gai. 1 ed. aed. cur.
Si venditor de his quae edicto aedilium continentur non caveat, pollicentur adversus eum redhibendi iudicium intra duos menses vel quanti emptoris intersit intra sex menses.
(transl. *Thomas*:) "Should the vendor not give an undertaking on the matters contained in their edict, the curule aediles promise against him an action for rescission within two months and an action for diminution [better: for the purchaser's interest (not: *quanti minoris sit*), J. P.] within six."

4. *Stipulatio duplae* and *stipulatio simplae*

In our sources, we find both *stipulatio duplae* and *stipulatio simplae* (even *stipulatio triplae* or *quadruplae* are possible)[11]. According to the dominant view, the different designation only concerns the amount of the vendor's liability in case of the so-called eviction: *duplam pecuniam dare* or *simplam pecuniam dare* means that the vendor has to pay either the double or the simple price to the purchaser, if a third party successfully sues the purchaser, invoking property of the purchased slave (case of eviction). Therefore, *dupla* and *simpla pecunia* exclusively concerned the vendor's liability for the purchaser's undisturbed possession of the slave (*habere licere*), i. e. in modern legal terminology, the liability for defects *in title*. Concerning defects *as to quality* (illness etc.), the wording of the *stipulatio duplae* and *stipulatio simplae* were basically identical: The vendor is promising his liability for the slave to be healthy etc. (*sanum esse … praestari*). Hence, he is liable to pay compensation.

We can find illustrating examples within the documentary practice from the first two centuries AD:

Erbe in den europäischen Kaufrechtsordnungen, eds. *Éva Jakab/Wolfgang Ernst*, Berlin et al. 2008, 123–137. *Jakab's* own theses on the impact of *stipulatio*, as pronounced in *Éva Jakab*, Praedicere und cavere beim Marktkauf, Munich 1997, can be considered as being disproved as well (particularly by *Kupisch* supra; *Dario Mantovani*, Le formule del processo privato romano, Padova 1999², 113 fn. 630, und *Donadio* supra); see also *Kazunori Uemura*, Zur Normstruktur des Edictum aedilium curulium. Exegese von D. 21,1,14,9 und D. 21,1,28, in: Aus der Werkstatt römischer Juristen, eds. *Ulrich Manthe* et al., Berlin 2016, 462–476, 469–474 (himself agreeing with *Kupisch*).

11 D. 21,2,56 pr. Paul. 2 ed. aed. cur.

TH 61 (Pompeii, 63 AD)	FIRA III 132 (Seleucia, 166 AD)	FIRA III 88 (Dacia, 142 AD)
[hunc hominem	**Eum puerum**	**Eum puerum**
san]um	**sanum**	**sanum**
furtis noxisque solutum		traditum
esse	esse	esse,
	ex edi[cto],	furtis noxaque solutum,
		erronem, fugitivum, ca-
[praestari		ducum non esse prestari,
et si qui]s eum hominem	**et si quis eum puerum**	**et si quis eum puerum**
		q(uo) d(e) a(gitur)
partemve quam eius	**partemve eius**	**partenve quam quis ex eo**
evicerit,	**evicerit,**	**evicerit,**
quo [minus L. Comi-]		q(uo) m(inus) emp-
nium Primum heredemve		torem s(upra) s(criptum)
eius habere [uti frui]		eunve, ad q(uem) ea res
possidere recte liceat,		pertinebit, uti frui habere
		possidereque recte liceat,
		tunc quantum id erit,
		quod ita ex eo evictum
		fuerit, t(antam)
simplam pecuniam	**simplam pecuniam**	**p(ecuniam) duplam**
	sine denuntiatione	p(robam)
r[ect]e [dari	recte dare	r(ecte) d(ari)
haec] ita uti adsolet recte		
praestari		
stipu[latus est] L.	**stipulatus est C. Fabul/**	**f(ide) r(ogavit) Dasius**
Comin-]ius Primus	**lius Macer**	**Breucus,**
spopondit P. Cornelius	**spopondit Q. Iulius**	**d(ari) f(ide) p(romisit)**
Popp[a]cu[s] [Erastus].	**Priscus:**	**Bellicus Alexandri,**
	… et tradedisse ei man-	
	cipium s(upra) s(criptum)	
	Eutychen bonis condi-	
	cionibus.	

In the first part of the *stipulatio*, the vendor is promising liability for defects as to quality: *sanum esse etc. praestari* – "to be liable for this slave (*homo*)/this young slave (*puer*) to be healthy etc."; in the second part (*et si quis ...*), he is promising to pay single the purchase price in TH 61 and FIRA III 132: *simplam pecuniam recte dari/dare* – "to pay duly single the money", while in FIRA III 88 he is promising to pay double the price: *pecuniam duplam probam recte dari* – "to pay duly double the money in good coin" in the case of eviction. We can translate the documents' common structure as follows: "To be liable for this slave to be healthy ... and to pay single / double the purchase price in case that someone will successfully claim the slave ..., the purchaser has taken the promise, the vendor has given the promise."

It should be emphasised that *dupla pecunia*/the *duplum* in FIRA III 88 is referring – grammatically unambiguously – to the eviction, *not* to defects as to quality. Back in 1927, *Otto Lenel* went even further: "There is no example of a formulation [of liability for defects as to quality] in duplum transmitted to us".[12] Meanwhile, this does not correspond to the evidence any more. We now know of two Greek documents dated to the middle of the second century AD, written at Side in the Roman province of Pamphylia (Southern Turkey). They refer the stipulated *dupla pecunia* both to the case of eviction and to the appearance of defects as to quality.[13] Both of them could have been written by a public scribe in the city archive of Side,[14] with nine years between them. We also have Theophilus' Greek *paraphrasis* of the Justinianic Institutes from the sixth century AD, talking – as an example (*λόγου χάριν*) – about the vendor's promise in the frame of the "aedilitian stipulation" to pay "the double" (*διπλάσιον*) in case of the appearance of a hidden defect (*πάθος κρυπτόν*) of the slave sold (Theophil., paraphr. 3,18,2).

Yet, several aspects make us believe that the Side documents are atypical deviations of the standard formula: On the one hand, even the smallest defect of the slave sold would cause the vendor's liability to pay double the price. On the other hand, nothing is said about where the slave himself would remain in such a case. If the Side documents were specimens of an established formula, one would expect that they would show an explicit ruling about the slave's restitution to the vendor – but they do not. However, slave vendors in Side seem to have lived with this ruling for years. Similar problems arise from the description given by Theophilus. Furthermore, if the designation as *stipulatio duplae* would concern the liability for defects as to quality, in a *stipulatio simplae* one would expect the promise of *simpla pecunia* in case of defects as to quality. But there is no surviving document

12 Otto Lenel, Das Edictum perpetuum. Ein Versuch zu seiner Wiederherstellung, Leipzig 1927^3, 562: "Ein Beispiel der Fassung in duplum ist uns nicht erhalten."

13 P. Turner 22 (142 AD); BGU III 887 = FIRA III 133 (151 AD); both in: *Johannes Nollé,* Side im Altertum. Geschichte und Zeugnisse II, Bonn 2001, 613–622.

14 *Nollé* (fn. 9) 616–617.

like that. Regarding defects as to quality, most of the surviving documents (with the only exception of the Side documents) show the promise of *praestari*, i. e. the promise to pay compensation for the purchaser's interest. So if the designation of a *stipulatio* accompanying sale would depend on the content of the promise regarding defects as to quality, all these documents would neither be called *stipulatio duplae* nor *simplae*, but "*stipulatio praestandi*" or "*stipulatio eius quod interest*". However, such a designation is nowhere to be found. Moreover, Paul is dealing with the question if based on *stipulatio duplae* one can claim *both* the repayment of the purchase price (the single one, of course) *and* a compensation, D. 21,1,58,1 Paul. 6 resp. If Paul and his readers called *stipulatio duplae* the promise to pay the double price in case of defects as to quality, Paul's said question would lose relevance. Therefore, the passage can be used as an argument that the standard content of the promise regarding defects as to quality is *praestari*, i. e. to pay the purchaser's interest. Finally, we learn from D. 21,2,31 Ulp. 42 Sab. that the *aediles*' model stipulation reads *sanum esse etc. praestari*. As seen above, their model stipulation is a *stipulatio duplae*. Therefore, the designation as *stipulatio duplae* or *simplae* does not concern the amount of liability for defects as to quality.

However, we have to insist that for the sale of slaves on the market the aedilitian edict is just providing conclusion of the *stipulatio duplae*. It is the *stipulatio duplae* that the purchaser can expect. If the vendor is only willing to give a *stipulatio simplae*, the purchaser has to be aware that the "risk management" regarding defects *in title* is deviating from the standard to his own disadvantage.

5. Non-mandatory Character of the Edictal Rulings

All the edictal duties can be excluded by a mutual agreement of both parties. The duty to give *stipulatio duplae*, as well as edictal liability because of missing information about defects, can be modified or completely abrogated by the parties:

> D. 2,14,31 Ulp. 1 ed. aed. cur.
> Pacisci contra edictum aedilium omnimodo licet, sive in ipso negotio venditionis gerendo convenisset sive postea.
> (transl. *G.M. MacCormack*:) "It is quite [better: at any rate, J. P.] lawful to make a pact contrary to the edict of the aediles, whether the agreement is made in the course of arranging the sale or afterward."

If the edictal rulings are completely excluded and no *stipulatio* is given, then there is no non-fault liability of the vendor, regarding defects as to quality; the purchaser cannot bring *actio redhibitoria* or *quanti minoris*, he cannot bring *actio ex stipulatu* nor claim rescission or compensation because of a missing *stipulatio*.

It seems likely that any renouncement of possible claims by the purchaser will have influence on the purchase price: "Under the edict", the slave will be more expensive than if the edict's rulings are abrogated.[15] However, to avoid his liability the vendor has to reach an explicit renouncement of the purchaser. Therefore, the purchaser must understand that he will be less protected than he would be according to the edictal standard. Hence, the edict could not prevent agreements about exclusion of liability from becoming customary on the slave market. Nevertheless, it seems that there were always slaves available on the market to be sold with full warranty.

6. *Simplariae venditiones* and Exclusion of *redhibitio*

According to modern scholarship the following statement by Pomponius is also to be located within the context of abrogating the edictal duties:

> D. 21,1,48,8 Pomp. 23 Sab.
> Simplariarum venditionum causa ne sit redhibitio, in usu est.
> (transl. *Thomas*:) "It is not our practice to allow rescission [better: it is our practice not to allow rescission, J. P.] in the case of sales where undertakings have been specifically excluded [better: in the case of 'simplarian' sales (since *simplarius* is a *hapax legomenon*), J. P.]."

Since late antiquity, the mentioned *simplariae venditiones* are identified as sales contracts with an exclusion of edictal liability, at least with an exclusion of *actio redhibitoria* by mutual agreement.[16] However, it is notable that such sales contracts were not called "simple" sales (that would be "*simplices venditiones*"), but "simplarian" or "singlarian" sales (*simplariae venditiones*). It is also notable that, according to the statement's linguistic structure, it is not the exclusion of rescission (*redhibitio*) that makes the sales *venditiones simplariae.* In fact, the practice of excluding *redhibitio* seems to align with contracts that *already have* the quality of being *simplariae*. Exclusion of *redhibitio* and qualification as *simplaria venditio* are two different aspects.

All over Latin literature, the word *simplarius,-a,-um* occurs only here. It is a so called *hapax legomenon*. Obviously a made-up word, it seems to be used in a very technical sense. It is deriving from *simplus,-a,-um*. Looking for parallels, the most similar kind of saying is *duplā emere* which occurs for example in:[17]

15 *Kupisch* (fn. 6) 41; *Uemura* (fn. 6) 464.

16 *Liber Syro-Romanus* 35,101; *Fritz Pringsheim*, The Greek Law of Sale, Weimar 1950, 483–484.

17 See also FIRA III 134 = SB III 6304 = CPL 193 (Ravenna, ca 151 AD), ll. 3–8 (Latin in Greek

D. 21,1,58,2 Paul. 5 resp.
Servum duplā emi …
(transl. *Thomas*:) "I bought for double his value [better: with *stipulatio duplae*, J. P.] …"

Duplā emere cannot be understood in any other way than "to buy with the conclusion of *stipulatio duplae*". The translation given by *Thomas* "to buy for double the value", creates an oddity[18]. *Duplā emere* means – *vice versa* – the very same as *duplā vendere*, which as a substantive would be *duplaria venditio*. Therefore, *simplaria venditio* is nothing else than *simplā vendere/emere*, the sale with the conclusion of *stipulatio simplae*. If we now project this interpretation onto the text of D. 21,1,48,8, the statement has to be read as follows:

"It is our practice not to allow rescission in the case of sales with *stipulatio simplae*."

a) *Usus* as established law

One could understand "our practice" as the practice of courts, the "settled jurisdiction".[19] That is how we have to understand *in usu esse* – for example – in:

D. 48,15,7 Her. 5 iur. epit.
Poena pecuniaria statuta lege Fabia *in usu esse* desiit.
(transl. *Robinson*:) "The money penalty laid down by the *lex Fabia has fallen out of use*."

Gai. 1,184
Olim cum legis actiones *in usu erant*, etiam ex illa causa tutor dabatur, … qui dicebatur praetorius tuto, quia a praetore urbano dabatur. Sed post sublatas legis actiones quidam putant hanc speciem dandi tutoris *in usu esse* desisse; aliis autem placet adhuc *in usu esse*, si legitimo iudicio agatur.
(transl. The Institutes of Gaius, eds. *W. M. Gordon/O. F. Robinson*, London 1988:) "In former times, when procedure by actions in the law *was in use*, a guardian was also appointed on the grounds, … He was called the 'praetorian' guardian, because he was appointed by the Urban Praetor. But after the abolition of the actions in the law, some jurists think that this kind of appointment of guardian has *fallen into disuse*; it is ac-

characters): *κουαμ ει δουπλα οπτιμις κον- / δικιωνιβους βενδιδι<<τ>> ετ τραδιδι* (= *quam ei duplā optimis condicionibus vendidi et tradidi* – "which I have sold to him with *stipulatio duplae* in best state/under best terms of contract").

18 Neither convincing is the explanation of sales "with double money" (i. e. with *stipulatio duplae*) in documents from Roman Egypt given by *Friedrich Preisigke*, Zum Papyrus Eitrem Nr. 5, Heidelberg 1916, 12, who believes that there are "two payers" making "double payment". See also infra at fn. 20.

19 *Jakab*, Praedicere und cavere (fn. 6) 187.

> cepted by others, however, that it *is* still *in use* if an action is brought in a statutory court."

"Not to allow rescission" would be a phenomenon that one had to assign to the lawyers, to the jurisdiction magistrate, or, more generally, to the existing *law*.[20] The phenomenon would have to be explained by a supplementary interpretation of contract ("*ergänzende Vertragsauslegung*"): If the vendor's liability in case of eviction, i. e. for defects in title, is reduced to *simpla pecunia* (by explicit mutual agreement), the same vendor shall be spared liability in form of *actio redhibitoria* (without being explicitly mentioned) in the case of defects as to quality. This would be coherent, if *actio redhibitoria* would always burden the vendor with more than the purchase price. Yet, according to our sources, this is not the case. In fact, the vendor has to repay the purchase price in exchange for receiving the slave. Further claims directed in the grant of compensation can only be brought up by the purchaser in form of retention, not in the way of *actio redhibitoria*.[21] If the vendor lets the slave remain with the purchaser, he cannot be forced to pay more than the purchase price that has been paid to him before. Therefore, the idea of supplementary interpretation of contract in case of *stipulatio simplae*, producing an exclusion of *actio redhibitoria*, is not easily to be assumed.[22]

b) *Usus* as Contract Practice

Yet *in usu esse ne sit redhibitio* can be understood in a different way as well: "Our practice" was the business custom, the common contract practice, as we can find it in other sources:

> Gai. 1,132
> Praeterea emancipatione desinunt liberi in potestatem parentum esse. ... Is eum iterum mancipat vel eidem vel alii (sed *in usu est* eidem mancipari) isque eum postea similiter vindicta manumittit ...
> (transl. *Gordon/Robinson*:) "Moreover, children also emerge from paternal power by emancipation. ... He again mancipates him, either to the same person or to someone else (but *it is usual* for him to be mancipated to the same person) who then again manumits him by rod ..."

20 See Syn. Bas. A, XII, 10 with gloss (r) (*Zepos* V 50).

21 D. 21,1,29,3 Ulp. 1 ed. aed. cur.

22 However, it remains possible that the promise of *simpla/dupla pecunia* for the case of eviction is working as a limit of compensation by supplementary interpretation of contract, see infra at fn. 20.

Gai. 2,181
Ceterum ne post obitum parentis periculo insidiarum subiectus videretur pupillus, *in usu est* vulgarem quidem substitutionem palam facere, id est eo loco, quo pupillum heredem instituimus ...
(transl. *Gordon/Robinson*:) "But in case our young son should seem to be exposed to foul play after his father's death, note that *the practice is* to make the ordinary substitution openly, that is, at the point where we appoint him heir."

Gai. 2,249
Verba autem utilia fideicommissorum haec maxime *in usu esse* videntur: peto, rogo, volo, fidei committo ...
(transl. *Gordon/Robinson*:) "In creating effective trusts the following words seem *to be* most *commonly used*: 'I call upon; I ask; I wish; I rely on your honour' ..."

Ne sit redihitio – "not to allow rescission", better: "that there shall be no rescission", would be the content of a typical parties' agreement: "In the case of sales with *stipulatio simplae*, it is our practice (to agree) that rescission shall not take place."

Hence, it is customary that the very same vendors who reduce their liability for defects *in title* to the repayment of *simpla pecunia* (thereby deviating in their own favour from the edictal standard) would also reduce their liability for defects *as to quality*, excluding rescission of the sale (that normally could be claimed based on the aedilitian edict, as well as based on the standard *stipulatio duplae*). To avoid any misunderstanding: Pomponius does not say that exclusion of *redhibitio* was customary in slave sales. What he says is still compatible with a business practice that uses *stipulatio duplae* and full warranty in the major part of sales contracts. The practice mentioned by Pomponius only concerns sales with *stipulatio simplae*. Based on his statement, we can only expect that in the city of Rome at the time of Pomponius slave sales with *stipulatio simplae* were normally, that means in the majority of cases, combined with an exclusion of *redhibitio* by agreement of the parties.

7. Documentary Evidence

Documentary evidence for this contract practice is not strong. There is not even one example from practice illustrating the *usus* as described by Pomponius. However, that does not mean a lot, since documents from practice are the typical subjects to all the lucky and unlucky ways of transmission. From the city of Rome and from the times of Pomponius we have no slave sales' documents at all.

a) Roman Egypt

Yet exclusion of giving back a slave or an animal sold is quite common in Greek documents from Roman Egypt. Objects are sold there: τοῦτον τοιοῦτον ἀναπόρριφον – "as they are, unrejectable".

Modern literature calls this the "*ἀναπόρριφον*-clause" (or "*τ. τ. ἀ.*-clause"): It is about the exclusion of the "rejection" of the sold object in the time after sale and delivery. In Latin legal terminology one would speak about the exclusion of *redhibitio*. If the *ἀναπόρριφον*-clause is found in slave sales contracts, there normally is an exception for the cases of epilepsy and leprosy – cases in which giving back the slave against repayment of the purchase price remains possible. For the rest, it is difficult to say if the *ἀναπόρριφον*-clause is necessary ("constitutive") to abrogate a statutory duty of the vendor to take back the defective object, or if the clause only has a clarifying ("declarative") character.[23] As an argument against any statutory, respectively edictal, duty to take back the defective object in Roman Egypt, i. e. against application of the aedilitian edict in one or another form in this province, one could use a fragment from proceedings of a trial from the mid second century AD, probably from Oxyrhynchus. A purchaser brings action against the vendor: He bought a slave girl that not only ran away from him shortly after the sale, but also took several goods away with her. Hence, the purchaser does not only claim the repayment of the purchase price, but also the compensation for his loss regarding the stolen goods. The vendor's attorney is refusing this claim. Here is what we read about his case:

P. Cair. Preis. 2.1,14–20 (ed. R. P. Salomons 2014)
… ἤκουσας τοὺς ἁπλῷ χρήματι πω [λοῦντας δοῦλον]
[ca 6 ἀν]ε υθύνους εἶναι, ἐπειδάν τις αὐτοῖς τοιοῦτ[ο ἔγκλημα ἐπενέγκῃ]
[οἷο]ν οὗτος· ἐὰν γὰρ μηδὲν ἐπερώτημα ᾗ ἐνγεγρα[μμένον ἀνεύθυνον]
[εἶναι τ]ὸν πράτην τῇ ἀποδώσει τῆς τειμῆς, ἐὰν ἁπ[λοῦν χρῆμα ᾗ ἐνγεγραμμένον]
[ca 7]ο μόνον πρᾶσις ἦν ἁπλῆ ἀνεύθυνος δ[ὲ ca 16 ὁ ὑπ']
[ἐμοῦ συ]νηγορούμενος, οὐδὲν γὰρ επ [ca 28]
[ca 4 ἁ]πλῆς πράσεω[ς …]

"… (The vendor's attorney says:) You have heard that those who sell [a slave] with simple money (= with *stipulatio simplae*) are unaccountable, whenever someone [brings such an action] against them as our opponent. For if no formal question (= no *stipula-*

23 Regarding the application of the aedilitian edict in Roman Egypt see – mostly convincing, but without concerning the following document – *Fabian Klinck*, "Vollharmonisierung" in der Antike – Zur Geltung des ädilizischen Edikts in den Provinzen, in: Methoden- und Verfassungsfragen der Europäischen Rechtsangleichung, eds. *Ioannis K. Karakostas* et al., Berlin 2011, 73.

> *tio*) has been inserted in the sales-contract, the vendor is unaccountable for the repayment of the purchase price. If simple money [has been inserted ---] only the sale was simple, not liable [--- m]y client, because nothing [--- s]imple sal[e ---]".

Without *stipulatio* – at least this is what the attorney wants the judge to believe – the vendor is not accountable for the "repayment of the purchase price". That means that there was no *redhibitio* without *stipulatio* in Roman Egypt. Under the aedilitian edict this would be incorrect for slave sales on the market.

What the vendor's attorney said about the liability under *stipulatio simplae* ("if simple money has been inserted") has forever been lost. However, according to him, it is not possible to bring an action "as brought by our opponent" in the actual case (which must be a case under *stipulatio simplae*). We have to be very precise: The opponent is claiming *both* the repayment of the purchase price, without giving back the slave girl (that is still on the run), *and* the compensation for the stolen goods. This is what is meant by "the action as brought by our opponent". It seems likely that the attorney tries to limit *every* liability of the vendor in cases of *stipulatio simplae* to the amount of the purchase price. The argument would be as follows: If in case of eviction (i. e. total loss of the object) the vendor has to pay only simple the purchase price (*simpla pecunia*), it would be odd if his strict liability for defects as to quality (including the slave's predisposition to escape) could go above *simpla pecunia*.[24] While the attorney's argument on *stipulatio simplae* remains unsure, the document speaks against statutory non-fault liability for defects as to quality of slaves sold in Roman Egypt, since in absence of a *stipulatio* the attorney denies every liability of the vendor. But we cannot be sure: It is not said whether the slave girl has been bought on the market. Even in Rome, statutory non-fault liability in form of the aedilitian edict applies only to slave sales on the market.

Furthermore, the *ἀναπόρριφον*-clause also occurs in documents of sale that would not be under edictal law anyway: handmills are documented to be sold with *ἀναπόρριφον*-clause,[25] as well as a part of a wooden oil press[26] and a fallen tree[27].

---

24 After all, also D. 21,1,58,2 Paul. 5 resp. in a similar case (the slave sold is escaping from the purchaser and taking away goods) emphasizes that the slave has been bought with *stipulatio duplae*. See supra at fn. 14.

25 See *Jakab*, Praedicere und cavere (fn. 6) 196 fn. 2.

26 BGU XV 2486,12 (93 AD).

27 P.Cairo SR 3049/11 (ca 130–138 AD), see *Bärbel Kramer*, Akanthus oder Akazie? Bemerkungen zu Bäumen, ZPE 97 (1993) 138–143 who points out (142) that all objects sold under the ἀναπόρριφον-clause besides slaves and animals are wooden and therefore subject to change. It seems convincing that either warranty or the ἀναπόρριφον-clause are used wherever defects hidden for the present can show up later.

Has the clause been introduced there erroneously by a scribe taking it from a formula for animal sales on the market?[28]

We have to leave the question open, whether the aedilitian edict was applicable in Roman Egypt. But even if there was no statutory law to be abrogated by the *ἀναπόρριφον*-clause, the clause still made sense. There can be a common business practice that at least knows cases of full warranty for all kinds of defects as to quality. Within such an environment, writers of documents can see the need to explicitly sign such cases without warranty or with reduced warranty by using the *ἀναπόρριφον*-clause. Even in Rome, in times before the enactment of the aedilitian edict, a business practice has to have existed for slave sales on the market that produced a standard of a vendor's full warranty. The *aediles curules* did nothing else than to fix the standard by their edictal stipulation model: "The model [of *stipulatio duplae* found in the aedilitian edict] basically corresponded to trade custom as used over centuries".[29] Hence, it is not surprising that deviations of the standard are made explicit even in regions where the aedilitian edict is not applicable.

Quite often, in documents with *ἀναπόρριφον*-clause we also find a clause about eviction; however, there is never a combination of the *ἀναπόρριφον*-clause and the promise to pay *double* the price in case of eviction. None of the documents of sales *διπλῷ χρήματι* ("with double money"), i.e. with the promise of paying double the price in case of eviction,[30] shows the *ἀναπόρριφον*-clause. On the contrary, they often show the vendor's explicit assertions about the absence of defects as to quality. On the other hand, we have a document where the sale is *ἁπλῷ χρήματι* ("with simple money"), i.e. under *stipulatio simplae*, and the vendor's liability for defects as to quality is reduced to the common minimum (epilepsy and leprosy) at the same time (SB XII 10894, Oxyrhynchus 140 AD).

b) Latin Documents

There are only few Latin documents about slave sales. Only three documents from Herculaneum (TH 60 and 61, ca 63 AD) and Seleucia (FIRA III 132, 166 AD) have a *stipulatio simplae*. None of them shows exclusion of *redhibitio*. However, regarding defects as to quality the vendor in FIRA III 132 only promises *sanum esse ex edicto* ("that the slave is healthy according to the edict"), but no liability is entered in case the slave is tending to escape, roving about or being charged with a tort action – which would be the rest of the edictal program

28 See again *Jakab*, Praedicere und cavere (fn. 6) 196 fn. 2 with further references.

29 *Klinck* (fn. 19) 72: "Das Muster entsprach im Wesentlichen jahrhundertealtem Handelsbrauch".

30 See supra fn. 14. *Jakab*, Praedicere und cavere (fn. 6) 208 expresses unfounded doubts.

(QVIS FVGITIVVS ERROVE SIT NOXAVE SOLVTVS NON SIT). This rest does not have to be excluded, since it seems likely that the aedilitian edict is not applicable in Seleucia. One can imagine that the vendor in this case simply does not have certain information about the slave's past. There is a risk that the slave still has another owner or that he already tried to escape from one of his former masters. So the vendor neither wants to be liable to more than the repayment of the purchase price in case of eviction (defects in title: *simpla pecunia*) nor beyond the actual health of the slave (defects as to quality: *sanum esse ex edicto*).

III. Conclusion

To sum up: The Romans know a vendor's non-fault liability for defects as to quality of slaves sold on the market. On the one hand, it is founded in the aedilitian edict. On the other hand, it can be created by the *stipulatio* that the vendor normally gives to the purchaser. Where the aedilitian edict is applicable, both edictal liability and conclusion of a *stipulatio* can be abrogated by an explicit mutual agreement. Where the edict is not applicable, there are no statutory duties to be abrogated. However, giving a *stipulatio* seems to be a common practice in all cases, and the standard seems to be the *stipulatio duplae* that is attested to be the edictal model of *stipulatio*. But we can also find the parties' freedom to reduce the vendor's liability, deviating from the standard, may it be statutory or customary, without excluding it as a whole. There is no hint that any part of the vendor's non-fault liability is compulsory law. If it is the compulsory character that makes modern consumer protection effective, at least the Roman law of "consumer protection" is not at the height of the European directive on the sale of consumer goods and § 476(1) BGB. Furthermore, the *aediles curules* (like the BGB until 2002) do not distinguish "consumers" from "entrepreneurs". Leaving aside that such concepts are foreign to Roman law (and ancient Latin language) – we will normally find a professional slave dealer on the Roman market as a vendor, yet we will not always find a "consumer" on the purchaser's side. Therefore, by qualifying the aedilitian edict as "consumer protection" no better understanding is gained of both Roman and modern law. The aedilitian edict, like §§ 434 and 437 BGB, offers nothing more than non-mandatory purchaser protection.

Pompeo Polito, Rome

Some Considerations on the Relationship between *res incorporales* and *Immaterialgüterrechte*

I. Introduction

If there is a field of nowadays law studies which seems to be so far away from Roman law, this field is, without any doubt, intellectual property law. If we just think that intellectual property is the core of current legal debates about phenomena like the internet, digitalization, social networks or the more recent bitcoin and block-chain, the law of Romans, apparently, has nothing to do with it.

Every work about the history or the origins of intellectual property law generally places, indeed, the birth of intellectual property[1] between the end of the 18th century and the beginning of the 19th century.[2] Moreover, if we read the official notion of intellectual property ("*Intellectual property refers to creations of the mind: inventions; literary and artistic works; and symbols, names and images used in commerce*")[3] we immediately realise that this is something referring to copyrights and patents, legal institutions completely ignored by the Romans.

Copyrights and patents are descendants of the technological progress; the first, in particular, being understood as exploitation right over one's literary work, is the outcome of the invention of printing. Only when printing became

---

1 The first known use of the term "intellectual property" dates to 1769, when a piece published in the *Monthly Review* used the phrase. See Oxford English Dictionary, Oxford 2010³, s. v. "intellectual property".

2 The "Statute of Monopolies" (1624) and the British "Statute of Anne" (1710) are identified as the origins of "patent law" and "copyright" respectively, firmly establishing the concept of intellectual property. See *Brad Sherman/Lionel Bently*, The Making of Modern Intellectual Property Law, Cambridge 1999, 207. The German equivalent was effective from the founding of the "North German Confederation" whose constitution granted legislative power over the protection of intellectual property (*Schutz des geistigen Eigentums*) to the confederation. When the administrative secretariats established by the "Paris Convention" (1883) and the "Berne Convention" (1886) merged in 1893 in Berne, they also adopted the term intellectual property in their new combined title, the "United International Bureaux for the Protection of Intellectual Property".

3 This is the notion of intellectual property given by the World Intellectual Property Organization, a self-funding agency of the United Nations. WIPO is the global forum for intellectual property services, policy, information and cooperation. See <http://www.wipo.int/about-ip/en>.

easier and cheap it had been possible to develop a literary market and then authors felt the need to prevent the exploitation of their works; even the right to sign one's own artistic work in order to attribute paternity over such work is a need felt by the artists only in 1178 AC.[4] Even if it is not unusual to read in Greek or Roman literature several authors' complaints about plagiarism or abusive exploitations of their works[5] – for these situations Roman law recognised a kind of protection for the author's moral rights, granting, in case of plagiarism, the use of the *actio iniurarum aestimatoria*[6] – the ancient world and Roman law, in particular, did not recognise any legal institution similar to the modern copyright.[7] If the Romans ignored patents and copyrights, why could it be useful even for intellectual property lawyers to study Roman law?

The connecting link between Roman law and modern intellectual property lies in the concept of a non-physical entity which characterises all the creation of the mind mentioned in the definition of intellectual property given by the WIPO. Such creations have been qualified by the juridical science between the

4 *Luigi Carlo Ubertazzi*, Diritto d'autore, parte I. Introduzione, in: Digesto delle discipline privatistiche. Sezione commerciale, Vol 4, Turin, 1989, 367: "*A partire dalla crocifissione firmata da Benedetto Antelami nel duomo di Parma gli artisti hanno cominciato un lento processo che li ha condotti ad uscire dall'anonimato del chiostro o della corporazione, a rivendicare pubblicamente la paternità delle proprie opere ed a prendere coscienza della loro peculiarità.*"

5 Hor., epist. 1,20,1–6; Mart. 1,52 and 1,53,11–12; Symm., epist. 1,31,2. Moreover it is important to highlight that originally *plagiarius* was somebody who enslaved the slave belonging to someone else but only with Martial this word meant appropriation of works belonging to someone else. In this regard see *Martin Schermaier*, Borrowed Plumes and Robbed Freedmen. Some Aspects of Plagiarism in Roman Antiquity, in: Judge and Jurist. Essays in Memory of Lord Rodger of Earlsferry, Oxford 2013, 244.

6 In this regard see *Rudolf von Jhering*, Rechtsschutz gegen injuriöse Rechtsverletzungen, in: Jahrbücher für die Dogmatik des heutigen römischen und deutschen Privatrechts, eds. *Carl Friedrich von Gerber* et al., Vol 23, Jena 1885, 155–338, 313–326. More recently about plagiarism in ancient Rome see *Schermaier* (fn. 6) 244, 245.

7 Despite there is literature denying the existence of copyright even in Roman law (*Russ Ver Steg*, The Roman Law Roots of Copyright, Maryland Law Review (2000) 522–552; *Ugo Bartocci*, Aspetti giuridici dell'attività letteraria in Roma antica. Il complesso percorso verso il riconoscimento dei diritti degli autori, Turin 2009; *Katharina de la Durantaye*, The Origins of the Protection of Literary Authorship in Ancient Rome, Boston University International Law Journal 25, 1 (2007) 37–111, we have to remember, together with the father of the Italian copyright law Eduardo Piola Caselli (*Eduardo Piola Caselli*, Codice del diritto d'autore, Turin 1943, 2) that the author could not have a right to receive an income by the sale of his work because the cost of the handmade publication was too high and the numbers of copies made very strict (for a detailed analysis of the sale of books in the ancient world see *Tönnes Kleberg*, Commercio librario ed editoria nel mondo antico, in: Libri, editori e pubblico nel mondo antico. Guida storica e critica, ed. *Guglielmo Cavallo*, Bari 2016[6], 27–80).

18th and the 19th century as *Immaterialgüterrechte*, "intangible things" or "*beni immateriali*", but this new category of goods has been elaborated as a reaction to the Roman legal institution of *res incorporales*.

More than thirty years ago, Giovanni Pugliese, an authoritative scholar, revealed in a long and detailed essay[8] that the Romans were the first to legally regulate entities which are not possible to see or to touch and the first to clearly describe how the creation of the legal category of *Immaterialgüterrechte*, "intangible things" or "*beni immateriali*", by the German jurists of the 19th century was influenced by the *res incorporales*.

Another analysis of the relationship between *res incorporales* and *beni immateriali* has been conducted, more recently, by Giovanni Turelli[9] who, from a scientific speculation perspective, found a connection that could be defined as "*affinità*" (contiguity) in an etymological sense (< lat. **ad-finis*) between ancient and modern categories. There is nothing more to add to such a brilliant analysis except the desire for a further investigation about the creation of the legal category of "goods", used in the legal language instead of the use of the terms "things" (*res*). Therefore, the following paper is just a proposal that may lead to further research in the future.

II. The Definition of *res incorporales*

The existence of entities which are not possible to see[10] or to touch is an ancient philosophical concept. The first organic theories in this regard have been elab-

8 *Giovanni Pugliese*, Dalle "*res incorporales*" del diritto romano ai beni immateriali di alcuni sistemi giuridici odierni, Rivista trimestrale di diritto e procedura civile (1982) 1137–1198.

9 *Giovanni Turelli*, '*Res incorporales*' e 'beni immateriali'. Categorie affini, ma non congruenti, Teoria e Storia del Diritto Privato (TSDP) 5 (2012) 1–30 (= in: "Afferrare… l'inafferrabile". I giuristi e il diritto della nuova economia industriale fra Otto e Novecento. Atti della giornata di studi storici e giuridici. Brescia, 11 maggio 2012, eds. *Alberto Sciumè* et al., Milan 2013, 71–87). By the same author see *idem*, Res incorporales, objetos corporales, objetos inmateriales: nota sull'itinerario moderno di un concetto antico, Roma e America: diritto romano commune, in: Rivista di diritto dell'integrazione e unificazione del diritto in Europa e in America Latina 37 (2016) 171–182, where the author examined the way in which, in the Latin-American legal experience (in particular in the thought of Dalmacio Vélez Sársfield), the distinction between *res corporales* and *res incorporales* has offered food for thought for the construction of the classification of "things" in the Argentine codification, from the *Código civil* of Venezuela to the current *Código Civil y Comercial de la Nación*.

10 On the criterion that identified the corporeal reality there was no agreement among the various philosophical schools; the concept of tangibility made right by the Roman jurisconsults comes from rather Aristotelian philosophy, while for the Stoics the criterion of the corporeality was given

orated by Plato and Aristotle and have reached the Roman thought through stoicism.[11] We could discuss several sources on that subject but the best witness regarding the existence of intangible things in Roman thought is the following text written by Cicero.

Cic. top. 5,26–27:
[...] Definitionum autem duo genera prima: unum earum rerum quae sunt, alterum earum quae intelleguntur.
[27] Esse ea dico quae cerni tangique possunt, ut fundum aedes, parietem stillicidium, mancipium pecudem, supellectilem penus et cetera; quo ex genere quaedam interdum vobis definienda sunt. Non esse rursus ea dico quae tangi demonstrarive non possunt, cerni tamen animo atque intellegi possunt, ut si usus capionem, si tutelam, si gentem, si agnationem definias, quarum rerum nullum subest corpus, est tamen quaedam conformatio insignita et impressa intellegentia, quam notionem voco. Ea saepe in argumentando definitione explicanda est.

" [...] But of definitions there are two principal kinds: one, of those things which exist; the other, of those which are understood.
[27] The things which I call existing are those which can be seen or touched; as a farm, a house, a wall, a gutter, a slave, an ox, furniture, provisions, and so on; of which kind of things some require at times to be defined by us. Those things, again, I say have no existence, which are incapable of being touched or proved, but which can be perceived by the mind and understood; as if you were to define usucaption, guardianship, nationality, or relationship; all things which have no body, but which nevertheless have a certain conformation plainly marked out and impressed upon the mind, which I call the notion of them. They often require to be explained by definition while we are arguing about them. "

Cicero distinguishes between things that exist and can be touched on the one hand and things that cannot be touched, but can be understood in your mind on the other hand; their existence lies in the notion of them we have in our mind. Reading this text we can say that Cicero defines concept as a thing because if you have a notion of something in your mind this thing exists even if it has no body.

by the effect, so that the voice would be corporeal because it produces effect on the auditory apparatus. See *Giuseppe Grosso*, Corso di Diritto Romano. Le cose. Con una "nota di Lettura" di Filippo Gallo, Turin 1941, reprint in: Rivista di Diritto Romano 1 (2001) 11.

11 About the influence of ancient Greek philosohy in Roman thought and then its influence in Roman law see *Mario Bretone*, I fondamenti del diritto romano. Le cose e la natura, Rome/Bari 1998, 123–143.

Despite the mention of usucaption or guardianship scholars agree that this text by Cicero contains no juridical definition of intangible things but just a philosophical reflection about them.[12]

Only knowing, however, such dichotomy[13] revealed by Cicero makes it possible to understand, how two centuries later the Roman jurist Gaius gave the first juridical definition of *res incorporales* in Western legal tradition:[14]

Gai. 2,12–14:1[15]

[12] Quaedam praeterea res corporales sunt, quaedam incorporales.

---

12 In this regard see *Giuseppe Falcone*, Osservazioni su Gai 2.14 e le *res incorporales*, Annali del seminario giuridico, Università degli studi di Palermo (AUPA) Vol LV (2012) 131–132.

13 According to *Pugliese* (fn. 9) 1138, fn. 2, indeed, the influence of Greek philosophy on Gaius through the mediation of Cicero's texts is indubitable.

14 *Vincenzo Arangio-Ruiz*, Istituzioni di diritto Romano, Naples 1994, reprint 2002, 162; *Pugliese* (fn. 9) 1138. For scholars thinking that the dichotomy between *res corporales* and *res incorporales* was probably elaborated by the Roman jurisprudence even before Gaius see *Turelli* (fn. 10, 2012) 4 fn. 6.

15 The literature about this text is enormous. The most relevant works, except the studies already cited, are: *Heinrich Pflüger*, Über körperliche und unkörperliche Sachen, ZRG RA 65 (1947) 339–343; *Raymond Monier*, La date d'apparition du "dominium" et de la distinction juridique des "res" en "corporales" et "incorporales", in: Studi in onore di Siro Solazzi, Naples 1948, 357–374; *Pierpaolo Zamorani*, Gaio e la distinzione tra "res corporales" e "res incorporales", Labeo 20 (1974) 362–369; *Ferdinando Bona*, Il coordinamento delle distinzioni "res corporales – res incorporales" e "res mancipi – res nec mancipi" nella sistematica gaiana, Prospettive sistematiche nel diritto romano, Turin 1976, 407–454; *Riccardo Orestano*, Gaio e le *res incorporales*, Diritto. Incontri e scontri, Bologna 1981, 297–314; *Pasquale Marottoli*, *Res incorporales* (Premesse), Roma 1989; *Franco Baldessarelli*, A proposito della rilevanza giuridica della distinzione tra *res corporales* e *res incorporales* nel diritto romano classico, RIDA 37 (1990) 71–116; *Jan Willem Tellegen*, 'Res incorporalis' et les codifications modernes de droit civil, Labeo 40 (1994) 35–55; *Alberto Burdese*, Considerazioni sulle "res corporales" e "incorporales" quali elementi del patrimonio (in margine al pensiero di Gaetano Scherillo), in: Gaetano Scherillo, ed. *Federico Pergami*, Atti del Convegno, Milano, 22–23 ottobre 1992, Bologna 1994, 23–42; *Mario Bretone*, Res incorporalis, in: Filellenismo e tradizionalismo a Roma nei primi due secoli dell'impero, Atti dei convegni Lincei, Rome, 1995, 1996, 117–142; *Bretone* (fn. 11) 143–149; *Wojciech Dajczak*, Der Ursprung der Wendung *res incorporalis* im römischen Recht, RIDA 50 (2003) 97–117; *Pascal Pichonnaz*, Res incorporales et possessio iuris. Questions choisies sur les relations entre choses et droits, Orbis Iuris Romani, Journal of Ancient Law Studies 9 (2004) 105–131; *Maria Floriana Cursi*, "Res incorporales" e modello proprietario nella tutela dell'informazione globale, in: Parola chiave: informazione. Appunti di diritto, economia e filosofia, ed. *Agata C. Amato Mangiameli*, Milan 2004, 173–206; *Giovanni Nicosia*, *Ea quae iure consistunt*, in: Scritti in onore di Generoso Melillo, ed. *Antonio Palma*, Vol 2, Napoli 2009, 821–836; *Christian Baldus*, Res incorporales im römischen Recht, in: Unkörperliche Güter im Zivilrecht, ed. *Stefan Leible* et al., Tübingen 2011, 7–31.

[13] Corporales hae sunt, quae tangi possunt, velut fundus, homo, vestis, aurum, argentum et denique aliae res innumerabiles.
[14] Incorporales sunt, quae tangi non possunt, qualia sunt ea, quae in2[16] iure consistunt, sicut hereditas, ususfructus, obligationes quoquo modo contractae. Nec ad rem pertinet, quod in hereditate res corporales continentur, et fructus, qui ex fundo percipiuntur, corporales sunt, et id, quod ex aliqua obligatione nobis debetur, plerumque corporale est, veluti fundus, homo, pecunia: Nam ipsum ius successionis et ipsum ius utendi fruendi et ipsum ius obligationis incorporale est. […]

"[12] Furthermore, some things are corporeal, some are incorporeal.
[13] Corporeal things are tangible, as land, a slave, clothing, gold, silver, and finally innumerable other things.
[14] Incorporeal things are intangible; such as those which have an existence simply in law as inheritance, usufruct, obligation, however contracted. It is irrelevant that an inheritance comprises corporeal things, and that the fruits of land enjoyed by a usufructuary are corporeal, and that the things owed to us by some obligation are mostly corporeal, such as land, a slave, money: for the right of succession, the right of usufruct and the right of obligation are incorporeal."

This text from the second book of Gaius' *Institutiones* is devoted to the regulation of things. After the distinction between *res mancipi* and *res nec mancipi* Gaius differentiates between things you can touch and things you cannot touch; the latter simply exist in law. We find this distinction very modern, because through such classification the things that are immaterial transition into the juridical world. Having noted this we have to focus our attention on two aspects in particular. Firstly, Gaius says that *res incorporales* are those things which *in iure consistunt. Consistere* in Latin means "to have foundation in something" and in this sense *res incorporales* are the things which find their existence only through the law.[17] *Res incorporales* are therefore a law creation. Secondly, we have to bear

16 The preposition *in* is not part of the original manuscript of Gaius' *Institutiones*, but has been added by editors because in the Justinian collection (D. 1,8,1,1 Gai. 2 inst.; Inst. 2,2,2) the text written by Gaius is reproduced with the preposition *in* before *iure consistunt*. According to *Falcone* (fn. 12) 130, however, the preposition *in* was part of the original text and probably disappeared just by accident during the text tradition.

17 In this sense *Orestano* (fn. 15) and *Bretone* (fn. 11), 141 who translates the sentence "Ea quae in iure consistent" as juridical existence while for *Filippo Gallo*, Recensione a "Mario Bretone, I fondamenti del diritto romano. Le cose e la natura, Rome/Bari 1998", IURA XLIX (1998) 137 such sentence would mean that *res incorporales* are the things that consist of rights. The same opinion of *Gallo* is shared by *Nicosia* (fn. 15) 831 who deems that the same sentence would have reflected a postclassic and Justinian view which tends to coincide the *res incorporales* with the rights.

in mind that this new distinction, made by Gaius for the first time in the history of law,[18] was the outcome of the new way of property transfer, the *traditio*, which superseded the old way, the *mancipatio*, completely. While the distinction between things was previously focused on *res mancipi* and *res nec mancipi*, it is now based on things you can touch and things you cannot touch because with *mancipatio*, indeed, it was not possible to transfer a *res* without touching it,[19] but then with *traditio* it became possible.[20] It is unquestionable that the definition of *res incorporales* is basically the definition of certain rights as for example the right of succession or the right of usufruct and therefore, in this sense, *res incorporales* have nothing to do, as we said above, with the modern intangible goods which are not defined as rights, but as objects of rights.

III. The Creation of a New Legal Category: The Intangible Goods

After the short analysis of Gaius' text, we can say that with the introduction of *res incorporales* this Roman jurist brought the concept of immateriality into the world of law although at his time and even for several centuries later there was not any immaterial entity to regulate.

Every single institution belonging to the wide field of intellectual property has its own specific history and development but, for sure, it was only after the

18 *Pasquale Voci*, Diritto Ereditario Romano, I, Milan 1967, 160–161, considering D. 8,1,14 pr. Paul. 15 Sab., hypothesizes a probable knowledge of the notion of *res incorporalis* by Sabinus.

19 In this regard it shall be enough just considering the definition of *mancipatio* given by the same Gaius who clearly explains that in order to do a *mancipatio* you have to hold the thing in your hand. Gai. 1,119: «*Est autem mancipatio, ut supra quoque diximus, imaginaria quaedam venditio; quod et ipsum ius proprium civium Romanorum est. Eaque res ita agitur: adhibitis non minus quam quinque testibus civibus Romanis puberibus et praeterea alio eiusdem condicionis, qui libram aeneam teneat, qui appellatur 'libripens', is, qui mancipio accipit, rem tenens ita dicit:* HVNC EGO HOMINEM EX IVRE QVIRITIVM MEVM ESSE AIO ISQVE MIHI EMPTVS ESTO HOC AERE AENEAQVE LIBRA; *deinde aere percutit libram idque aes dat ei, a quo mancipio accipit, quasi pretii loco.*» – «Mancipation, as before stated, is an imaginary sale, belonging to that part of the law which is peculiar to Roman citizens. It consists in the following process: in the presence of not fewer than five witnesses, citizens of Rome above the age of puberty, and another person of the same condition, who holds a bronze balance in his hands and is called 'the balance holder', the alienee holding a bronze ingot in his hand, pronounces the following words: THIS MAN I CLAIM AS BELONGING TO ME BY THE RIGHT OF THE CITIZENS OF ROME AND BE HE PURCHASED TO ME BY THIS INGOT AND THIS SCALE OF BRONZE. He then strikes the scale with the ingot and he delivers the ingot to the mancipator as in place of the purchase price."

20 See *Zamorani* (fn. 15) 368–369.

industrial revolution that jurists tried to find a legal category able to collect all the "creation of the mind"; at the beginning of this classificatory attempt[21] these institutions have been qualified as *res incorporales*. Even the adjective "incorporeal", thanks to the tradition of *res incorporales*, seemed to be a useful adjective to identify the new legal entities of the industrial revolution.[22] Among several authors of the 18th century who made use of *res incorporales* in order to collect patents or trademarks[23] we cannot avoid quoting the father of the BGB, *Bernhard Windscheid*, who in his famous *Lehrbuch des Pandektenrechts* clearly wrote that in a "modern sense" *res incorporales* are even the scientific and artistic works.[24] We should ask ourselves now why if *res incorporales* seemed to be so useful to collect and identify the creations of the mind we have seen listed in the definition of intellectual property given by the WIPO nowadays nobody speaks of *res incorporales* but of immaterial goods. The reason is that *res incorporales* in Roman law were defined as rights while the new legal entities of copyrights or patents were not defined as rights, but as object of rights.[25]

This is why[26] *Josef Kohler*[27] reacted by elaborating the category of *Persönlichkeitsrechte* (*Individualrechte*, personality rights) on one hand and introducing the category of *Immaterialgüterrechte* (rights on intangible goods) on the

21 This process and attempts have been clearly described by *Pugliese* (fn. 9) 1159–1198, who also made a distinction between the continental experience and the English law tradition.

22 In this regard we cannot avoid reminding that Napoleon, during a session of the State Council said: "*Une propriété littéraire est une propriété incorporelle.*" (See *Laura Moscati*, Napoleone e la proprietà intellettuale, Rivista di diritto civile 52 [2006] 179).

23 All mentioned and analysed by *Pugliese* (fn. 9) 1160 fn. 30.

24 *Bernhard Windscheid*, Lehrbuch des Pandektenrechts in drei Bänden Vol 1, Stuttgart 1879[5], 419. Some years later *Ernst Immanuel Bekker*, System des heutigen Pandektenrechts, Vol I, Weimar 1886, reprint Aalen 1979, 288 writes: "Der Ausdruck *res incorporalis* ist ein unnützes Stück der Römischen Rechtssprache; daher wir wol befugt sind den Namen 'unkörperliche Sache' auf einen völlig neuen Begriff anzuwenden."

25 In every creation of the mind we distinguish two different entities: In a literary work for instance we have the book made of pages of paper and the story told by the book; the first is the *corpus mechanicum*, the latter is the corpus mysticum and the object of right is, obviously, the latter. The distinction between corpus *mysticum* and *corpus mechanicum* has been elaborated by the philosopher Immanuel Kant. See in this regard *Riccardo Pozzo*, Immanuel Kant on intellectual property, Trans/Form/Ação 29 (2006), 11–18.

26 According to *Adriano Vanzetti*, Funzione e natura giuridica del marchio, Rivista del diritto commerciale, LIX (1961) 43; *Pugliese* (fn. 9) 1187, fn. 74.

27 *Josef Kohler*, Deutsches Patentrecht. *Systematisch bearbeitet unter vergleichender Berücksichtigung des französischen Patentrechts*, Mannheim 1878; *Idem*, Das Autorrecht. Eine zivilistische Abhandlung. Zugleich ein Beitrag zur Lehre vom Eigenthum, vom Miteigenthum, vom Rechtsgeschäft und vom Individualrecht, Jahrbücher für die Dogmatik des heutigen römischen und deutschen Privatrechts, Vol 18, 1880, 129–478.

other hand. The first category corresponds to the modern category of personal rights, and in it Kohler, subtracting them from a concept of property that was in fact property on *iura*, and as such deprived of its own content, placed the right to bodily integrity, freedom, name, and next to these the right on distinctive signs. The second category went decidedly back to the traditional concept of property, taking the form of an absolute right over a new immaterial economic good, of which the legal system guaranteed to its author the exclusive economic exploitation and included the works of art and literature, as well as inventions and models. The construction of Kohler with the categories of the rights of personality and the rights on intangible goods provided the conceptual tool for the dogmatic arrangement of the matter, and in fact it was received almost universally, even if soon with considerable modifications. One modification particularly was to subtract the right to the trade mark from the category of personality rights, where Kohler had placed it, and to include it in the category of rights on intangible assets, thus succeeding in consolidating the now-established habit of talking about property of the brand, and at the same time to perpetuate the juxtaposition between brands and patents summarised in the suggestive term of industrial property.

IV. Conclusions

What we have written above, as we have said at the beginning of this paper, is absolutely nothing different from the wider and more detailed analysis of *Giovanni Pugliese*. However, we think that it is not possible to understand how we switched from *res incorporales* to intangible goods without investigating how, in the western legal tradition, we switched from the Roman law concept of *res* to the modern concept of goods. The second book of the first Civil Code (the French Civil Code, published in 1804) indeed, was devoted to the discipline of goods (*des biens*) and not of things, and from that time *res* (or things) slowly disappeared in the legislators' lexicon. *Res* were a key point of the Roman law system (*personae/res/actiones*), but the first Civil Code that implemented its tradition used the term "goods" (*biens*) instead of *res* (*choses*). The introduction of the term "goods" into the legal lexicon is given, according to *Salvatore Pugliatti*,[28] by the birth of economic science; the term "goods" was according to him adopted by the juridical lexicon through economy. A "good" qualifies, indeed, not just a simple thing but something that is possible to exploit and in this sense

28 *Salvatore Pugliatti*, Beni (teoria generale), Enciclopedia del Diritto, Vol 5, Milan 1959, 164–188, 167–169.

a "good" seems to be much more useful than the term *res* to qualify a creation of the mind. As we said above, however, this might be the object of wider research in the future.

Cornelius G. van der Merwe, Stellenbosch*

The Practical Application of Roman Law Principles Relating to the Acquisition of Movable Property by *accessio* and *specificatio* in Modern South African and Scots Law

I. Introduction

The legal systems of both South Africa and Scotland rank amongst the so-called mixed legal systems of the world, consisting of a mixture of civil and common law with private law mostly based on civil law principles and public and procedural law based on common law principles.[1] The reason why this happened in South Africa was that when Britain took over the government of the Dutch Colony of the Cape in 1806, it allowed the Dutch citizens to retain their private law of property, contract and tort (delict) based on the writings of the Roman-Dutch jurists of the 17th and 18th century,[2] while public and procedural law and the administration of the courts were based on the common law of the new sovereign.[3] Interestingly, the Scots law students of the 17th and 18th century preferred to study in Orléans in France and Leiden in the Netherlands rather than at Oxford and Cambridge. On their return to Scotland, they wrote books based on the Ro-

---

* University of Stellenbosch.

1 See in general: Mixed Jurisdictions Worldwide. The Third Legal Family, ed. *Vernon Valentine Palmer*, Cambridge 2012²; *Cornelius G. van der Merwe*, The Origin and Characteristics of the Mixed Legal Systems of South Africa and Scotland and their Importance in Globalisation, Fundamina 18 (1) 2012, 92–114.

2 Some of the most important Roman-Dutch jurists of the 17th and 18th century are *Hugo Grotius* (1583–1645), Inleidinge tot de Hollandsche Recht-geleerdheid (1620) and De Iure Belli ac Pacis (1625); *Arnoldus Vinnius* (1588–1657), Institutionum (1642); *Simon van Leeuwen* (1626–1682), Censura Forensis (1662) and Roomsch Hollandsch Recht (1686); *Ulricus Huber* (1636–1694), Praelectionum Juris Civilis (1698) and Heedensdaegse Rechtgeleertheyt (1692); *Johannes Voet* (1647–1713), Commentarius ad Pandectas (1698–1704); *Gerardus Noodt* (1647–1725), Commentarium, ad Lib. X Tit. IV, Ad exhibendum; *Dionysius Godefridus van der Keessel* (1738–1816), Theses Selectae (1800) and Praelectiones Iuris Hodierni (manuscript published in 1967); *Van der Linden* (1756–1835), Koopmans Handboek (1806).

3 See *Van der Merwe* (fn. 1) 94–95.

Fig. 1: Illustration of the scenario; photo by Hayes Potter on Unsplash, markings by author. <https://unsplash.com/photos/dHuKem53HOw.>

man-French and Roman-Dutch law that they studied in Europe and these books became and remain, besides case law, a very important source of Scots private law.[4] Because of their proximity to England, the prime trading nation of the world at that time, the Scots commercial law, together with their public law and procedural law and the administration of the courts were and still are strongly based on English common law.[5]

---

4 These writers are referred to as the institutional writers because the early writers modelled their works on the Institutes of Justinian. The most important institutional writers are *Sir Thomas Craig,* Ius Feudale (1606, but only printed in 1655); *Viscount Stair,* Institutions of the Law of Scotland (1657); *George Mackenzie,* Institutions of the Law of Scotland (published in 1684 with eight editions between then and 1758 and eventually, in 1754); *Andrew McDouall/Lord Bankton,* An Institute of the Laws of Scotland in Civil Rights (in three volumes published between 1751 and 1753); *John Erskine,* Principles of the Law of Scotland (1754) and An Institute of the Law of Scotland (posthumously 1773); *Baron David Hume* in his Lectures, 1786–1822 (published after his death by *George Campbell/Henderson Paton* [eds.], Baron David Hume's Lectures 1786–1822, Vol 5 [1939], Vol 15 [1952], Vol 18 [1957], Vol 19 [1958]; and *George Joseph Bell,* Principles of the Law of Scotland (1829) and Commentaries on the Law of Scotland and the Principles of Mercantile Jurisprudence [first published in 1770, but later expanded, thus 1770–1843]). For more details on these writers, see *Van der Merwe* (fn. 1) 108–109.

5 See *Van der Merwe* (fn. 1) 110–111 regarding the English influence on Scots law.

One of the areas of law least influenced by common law principles was property law[6] and especially the law relating to the acquisition of movable property. The aim of my contribution is to examine the application of the Roman rules on accession (the joining together of movables) and specification (the production of a new product) to an almost identical case scenario in South African and Scots law. The scenario relates to the joining together of the front part of the wreck of one motor car to the rear part of the wreck of another motor car to produce a new built-up motor car at a scrap yard of a panel beating business. In the South African case, the front part of the wreck of a 1985 BMW was joined to the rear part of the wreck of a 1988 BMW to produce a built-up BMW. In Scotland, a new built-up Ford was constructed from the same parts of the wrecks of two Ford motor vehicles belonging to different owners. In the South African case, it was assumed that this was an instance of accession. By contrast, the Scottish case was argued based on specification.

II. South African Case: "Khan v Minister of Law and Order"

In "Khan v Minister of Law and Order",[7] Khan purchased a wreck of a 1985 model BMW at a scrap yard and arranged with a panel-beater[8] to rebuild the wreck so as to appear to be not a 1985 model but a 1988 model BMW. This the panel-beater did by cutting the 1985 wreck through in front of the windscreen pillars and by joining the rear portion of a wrecked 1988 model BMW to the front portion of the 1985 wreck. The new composite vehicle was then sprayed the colour of the 1988 portion, namely dolphin grey, fitted with a gearbox supplied by the panel-beater and registered as a built-up car. The 1985 jet engine was modified to make it function like an engine of a 1988 model BMW. The police seized the built-up vehicle as a stolen vehicle in terms of the South African Criminal Procedure Act[9] which allows seizure of vehicles involved in a probable crime (theft) on behalf of the Minister of Law and Order.[10] Khan contended

6 See *Palmer* (fn. 1) 169 and 257 regarding South Africa and Scotland respectively.

7 1991, 3 SA, 439 (T).

8 The Concise Oxford dictionary defines a panel-beater as a workman who beats out metal panels of motor vehicles.

9 Act 51 of 1977.

10 In terms of S 20 (1) of the Criminal Procedure Act 51 of 1977, the State may seize an article which is concerned in or is on reasonable grounds believed to be concerned in the commission or suspected commission of an offence; which may afford evidence of the commission or suspected commission of an offence, or which is intended to be used or is on reasonable grounds believed to be intended to be used in the commission of an offence.

that the seizure was unlawful and claimed the return of the built-up BMW.[11] On evidence, it was found that the rear portion of the built-up BMW including the interior could positively be identified as having been stolen, but that the engine and inner panels were probably part of the 1985 BMW wreck bought by Khan.[12]

It was argued on behalf of Khan that the components and rear portion identified as having been stolen, had acceded to the applicant's car. The front part of the built-up car attracted the rear part of the car to it by accession and that Kahn was, therefore, the owner of the car and entitled to have the car returned to him. The court then proceeded to apply the doctrine of accession namely that where one movable is joined to another in such a manner as to form an entity, the owner of the principal thing becomes the owner also of the thing joined to it (the accessory). The court reasoned that the decision as to which of the components is the principal thing ordinarily is a matter of pure and simple common sense. Having reviewed the guidelines given by Van der Merwe,[13] several Roman-Dutch authorities[14] and applicable case law,[15] the court settled on the so-called identity test as the applicable test. In terms of this test, the component that by its character, form and function gives the composite entity its final identity must be considered the principal thing.[16] Applied to the facts of the present case, the court concluded that the built-up vehicle was a 1988 model, to which a 1985 engine modified to conform to a 1988 engine was added and to which small portions of a 1985 body were added. Under the circumstances, the car could not be said to be that of the applicant (Khan), due to the fact that the stolen parts were added to his 1985 wreck. The court emphasised that it happened the other way round: the rear part of the built-up car (which was in fact the stolen 1988

11 S 31(1) of the Criminal Procedure Act 51 of 1977 provides that if no criminal proceedings are instituted in connection with any article referred to in section 30 *(c)* or if it appears that such article is not required at the trial for purposes of evidence or for purposes of an order of court, the article shall be returned to the person from whom it was seized, if such person may lawfully possess such article, or, if such person may not lawfully possess such article, to the person who may lawfully possess it.

12 At 442 E.

13 *Cornelius G. van der Merwe,* Sakereg, Durban 1989^2, 230–231.

14 *Grotius* (fn. 2, Inleidinge) 2,9,1 as commented on by *Gerlach Scheltinga* (1708–1765), Dictata ad Grotium Inleidinge (manuscript 1752); *Voet* (fn. 2) D. 41,1,14 and *Huber* (fn. 2, Heedensdaegse Rechtgeleertheyt) 2,6,2. Interestingly, the court remarked that the criterion used by Grotius, namely *waerdiger*, could mean both, "more valuable" as well as "worthier" in the sense of that portion of the whole which gives the composite product its identity. He also pointed out that one of the examples given by Huber, namely the diamond added to the ring, clearly indicates that Huber applies, in essence, the character, form and function test.

15 "Cooper v Jordan" (1884) 4 EDC 181; "Doli v Mamkele" 1926 EDL 269; "Aldine Timber Co v Hlatwayo" 1932 TPD 337; "JL Cohen Motors (SWA) (Pty) Ltd v Alberts" 1985 (2) SA 427 (SWA).

16 At 443 B-D.

model) was the principal part which by its form, character and function gave the built-up car its identity.[17]

In an *obiter dictum*, the court remarked that it was not entirely certain that "Aldine Timber Co. v Hlatwayo"[18] (a decision of the Transvaal Provision Division of the Supreme Court) was not as argued by Van der Merwe and De Waal[19] rather a case of *specificatio* than of *accessio*. The facts of the case are as follows. The son of *Hlatwayo* was donated a stand in a black area of the town by his grandfather on which a movable wood and iron shed was erected. The father then pulled down the shed and proceeded to erect a new and larger building measuring 30 by 30 feet out of the materials so obtained together with new materials bought from Aldine Timber Co. for £121 on an installment sale. The new shed was more than twice as large as the old shed and the value of the new materials bought was far in excess of the value of the materials obtained from the old demolished shed. The father paid a deposit and some installments which left a deficit of £98. Aldine Timber Co. then attached the new shack and the son instituted interpleading proceedings for an order that the building was wrongfully attached. The court decided that the onus of proof was on the son to proof that the attachment was unlawful. The court then decided that the work done on the old material was not in the nature of *specificatio* because no new species has been created and the original article has not ceased to exist as such as in the case of turning grapes into wine and corn into bread. The court then applied the doctrine of accession and finding that the father did not intend to improve the son's property, held that the less valuable materials (£40) acceded to the more valuable materials (£121) and that the new building was, therefore, the property of the father. The court, therefore, decided that the son has not discharged the onus and that the property was executable.

III. Requirements for Accession of Movables

Accession as a mode of acquisition of ownership was not used in the *Corpus Iuris Civilis* but is a term coined by modern Romanists. The Romans followed by the Roman-Dutch authorities and the Scottish institutional writers, distinguished various

17 At 443 E-G. The court thus concluded on evidence that the composite vehicle was not a relatively expensive engine surrounded by panelling and the body of a 1988 BMW but rather a 1988 BMW in which a converted 1985 model engine was placed.

18 1932 TPD 337 at 341–342.

19 *Cornelius G. van der Merwe/Marius De Waal*, Accessio deur die verbinding van roerende sake in historiese perspektief, THRHR (Tydskrif vir Hedendaagse Romeins-Hollandse Reg, Journal of Contemporary Roman-Dutch Law) (1986) 66–70.

forms of joining movables belonging to different persons so as to form a composite thing namely *adjunctio* (welding a foot to a statue or a handle to a cup);[20] *textura* (weaving golden threads into a garment);[21] *ferruminatio*[22] (welding different metal objects together by using the same metal as opposed to *plumbatura*[23] soldering objects together); *scriptura* or *tabula* (writing on parchment)[24] and *pictura* (painting on canvas).[25] Interestingly there was a dispute among Roman jurists again taken over by Roman-Dutch and institutional Scottish writers as to whether *pictura* was a form of *accessio* or *specificatio.*[26]

The accepted requirements for accession of movables are the following:

First, there must be a physical or functional attachment of movables belonging to different persons in such a manner that the one is considered to become subsumed into the other.[27] The attachment must be such that physical separation is either impossible or impossible without causing serious damage to the property.[28] It is generally accepted that the aim of this rule is to preserve the economic entity created by the combination.

Second, it must be possible to distinguish between a principal component and an accessory.[29] Various factors have been used in the past to determine the principal component of the composite thing for instance value, bulk, whether the one is only a decoration of the other and whether the one cannot exist without the other. Ultimately is was accepted as in "Khan v Minister of Law and Order", that the component which due to its form, character and function gives the resulting combination or attachment its identity, must be considered the principal thing which subsumes the accessory attached to it.[30]

---

20 D. 6,1,23,5 Paul. 21 ed. (In Roman times the statues were of gold, silver, bronze or iron and not of marble).

21 Inst. 2,1,25; *Grotius* (fn. 2, Inleidinge) 2,10,4; *Van Leeuwen* (fn. 2, Roomsch Hollandsch Recht) 2,5,3; *Huber* (fn. 2, Heedensdaegse Rechtsgeleertheyt) 2,6,2; *Voet* (fn. 2) D. 41,1,22.

22 D. 41,1,26 pr. Paul. 14 Sab.; *Voet* (fn. 2) D. 41,1,27.

23 *Voet* (fn. 2) D. 41,1,27.

24 Gai. 2,77; Inst. 2,1,33; D. 6,1,23,3 Paul. 21 ed.; *Grotius* (fn. 2, Inleidinge) 2,8,3; *Van Leeuwen* (fn. 2, Roomsch Hollandsch Recht) 2,5,4; *Huber* (fn. 2, Heedensdaegse Rechtgeleertheyt) 2,6,7; *Voet* (fn. 2) D. 41,1,26; *Van der Keessel* (fn. 2, Praelectiones) 2,8,23 (*dubitante*).

25 D. 6,1,23,3 Paul. 21 ed.; *Grotius* (fn. 2, Inleidinge) 2,8,3; *Voet* (fn. 2) D. 41,1,26; *Van Leeuwen* (fn. 2, Roomsch Hollandsch Recht) 2,5,4 requires that the painter must act in good faith.

26 Inst. 2,1,34; *Van der Keessel* (fn. 2, Praelectiones) 2,8,3.

27 See for instance *Noodt* (fn. 2) 151: *Quotiens res mea tuam trahit per praevalentiam, dominum rei tuae extingui et ad me transire.*

28 *Stair* (fn. 4) II,I,39.

29 *Bell* (fn. 4, Principles) 1298 noted: "Of two things having intimate connection, the property of the principal draws after it that of the accessory; the only difficulty is to fix which is the principal."

30 D. 34,2,19,13 Ulp. 20 Sab. and D. 34,2,19,20 Ulp. 20 Sab.; *Van der Linden* (fn. 2) 1,7,2.

Fig. 2: Illustration of the scenario ;photo by Wade Lambert on Unsplash, markings by author. <https://unsplash.com/photos/XNpa4Er8N2o>

Third, the human effort involved in the attachment must not result in the production of a new entity (*specificatio*).

At this point, it seems appropriate to mention that it is generally accepted that good faith is not a requirement for acquisition of ownership by accession.[31] If A builds a stolen engine into his motor vehicle, he will become the owner of the engine. Bad faith therefore has no relevance other than to the question of compensation. The rationale for this result is eloquently stated by Huber[32] as "that the law wanted to avoid uncertainty of ownership with regard to the same thing".

IV. Scottish Case: "McDonald v Provan"

Now let us proceed to the Scottish case "McDonald v Provan".[33] In this case, Feldman or his associate had stolen a Ford vehicle from its true owner and had

31 *Stair* (fn. 4) II,I,39.

32 *Huber* (fn. 2, Heedensdaegse Rechtsgeleertheyt) 2,6,2: "Because the law wanted to avoid that uncertainty of ownership with regard to the same thing."

33 1960 SLT 231 at 262.

arranged to have the front part of the stolen Ford, including half the chassis, the engine and the gear box, welded to the rear portion of another Ford vehicle. He then sold the composite vehicle to Provan, a motor dealer (defendant, designated defender in Scots law) who acquired the built-up vehicle *bona fide*. Provan then sold the vehicle to McDonald (plaintiff, designated pursuer in Scots law). Some three months after the sale had been completed and the vehicle handed over, the police removed it from McDonald's possession as stolen property. McDonald then claimed damages from Provan primarily on the ground that Provan was in breach of the implied warranty of ownership under section 12 (1) of the Sale of Goods Act, 1893. Provan contended that the composite vehicle which they had sold was a new entity constructed and acquired by Feldman in terms of the doctrine of *specificatio* and having acquired the built-up vehicle free from the taint of theft, they had the right to sell it to McDonald. If so, it followed that Feldman was able to transmit the ownership of the composite vehicle to Provan and Provan, therefore, had a right to sell it to McDonald. They were consequently not in breach of the implied condition laid down in section 12 (1) of the Sale of Goods Act, 1893.

Lord President Clyde reasoned that Provan's case depended upon him being able to establish that Feldman's operations on the two vehicles resulted in law in the creation of a new entity free from any of the defects in title which affected either of the vehicles from which it was constructed. To achieve this result, Provan invoked the doctrine of *specificatio* adopted by the law of Scotland from Roman law. The doctrine deals with cases where a new species or object is created by some process of manufacture. On the authority of two Scottish institutional writers[34] Lord President Clyde then pointed out that a distinction must be drawn between two different kinds of manufacturing processes which in fact emphasises the requirement of irreducibility which must be complied with. He explains that if the manufactured object can be reduced once again to the materials or matter of which it was made, as for instance a tankard made of gold which can be melted down to raw gold again, the law regards the new product as still belonging to the owner of the original material although the form and shape of that original material had been altered. By contrast, where the manufactured object cannot be so reduced, as for instance wine made out of grapes, the property in the manufactured article belongs not to the owner of the grapes but to the maker of the wine. In applying the test of irreducibility to the facts of the present case, Lord President Clyde concluded:

34 *Stair* (fn. 4) II,I,41 and *Erskine* (fn. 4, Institute) II,I,16.

> *Prima facie* at least if a vehicle can be constructed by welding together the front half of one vehicle and the rear half of another, it would appear to be equally practicable to cut them into two once more. If so, the defenders could not successfully contend that Mr Feldman created a new entity which wholly belonged to him as its maker.[35]

Lord President Clyde then moved on to two further requirements for *specificatio*. First he assumed in favour of Provan that Feldman complied with the requirement that a *nova species* must have been created by Feldman. He assumed that Feldman had indeed created a new product by using stolen material and in addition material to which he had some right. This brought him to dwell upon the requirement of *bona fides*. He explained that *specificatio* is an equitable doctrine which on the authority of the Scottish institutional writer Bell[36] can only be invoked where there is complete *bona fides* on the part of the manufacturer. In the present case Lord President Clyde concluded that the manufacturer was not constructing the new vehicle in *bona fide*. On the contrary, a substantial portion of it was stolen by Feldman from its rightful owner. This in itself excluded the doctrine of *specificatio* and confirmed the other well-established principle of Scots law whereby the true owner of stolen property is entitled to follow and to recover his property into whomever's hands it may have landed.[37] Consequently, Provan never acquired ownership in the composite vehicle and was thus not in the position of having an unqualified right to sell it to the pursuer. Provan, therefore, acted in breach of the implied warranty of ownership under section 12 (1) of the Sale of Goods Act, 1893.

V. Requirements for Specification Revisited

In this section, the requirements for *specificatio* some of which were touched upon by Lord President Clyde will be assessed critically. To start with it is appropriate to mention that the term *specificatio* is a contraction of the Roman phrase *speciem ferre*, used for various instances where goods with a new identity were produced from raw material belonging to third persons. The term specification was first coined in the *Brachylogus*, a textbook for students based mainly on Justinian's Institutes compiled during the 12th century before the time of the glossators.[38] The

35 At 232.

36 *Bell* (fn. 4, Principles) 1298.

37 *Bell* (fn. 4, Principles) 1318.

38 See *Hermann Fitting*, Über die sogenannte Turiner Institutionenglosse und den sogenannten Brachylogus, Halle 1870, reprint Amsterdam 1967, 39.

first requirement which was assumed by Lord President Clyde to be present in "McDonald v Provan", was that a *nova species* or a product with a new identity must have been manufactured by the maker.[39] In Scots law, it has been accepted that a product with a new identity must have been produced which is so different that it can no longer be vindicated by the owner of the raw materials.[40] Mere repairs of a motor vehicle or the restoration of a painting would not constitute a *nova species*. Thus repairing a ship constantly with new planks until the entire ship has been renovated would not constitute a *nova species*. There must have been some creative labour on the materials which gives the worked over materials a new identity. Initially, it was assumed that a new species is only created if a thing with a new name has emerged. In recent times it has been realised that this is not necessarily the case and in a German decision of the Appeal Court of Cologne it was decided that a motor cycle assembled from different parts of old motor cycles constituted a new thing compared to its constituent parts. The motor cycle produced was a new model and needed special authorisation of the Technical Inspection Agency.[41] On the analogy of this case, it can be argued that the production of the 1988 model BMW from the materials of the 1985 wreck and the 1988 wreck indeed produced a *nova species*.[42] Similarly, the production of a new Ford model from the materials of the two Ford wrecks and the production of a new iron and wooden shed from the demolished old shed and new materials bought from Aldine Timber Co. indeed constituted a new species.[43] The first requirement as assumed by Lord President Clyde was thus complied with.

---

39 For a detailed discussion of this requirement see *Cornelius van der Merwe*, Nova species. Roman Legal Tradition 2 (2004) 96–114. This was expertly supplemented by *Ernest Metzger*, Acquisition of Living Things by Specification, Edinburgh Law Review 8 (2004) 115–118.

40 *David L. Carey Miller/David Irvine*, Corporeal Moveables in Scots Law, Edinburgh 2005², 87 citing "Northwest Securities Ltd v Barrhead Coachworks" 1976 SC 68 at 72 in support.

41 OLG Köln, Decision of 23. August 1996 – 11 U 39/96 – juris, *Oberlandesgericht Köln* (Higher Regional Court Cologne) 1996, NJW 1997, 2187–2188. See at par 7: "Vor diesem Hintergrund wurde im vorliegenden Fall durch den Zusammenbau des Motorrads aus den verschiedensten Einzelteilen eine neue Sache hergestellt. Dies zeigt sich unter anderem daran, dass unstreitig das vom Streitverkündeten zusammenmontierte Motorrad 'wie ein neues Modell' einer besonderen TÜV-Zulassung bedarf. In dem im Strafverfahren eingeholten Gutachten wird das Motorrad nämlich als 'Eigenbau' im zulassungsrechtlichen Sinne qualifiziert. Das individuell zusammengebaute Motorrad hat eine ganz andere wirtschaftliche Qualität als die Summe der losen Einzelteile. Die Trennung der eingebauten Teile würde zur Zerstörung eines funktionstüchtigen Motorrads führen, das gerade durch die besondere Zusammensetzung seiner Bestandteile seinen individuellen Charakter gewonnen hat. Der Kläger hat […] zutreffend darauf hingewiesen, dass in den einschlägigen Käuferkreisen gerade der unverwechselbare Eigenbau aus 'Harley-Davidson'-Teilen besondere Wertschätzung genießt."

42 See *Van der Merwe and De Waal* (fn. 19) 69–70.

43 See the facts of "Khan v Minister of law and Order", "McDonald v Provan" and "Aldine Timber

The second requirement is a relic of the *media sententia* probably adopted by Justinian to reconcile the views of the law schools of the Sabinians and the Proculians. The Sabinians were of the opinion that the essence of a thing consists in the *matter* or raw material of which the thing is made, while the Proculians held the view that the essence of a thing is constituted by its *form*. The reconciliation of these points of view, led to an acceptance of the so-called middle opinion of Justinian and framed the reducibility test. This test involves that if the final product is reducible to its former raw material constituents, the final product would remain the property of the owner of the materials whereas if it is not so reducible the maker would acquire the final product by *specificatio*. The easy acceptance by Lord President Clyde that the new composite Ford can easily be reduced to its former constituents by cutting them apart again, does not fit in with the Roman law examples of goblets, a tankard or a plate produced from someone else's gold or other precious metals which can easily be melted down to its original materials. A further argument against Lord President Clyde is that the Institutes of Justinian, echoed by some *ius commune* writers, stipulates that if a new thing is produced partly from the material of the producer and partly form the material of a third party, the new article would be awarded to the producer thereof even if the materials were easily reducible to their former state.[44] Finally the requirement of irreducibility based upon outdated concepts of Greek philosophy, has been discarded by most European Civil Codes in favour of a criterion based either on the increased value of the final product as compared to the value of the original raw materials or the amount of labour put into the production by the producer.[45]

Company v Hlatwayo" above. See also the following passage in OLG Cologne, Decision of 23. August 1996 at par 8: "Der Rahmen des Motorrads kann nicht als Hauptsache im Sinne dieser Bestimmung angesehen werden. Dies folgt schon daraus, dass der Wert des Rahmens gegenüber dem des gesamten Motorrads eine untergeordnete Bedeutung hat. Nach der Verkehrsanschauung ändert der Austausch dieses Rahmens das Motorrad nicht soweit, dass eine vollkommen neue Sache entsteht. Denn zulassungsrechtlich müsste beim Einbau eines neuen Rahmens diesem die Fahrgestellnummer des Motorrads gegeben werden, in das er eingebaut wird."

44 Inst. 2,1,25; *Theophilus* ad Justinian 2,1,25; *Voet* (fn. 2) *D.* 41,1,21: This occurs when a person has made a new species partly from his own and partly from another's material, say mead from wine and another's honey or a garment from his own and another's wool, the new species then belongs to the maker whether or not it can be brought back to the former material. *Harald Elbert*, Die Entwicklung der Spezifikation im Humanismus, Naturrecht und Usus modernus, Cologne 1969, 64, note 1 cites eighteen authorities, *inter alia*: *Joachim Mynsinger* (1514–1588), Apotelesma (1633) scholia: b ad Inst., 2,1 § *quod si partem; Samuel Strykius* (1640–1710), Specimen usus moderni (1729), Continuatio IV Lib. XLI Tit. 1 § XXIV.

45 This has been explained in an erudite article by *Douglas J. Osler*, Specificatio in Scots Law, in: The Civil Law Tradition in Scotland, ed. *Robin Evans-Jones*, Edinburgh 1995, 100–127.

The third requirement also recognised by Lord President Clyde is *bona fides*.[46] In "McDonald v Provan" Lord President Clyde argued that Mr Feldman did not construct the built-up Ford in *bona fide* due to the fact that a substantial portion of it was stolen property. This excluded the doctrine of *specificatio* and introduced the other well-established principle of Scots law whereby the true owner of stolen property is entitled to follow and to recover his property into whomever's hands it may have gone.[47] The idea is that a *vitium reale* (an indelible blemish) attaches to the property which prevents it from being acquired in ownership except by the original owner.[48]

The fourth requirement is that the producer must have acted in his own name (*suo nomine*) and not on behalf of another (*alieno nomine*). In the event that the producer produces the new entity on behalf of another, the person on whose behalf he or she has acted, would acquire the new object by *specificatio*. This is exactly what happened in "Khan v Minister of Law and Order". The panel-beater did not produce the 1988 BMW in his own name but in the name of Khan who commissioned him to put together a new built-up 1988 BMW.

VI. Arguments against the Requirement of Good Faith for Acquisition of Ownership by *specificatio*

In my opinion several arguments can be advanced against *bona fides* being a requirement for acquisition of ownership by *specificatio*. Firstly, it is accepted that *bona fides* was not a requirement for *specificatio* in Roman law. Neither Gaius' nor Justinian's Institutes mentioned it as a requirement, something so crucial that one would have expected it to be mentioned in textbooks for students. Furthermore, the owner of the materials is not awarded any of the proprietary remedies for recovery of his material. Although one text mentioned that the *actio*

46 For a detailed discussion of the requirement of *bona fides*, see *Cornelius G. van der Merwe*, A Re-Assessment of the Requirements of Specificatio, in: Northern Lights. Essays in Private Law in Memory of Professor David Carey Miller, eds. *Douglas Bain* et al., Aberdeen 2018, 217–243.

47 *Bell* (fn. 4, Principles) 1318.

48 The counter-argument is put forward in the OLG Cologne Decision of 23. August 1996 – 11 U 39/96 – juris par 13: "Der Kläger vermag nicht mit seiner Auffassung durchzudringen, der Verarbeitung komme allein deshalb kein Wert zu, weil die Einzelteile angeblich gestohlen worden sind. § 950 BGB ermöglicht vielmehr nach allgemeiner Auffassung auch den Eigentumserwerb an gestohlenen Sachen (BGHZ 55, 176 [178]; Staudinger-Gursky, BGB, 13. Auflage, § 950 Rn. 16). Der originäre Eigentumserwerb durch Verarbeitung tritt unabhängig davon ein, ob der Hersteller bösgläubig ist oder abhanden gekommene Einzelteile verarbeitet hat (BGH MDR 1989, 989). Auch auf einen rechtsgeschäftlichen Erwerbswillen des Herstellers kommt es nicht an."

ad exhibendum could be instituted for recovery of the value of the materials, this text could be explained in a different way as only the erstwhile owner being entitled to institute such an action.[49] On the contrary various personal remedies based on theft, unjustified enrichment and even delict could be brought by the owner of the materials who suffered damage or loss on account of his or her materials being transformed into something new which can no longer be vindicated. Secondly, of the Scots institutional writers there are only Bell[50] and William Forbes[51] who accept unequivocally that 'if the materials, as a separate existence, be destroyed *bona fide*, the property is with the workman' without explaining why *bona fides* is required. The rest of the institutional writers, for example Stair[52] and Erskine[53], are equivocal about the requirement of *bona fides*. Again, the majority of Roman-Dutch authorities, amongst others Grotius,[54] Vinnius[55] and Van der Keessel[56], accept *bona fides* as a requirement for acquisition of ownership by *specificatio*. The only Roman-Dutch author who attempts to explain why this is so is Noodt[57] who declares: the *mala fide* producer is not allowed to profit from his dishonesty (*improbitate sua*). On the contrary Johannes Voet[58] states clearly that in the case of *specificatio* good or bad faith does not affect the question of ownership and that only the remedies differ. Voet explains:

> (I)t does not matter whether he was in good or bad faith and thought the material to be his own, or was aware that it was another's. In both cases he is rendered owner of the new type, for the reason that a thing is so changed that it cannot be brought back to its former material is understood as having been wiped out. Good or bad faith on the part

49 D. 10,4,12,3 Paul. 26 ed. See *Van der Merwe* (fn. 46) at fn. 74–77.

50 *Bell* (fn. 4, Principles) 1298.

51 Professor of Law at the University of Glasgow (1714–1746), Great body of the Law of Scotland.

52 *Stair* (fn. 4) II,I,41.

53 *Erskine* (fn. 4, Principles) II,I,16 argues that where the new species cannot be reduced to its former constituents, there is no room for the legal fiction that the former subjects are still taken to exist; as in wine, which, as it cannot again be turned into the grapes of which it was made, becomes the property not of the owner of the grapes but of the maker of the wine. This implies that the effect of specification is for ownership to pass to the producer as a matter of proprietary consequence. See also *Carey Miller/Irvine* (fn. 40) 90.

54 *Grotius*, (fn. 2, Inleidinge) 2,8,2.

55 *Vinnius*, (fn. 2) 2,1,25, note 2.

56 *Van der Keessel* (fn. 2, Praelectiones) 2,8,2.

57 *Noodt* (fn. 2) 247: *Eum recte de improbitate sua lucrum facere & accipere actionem quam non habuit, non oportet.*

58 *Voet* (fn. 2) D. 41,1,21.

of the maker cannot have the effect that the actual former thing appears to a greater or lesser degree to be still in existence.[59]

With regard to the difference in actions, Voet declares that maker in good faith can only be sued by the *actio in factum* under the Aquilian law as one who has caused the loss by his negligence; whereas the maker in bad faith is also held liable in the penal and personal actions based on theft as well as the *actio ad exhibendum* for fraudulently ceasing to possess the material of the owner of the material.[60]

A third argument against requiring *bona fides* for acquisition of ownership by *specificatio* is that *bona fides* is not a requirement according to any of the three rationales which figure as bases for the acquisition of ownership by means of *specificatio*.[61] In terms of the accession theory which holds that the matter or raw materials as accessory accedes to the form as principal,[62] *specificatio* is classified by some Roman-Dutch writers as industrial accession. Once classified as a form of accession, we have seen that *bona fides* does not figure as a requirement for acquisition of ownership. According to the occupation theory, the matter from which the final product was reduced has perished once it had been changed into another species. The new product is thus a *res nullius* susceptible of being acquired by the first taker. Even though there are difficulties with the occupation theory,[63] it is clear that *bona fides* on the part of the first taker is not required. According to the production or labour theory, the maker acquires the final product due to the labour, toil and workmanship skills put into producing the new product. A corollary to this theory is that the workman should be rewarded for the time and skills put into creating the product by the acquisition of ownership in the final product. This gave rise to the theory being designated the reward theory. This theory does not derive from Roman law since labour as such was

59 Translation by *Percival Gane*, The Selective Voet, Vol 6, Durban 1957, 204–205. This accords with the reasoning that the object has been altered to such an extent that it can no longer be vindicated by the owner of the raw matter. The unethical production of the new entity does not affect the proprietary consequence that the maker becomes the owner of the new entity.

60 *Voet* (fn. 2) D. 41,1,21.

61 For the various rationales advanced as basis for the acquisition of ownership by specification, see *Van der Merwe* (fn. 46) 218–230.

62 The main objection to this theory is that it is unacceptable that corporeal substances such as raw materials can be attached to an incorporeal entity such as form so as to produce a new composite object.

63 One difficulty with this theory is that the maker never consciously takes possession with the intention of becoming the owner and that in long fabrication processes the maker may not be the first on the scene to occupy the final product. The other difficulty is that the sources only speak of virtual or quasi destruction and not total destruction of the substance of the raw material.

not highly regarded due to the fact that it was mostly performed by slaves. It has been criticised on the ground that not all labour for instance the repair of a motor vehicle and the dyeing of wool are rewarded in this manner. Even so it is acknowledged that the ethical value of manual labour has been glorified since the time of Adam and Eve who had to toil for their food on the sweat of their brows after they had been banished from paradise. And this ethical force of labour has been reinforced by the puritanical writings of Calvin and political philosophers like Locke. Even after the Industrial Revolution mankind was exhorted to work with the machinery and in the succeeding ages the labour theory gained pre-eminence in Socialist and Communist philosophy.[64] But at some stage there was a movement towards rewarding only honest labour on the principle that no one should be allowed to benefit from his own wrongdoings. Even so, the labour theory does not shy away from rewarding even the *mala fide* producer with the ownership of the final product.

A final argument against requiring *bona fides* for the acquisition of ownership by *specificatio*, is the fact that the *Motive* and the *Protokolle* accompanying the drafts of the German Civil Code contain sound reasons why *bona fides* should not be so retained. The central argument is that in order to preserve freedom and unrestricted commerce in goods, the producer should be awarded ownership of the goods even if he has produced them *mala fide*. The producer who is perceived by the general public as the owner in accordance with the publicity principles is in the most favourable position to use and deal with the goods.[65] As commerce treats goods which have been transformed by specification as new, it is theoretically justified that ownership in the new product should vest in the producer. To make the proprietary consequences of *specificatio* dependent on subjective elements such as good faith, creates uncertainty in commerce. *Specificatio* differs from the reasons underlying acquisition by prescription which calls for exceptional protection of the owner of stolen property. This is not needed in the case of acquisition by specification. Furthermore, to require good faith for *specificatio* can lead to unfair practical results as in the case of a painter who in a moment of inspiration uses the canvas of another to produce a splendid painting. Again, the owner of the material may not actually want to become the owner of the final product for instance where a kite is made of an expensive damask table cloth stolen from its owner. Finally, the owner of the material is adequately protected by the remedies awarded to him or her namely a claim for unjustified

64 See *Hans-Dietrich Müller*, Wie verhält sich der § 950 BGB zu dem Satz, dass jeder Arbeiter Eigentümer des Arbeitsproduktes werden soll?, Jena 1930, 102.

65 Motive zum Entwurf eines BGB für das Deutsche Reich, Band III Sachenrecht, Berlin 1888, 361.

enrichment and a delictual claim for losses suffered for being deprived of the possession and ownership of his or her materials.[66]

VII. Conclusion: Back to the Requirements of Specification

I would accept the first rule of the "Draft Common Frame of Reference" which states that the producer of new goods out of materials owned by another becomes the owner of the new goods.[67] But I would stop there. I would not qualify this rule by taking account of the relative value of the materials and the workmanship involved in the production of the new entity or the *bona fides* of the parties. I do not accept the reversibility test embodied in the *media sententia*, because this compromise solution introduced by Justinian is based on Greek philosophical ideas about the essence of matter and form. I also do not accept the relative value test initiated by Connanus which replaced the reversibility test in modern European codifications with variations on the role played by value of the matter and of the workmanship involved.[68] My main criticism here is that these nuances force jurisdictions to select either the craftsman or the owner of the matter as the owner of the final product. As such selection can be difficult and disputed, this flies in the face of the purpose of the law of property to clearly identify the holders of property rights in goods so as to promote certainty in commercial transactions. Once a *nova species* is created, it should automatically go the producer, irrespective of the value of the raw materials or the value of the labour involved.

With regard to the question of *bona fides*, one has to conclude that the historical controversy surrounding this issue has left us with an uncertain outcome. I have already set out the arguments in favour of relinquishing the requirement of *bona fides*. In my opinion the most persuasive argument is that in the interest of legal certainty one has to allocate the *nova species*, which is recognised as a new individualised object in commercial traffic to the person who has the

66 Protokolle der Kommission für die zweite Lesung des Entwurfs eines BGB, bearbeitet von *Alexander Achilles / F. Albert Gebhard/Peter Spahn*, Berlin 1897–1899[3], 646; *Friedrich Ebert*, Die Verarbeitung fremder Stoffe, Jena 1914, 59–60. See further *Van der Merwe* (fn. 46) 240–242.

67 Principles, Definitions and Model Rules of European Private Law (DCFR), eds. *Christian Bar/Erich Clive*, Munich 2019, 5:059 VIII – 5:201(1).

68 See *Bell* (fn. 4, Commentaries) I 276. See also I 295 note 1: "Neither the system of the Proculeiani, nor that of the Sabiniani, nor the middle opinion of Justinian's lawyers, have been universally approved abroad. […] It was not to be expected that a rule founded on this kind of subtlety should be tamely acquiesced in by modern nations, to whom the Roman law was rather a fountain than a code of law", (The emphasis is my own.).

closest connection with the new entity namely the producer, irrespective of his or her *bona* or *mala fides*. The attribution of the consequences of production to the producer is based on the need of the law of property for legal certainty as to ownership and thus the immediate release of the *nova species* into commercial traffic.

In the light of the foregoing, it is unfortunate that the advocate arguing on behalf of Khan in "Khan v Minister of Law and Order" did not base his case on acquisition of ownership of the 1988 built-up BMW on *specificatio*. He could have argued that the fact that the *nova species* into which the wrecks of the two BMW's were transformed still produced an entity with the same name, namely a BMW, does not mean that an object with a new identity has not been formed. Again, he could have relied on the passage of Johannes Voet to show that it was not generally accepted in Roman-Dutch law that *bona fides* was a requirement for acquisition of ownership by specification. Similarly, one could argue that in "McDonald v Provan" Lord President Clyde correctly assumed that a *nova species* had been formed, that he erroneously applied the irreversibility test to a situation that does not fit the Roman examples, that he should have taken into account that the Scottish institutional writers did not unequivocally support the requirement of *bona fides* and that he should have been mindful of the fact that support for *bona fides* would undermine the legal certainty on which modern commerce is based.

As far as the rationale for awarding the final product to the *specificans* is concerned, changing modern circumstances have eclipsed the labour theory. Today goods are seldom produced by single craftsmen. The distillation of grapes into wine is managed by major distilleries, while large-scale factories specialise in the mass production of bulk commodities. In assembly-line production the labour produced by humans is mostly an insignificant part of the production process, overshadowed by the role of machinery and the capital investment of the entrepreneur in establishing suitable conditions for the production process. The crucial question now is: Who is the producer?

This brings us now to the requirement that the new entity must have been produced *suo nomine*.[69] It stands to reason that the tailor or seamstress who receives a commission from a large factory to fashion cloth into garments would not acquire ownership in the garments they produce, but that the producer

69 The following Digest texts deal with *suo nomine*: D. 41,1,7,7 Gai. 2 cott.; D. 12,1,31,1 Paul. 17 Plaut. and D. 41,1,25 Call. 2 inst. For numerous references to *suo nomine* in the *ius commune* see *Elbert* (fn. 44) 169–172. See also *Ben Stoop*, Non solet locatio dominium mutare: Some Remarks on Specification in Classical Roman Law, Tijdschrift voor Rechtsgeschiedenis, 66 (1998) 3–24.

would be the factory.[70] The *suo nomine* requirement could even supply an answer to the case where the parties addressed the question of ownership in the transaction giving rise to the production. A typical modern scenario is where the supplier of goods or materials (for example a saw mill or wine farmer) has contracted with the buyer (a furniture factory or a distillery) on the basis that, pending full payment of the purchase price, the seller's (saw mill or wine farmer's) title in the goods (timbers or grapes) will be retained in anything made or produced (furniture or wine) by the buyer.[71] In such a situation one might have to conclude that the factory or distillery was, in fact, producing not *suo nomine* but *alieno nomine* on behalf of the saw mill or the farmer.[72] This shows that one must be very wise in adjusting the idyllic examples of Roman law to the practicalities of modern commerce.[73]

70 *Jean Sonnekus*, Opbou van motorwrakke, *accessio* en *specificatio*, Tydskrif vir die Suid-Afrikaanse Reg (1991) 706–11.

71 *Carey Miller/Irvine* (fn. 40) 85–86. This question was raised in "Kinloch Damph Ltd v Nordvik Salmon Farms Ltd" Outer House, Court of Session, 30 June 1999 unreported, commented on by *Ernest Metzger* (fn. 39) 118.

72 This would have serious repercussions if completed furniture or distilled wine is still on the site when the factory or the distillery goes bankrupt.

73 The author gratefully acknowledges the financial assistance of the South African National Research Foundation for my research projects. A special note of gratitude is also due to the Scottish MacCormick Fellowship programme and the German Alexander von Humboldt Foundation for making it possible for me to conduct research on original modes of acquisition of property at Edinburgh Law School and the Max Planck Institute for Comparative and Private International Law in Hamburg during the European summers of 2013 and 2014 respectively and finally to John Townsend, my former assistant student at the University of Aberdeen, who improved the readability of the text.

PART TWO: ROMAN LAW IN MODERN LEGAL REASONING

Frits Brandsma, Groningen

Law in Daily Life

Parking Fines and Roman Law

I. Introduction

On April 15th, 2013 at 2.29 p.m., a man with the unfortunate name of Beavis parked his vehicle in a car park called the "Riverside Retail Park" in Chelmsford, a town north-east of London. The car park was managed by ParkingEye Ltd. for its owner British Airways Pension Fund. At the entrance of the car park, as well as at around twenty other places on the property, signs had been placed. These stated that the maximum allowed parking time on the car park was two hours – and a maximum of four hours for members of the fitness centre. In case of a violation of the permitted parking time, a so-called parking charge of £85 was levied. Mr Beavis returned to the car park after two hours and fifty-six minutes. Mr Barry Beavis was the owner of a fish and chip shop called "The Happy Haddock" and is unlikely to have been a member of the fitness centre. Therefore, he had parked for almost one hour longer than was permitted. ParkingEye was able to obtain Beavis' name and address from the Driver and Vehicle Licensing Agency. A demand was sent to Beavis' address for the payment of £85. However, he did not pay the fine, not even after he received a reminder. Subsequently, ParkingEye started proceedings in the County Court. Normally, the claim would be dealt with in the so-called small claims procedure, but because Beavis raised a number of objections on principle, the case was transferred to the Designated Civil Judge for East Anglia, Judge Moloney QC. Judge Moloney rejected Beavis' objection.[1] Like other people with objections on principle, Beavis did not stop here but appealed.[2] The three justices of the Court of Appeal also saw no reason to find in Beavis' favour. Therefore, the case of a parking fine of £85 ended up in front of no fewer than seven members of the United Kingdom Supreme Court.

---

1 In an 'unreported judgment' dated May 19th 2014 in Chelmsford County Court (according to the Court of Appeal; the digital version of the judgment calls it Cambridge County Court), to be found at: http://www.debtrecoveryplus.co.uk/debtor/ParkingEye v Beavis and Wardley Judgment.pdf (11/5/2017); see also http://www.parkingcowboys.co.uk/wp-content/uploads/2014/11/Judgment_1905-OCRD_2.pdf (3/1/2019).

2 ParkingEye Limited – and – Barry Beavis, [2015] EWCA Civ 402, [2015] WLR(D) 190.

Usually, the Supreme Court decides cases with just five members, but in cases, which possibly demand decisions to be made based on principle, a chamber of seven members can be installed.

The oral consideration of the case "ParkingEye vs. Beavis" took place on 21, 22 and 23 July 2015. Mr Beavis had travelled to London by train, because – as he said – "I wasn't going to pay to park." On the 4th of November 2015, the Supreme Court rendered its judgment.[3] The court again did not find in Beavis' favour, in a judgment of no less than 123 pages.[4] Six members of the Court formed a clear majority. One member gave a dissenting opinion. Beavis' principal objection concerned the penal character of the amount that ParkingEye demanded of him. The English law was indeed rather strict with regards to penalty clauses in agreements. The court seized the opportunity to revise the rules regarding penalty clauses in English law. The first sentence speaks for itself: "The penalty rule in England is an ancient haphazardly constructed edifice which has not weathered well."[5]

II. Law in Daily Life

It is in these kinds of everyday matters that important legal questions can be hidden. I have had the privilege to be taught by professors who knew how to employ these everyday matters in their teachings of Roman law. With just one such example, they would bring a legal doctrine to life to their students. They had a predecessor in this, and a prominent one, Rudolf von Jhering. In 1870, Jhering published "Die Jurisprudenz des täglichen Lebens" and this volume was reprinted again and again.[6] In the introduction, Jhering noted the following regarding the purpose of his work:[7]

> "Im täglichen Leben kommen viele Rechtsverhältnisse und Rechtsgeschäfte vor, die wegen der Geringfügigkeit des Gegenstandes kaum je zu einem Prozess führen, die sich

---

3 "ParkingEye Limited v Beavis": 162 Con LR 1, [2015] 3 WLR 1373, [2015] UKSC 67, [2016] AC 1172, [2016] 1 Lloyd's Rep 55, [2016] CILL 3769, [2016] RTR 8, [2016] BLR 1, [2015] WLR(D) 439.

4 The judgment also covers "Cavendish Square Holding BV v Talal El Makdessi".

5 Cf. on this case also *Frits Brandsma*, Beavis zonder Butt-Head, Groninger Opmerkingen en Mededelingen XXXIV (2017) 3.

6 At that time part of *Rudolf von Jhering*, Civilrechtsfälle ohne Entscheidungen, Jena 1870. The first separate edition is *idem* (ed.), Die Jurisprudenz des täglichen Lebens, Jena 1873. The last edition, revised by *Paul Oertmann*, is of 1927^{15}.

7 *Von Jhering* (fn. 6) Jena 1873^{2}, III.

aber gleichwohl für den juristischen Unterricht mit hohem Nutzen verwenden lassen, weil sie dem Anfänger Anleitung geben, auch die Vorfälle des gewöhnlichen Lebens mit juristischem Auge zu betrachten."

"In daily life, many legal relations and legal acts take place that, due to the trivial nature of the matter, will never lead to a trial, but that one can very well use for legal education because they guide the novice in how to view the events of daily life in a legal perspective." Jhering had not anticipated the case of Mr Beavis, who, despite the "trivial nature of the matter" chose to fight his case in front of a judge. We are grateful to Barry Beavis and others who fight for their principles.[8]

What was the matter in the Beavis case? How could Beavis' parking and the fine that was imposed on him for overstaying be legally qualified? Not a lot of thought was given to this in the judgment of the Supreme Court, although an extensive and interesting discussion was held on this during the oral treatment of the case. For further details on this matter I refer interested readers to YouTube where the United Kingdom Supreme Court posts videos of oral treatment of cases and oral judgments.[9] Practically all judges that were involved in the case assumed that by parking, Barry Beavis had entered into a contract with ParkingEye and that the regulations on the signs in the car park applied. It was not the first time English judges applied a contractual theory to parking in a car park. Lord Denning, for instance, used his literary gifts to describe the parking of Mr Thornton – "a free-lance trumpeter of the highest quality" – at a multi-storey automatic car park where a ticket was issued by an automatic machine.

> The customer pays his money and gets a ticket. He cannot refuse it. He cannot get his money back. He may protest to the machine, even swear at it. But it will remain unmoved. He is committed beyond recall. He was committed at the very moment when he put his money into the machine. The contract was concluded at that time. It can be translated into offer and acceptance in this way: the offer is made when the proprietor of the machine holds it out as being ready to receive the money. The acceptance takes place when the customer puts his money into the slot.[10]

---

8 Another principled man is Sven Klaus Tederahn, whose parking debt of around € 13,15 led to a preliminary ruling by the Second Chamber of the Court of Justice of the European Union on the 9th of March 2017: ECLI:EU:C:2017:193. He is still pursuing, no doubt, his case in the courts of Croatia. Cf. e. g. *Burkhard Hess*, Factual Contracts in European Law? Critical Reflections on the Conclusions of AG Bobek of October 27, 2016 in Case C-551/15 Pula Parking/Tederahn, on <conflictoflaws.net/2016> (11/5/2017).

9 See <https://www.youtube.com/user/UKSupremeCourt> (11/5/2017).

10 "Thornton v Shoe Lane Parking Ltd.", Court of Appeal, 18 December 1970, [1971] 2 Q.B. 163, at 169.

The parties themselves in the Beavis case also assumed a contract had been entered into and Beavis had a good reason to do so. However, one member of the Court of Appeal doubted that this was the correct premise for the case and wondered whether it was not rather a matter of giving permission by or for the landowner to enter the property for a maximum of two hours.[11] After the expiry of this period, the stay on the property would be contrary to the will of the owner and result in trespass, a wrongful act that required compensation. In that case the fine would have been problematic, because ParkingEye could not prove it had suffered a loss. The company itself was not the owner of the car park.

III. The Hamburg Car Park-Case

Already in 1956, a similar case had been discussed in much more detail by the German *Bundesgerichtshof* in the so-called "*Hamburger Parkplatzfall*" (the case of the Hamburg car park).[12] In 1953, the Hanseatic city of Hamburg had earmarked part of the city hall square as a car park. The city had entitled a Hamburg businessman to have the car park guarded against a fee to be paid by the parking public. The parking spaces were delineated by white lines on the city hall square and were indicated by signs with the inscription "*parkgeldpflichtig und bewacht*" ("parking fee is to be charged and parking spaces are guarded"), a somewhat shorter notice than that on ParkingEye's signs. The German counterpart to Barry Beavis was a lady of whom we, unfortunately, do not know the name, because the tendency of making the parties anonymous already existed in German court judgments at the time. She parked her vehicle in the car park several times between the 3rd of September and the 12th of October 1953. Every time, she told the employees of the German businessman who guarded the car park that her vehicle did not need to be guarded and that she refused to pay. The parking fee amounted to 20 Pfennigs for the first hour, 30 for the second hour and 50 Pfennigs for each subsequent hour. The businessman demanded payment of 25 DM. Still the woman refused to pay. She clearly had some principles of her own. The businessman went to court and based his claim on three, or rather two, legal grounds. If it could not be said that there was a contract – he did not believe there was –, then the defendant would have been unlawfully enriched with the amount demanded. Or, because *Frau* Beavis had parked her vehicle at the car park, the opportunity to make the parking space available to other users who were willing to pay would have been unlawfully taken away

11 *Lord Justice Moore-Bick*, (fn. 2) nr 23.

12 BGH, 14 July 1956 – V ZR 223/54. BGHZ 21, 319; NJW 1956, 1475.

from the businessman. The case went to the *Landgericht* (County Court) *Hamburg* that found in favour of the businessman and the *Oberlandesgericht* (Court of Appeals) *Hamburg* that found in favour of the woman. The case ended in the German *Bundesgerichtshof* (Supreme Court).

This court rejected the claim of an unlawful act – a delict or tort – because the plaintiff should have delivered proof that he had had to reject other users who were willing to pay because the parking space was used by the defendant. The claim of unlawful enrichment encountered the objection that the enrichment of the defendant did not match the requested amount, that it was hard to establish – for instance, how much petrol had she saved by not having to park elsewhere – and the enrichment had to have been at the expense of the plaintiff.

IV. "The not Unrealistic Road": Contract

That left the contractual basis, which the plaintiff hardly had chosen because he did not believe it could be successful. The Court considered that the search for a solution to the dispute in other ways than the contractual one would lead to results that were "*wirklichkeitsfremd*" ("unrealistic"). However, for the not unrealistic option, the Court needed four paragraphs, given more or less as *obiter dicta*, because the plaintiff himself did not expect much from that option. Whether the way the Court went about the case was or was not *wirklichkeitsfremd*, I will leave for you to decide. It mentioned a contractual relationship, although it did not assume a contract through an agreement of the parties. It mentioned "*faktische Vertragsverhältnisse*" ("actual contractual relations"). The doctrine of actual contractual relations was developed by Haupt at the beginning of the twentieth century because of the tram railways.[13] That case was the first one that Jhering presented in his *Jurisprudenz des täglichen Lebens*: "Um nach der Eisenbahn zu fahren, steigen wir in einen an unserer Wohnung vorüberfahrenden Wagen der Strassenbahn, ohne ein Wort zu verlieren. Hat dies Einsteigen eine juristische Bedeutung und welche?"[14] ("To travel to the railways, we board

13 *Günter Haupt*, Über faktische Vertragsverhältnisse, in: Festschrift der Leipziger Juristenfakultät für Heinrich Siber zum 10. April 1940, Vol II, Leipzig 1941, 5 ff. Cf. *Hans Hattenhauer*, Grundbegriffe des Bürgerlichen Rechts, Munich 1982, 70 ff., about the influence of the period in which Haupt published his theory: "Die im Jahre 1941 herrschende Lehre vom absoluten Vorrang der völkischen Gemeinschaft liess den Rechtsbegriff der Person und der Kraft ihres Willens endgültig überwunden erscheinen." ("The doctrine of the absolute priority of the people's community prevailing in the year 1941 appeared to overcome finally the legal concept of the person and the power of its will.").

14 *Rudolf von Jhering* (fn. 7) 5.

a tram that passes our house without saying a word. Does this act of boarding have any legal meaning, and if so, which?"). The aforementioned Haupt turned away from the view that agreements only came into being through offer and acceptance. That view did not correspond with the reality of life. In addition, there were actual contractual relations that were not based on the entering into an agreement but on a social "*Leistungsverpflichtung*" ("duty to serve"). For instance, a similar relation concerning the use of a tram did not come into being due to an agreement between the tram company and the passenger, but because the passenger boarded the tram. This doctrine was further developed into the doctrine of Larenz who mentioned "*Schuldverhältnisse aus sozialtypischem Verhalten*" ("contractual relations out of socially typical behaviour").[15] Larenz posed that the high volume of traffic in modern society brought with it legal relations that could only be explained by a pure factual public offer of a service and a pure factual use of this service by the public. For lack of a conscious declaration of a legally relevant intention, such behaviour should not be explained as mutual expressions of intentions, but as an event that through its socially typical meaning had the same legal effects as a contract. The formation of a contractual relation in these kinds of cases was not the legal effect that was intended or was declared through the "actual actions" (this tautology was actually used in the German text: "des tatsächlichen Handelns") of the passenger. But the legal effect of this relation was, according to generally accepted practice, without any doubt the result of this action.

The *Bundesgerichtshof* embraced this doctrine of the socially typical behaviour and applied it to the "*Hamburger Parkplatzfall*". Whoever uses a parking place for which payment is requested, enters into a contractual relation that requires payment. The deviating attitude of the parking place user was not conclusive, not even if this was expressed by the "*parklustige Kraftfahrer*" ("the vehicle driver who likes to park") towards the guard of the car park when parking. Only this view could lead to the result that the user of the parking place was subject to the regulations, which had been established legally for its use.[16]

---

15 *Karl Larenz*, Lehrbuch des Schuldrechts, Band 1: Allgemeiner Teil, Munich 1953, 27 ff.; *idem*, Die Begründung von Schuldverhältnissen durch sozialtypisches Verhalten, Neue Juristische Wochenschrift 1956, 1897.

16 The senate of the *Bundesgerichtshof* deciding this case, was presided by Justice Tasche. He had written an essay in 1942 in which he applied Haupt's doctrine of the actual contractual relations to void contracts. *Friedrich Tasche*, Vertragsverhältnis nach "nichtigem" Vertragsschluss?, Jherings Jahrbücher 90 (1942) 101. Cf. on the influence of Tasche on this judgment e. g. *Peter Lambrecht*, Die Lehre vom faktischen Vertragsverhältnis, Entstehung, Rezeption und Niedergang, Tübingen 1994, 108.

English does not have the same means of expression as German, because of which I have had to simplify the previous account to some extent, but even so, it remains a juggling with words. It appears to me that the reasoning was of the following kind: Why is the user of the parking place liable? Because it is desirable that she is liable. This all is of course wrapped in the relevant jargon, which is not only the prerogative of the social sciences. It reminded me briefly of an informative little book that I recently bought because of the tantalising title. It is called "Learn to Write Badly: How to Succeed in the Social Sciences".[17] In this case, I call for social sciences to read legal sciences! Fortunately, the verdict of the *Bundesgerichtshof* received its portion of criticism. One of the critics, Küchenhoff by name, asked for the classic theory of contracts to be defended, with the words: "*Heraus zum Kampf mit uns allen*" ("Let's all go out and fight").[18]

V. Roman Law and Tacit Agreements

What would a Roman lawyer have thought of these legal gems?[19] Undoubtedly, he would have raised his eyebrows. Paul, for instance, said in D. 2,14,2, appealing to Labeo, "that one can enter into an agreement by accepting a thing, by letter or by means of a messenger between absent parties":[20]

> Paulus libro tertio ad edictum
> pr. Labeo ait convenire posse vel re: vel per epistulam vel per nuntium inter absentes quoque posse. Sed etiam tacite consensu convenire intellegitur.
> 1. Et ideo si debitori meo reddiderim cautionem, videtur inter nos convenisse ne peterem, profuturamque ei conventionis exceptionem placuit.

---

17 *Michael Billig*, Learn to Write Badly: How to Succeed in the Social Sciences, Cambridge 2013.

18 *Günther Küchenhoff*, Faktische Vertragsverhältnisse und faktische Arbeitsverhältnisse?, in: Recht der Arbeit 1958, 121 ff., 127. Cf. also e. g. *Werner Flume*, Rechtsgeschäft und Privatautonomie, in: Hundert Jahre deutsches Rechtsleben, Festschrift zum hundertjährigen Bestehen des deutschen Juristentages 1860–1960, Vol 1, Karlsruhe 1960, 135, and *idem*, Das Rechtsgeschäft und das rechtlich relevante Verhalten, Archiv für die civilistische Praxis (AcP) 161 (1962) 52.

19 See e. g. *Carlo Augusto Cannata*, Das faktische Vertragsverhältnis oder die ewige Wiederkunft des Gleichen, Studia et Documenta Historiae et Iuris, 53 (1987) 297 ff. Cf. *Benedikt Kühle*, Der Dualismus von ausdrücklicher und stillschweigender Willenserklärung, Frankfurt a. M. 2009, 7 for a discussion of the explicit and tacit declaration of the will among the pandectists.

20 Translations have been taken from *Theodor Mommsen/Paul Krueger/Alan Watson*, The Digest of Justinian, Philadelphia 1985.

Paul, Edict, book 3
"pr. Labeo says that we can agree either by handing something over or by means of a letter or messenger when we are absent. But there is also understood to be agreement by implication.[21]
1. And, therefore, if I return a *cautio* to my debtor, we are held to have agreed that I will not sue and it has been settled that a defense based on the agreement will be available to him."

One even accepts that tacit consent can lead to an agreement. Therefore, it is accepted that if I return the "IOY" to the debtor, it is then agreed between us that I will not initiate a claim and that, as per the current doctrine, the plea of the concluded agreement will support his case. The doctrine of the tacit statement of intention has its impact in this text, amongst others. One does not have to have explicitly stated that one intends to enter an agreement. This intention can also be inferred from the behaviour of the person in question. Another example of the application of this doctrine is given by Florentinus, who discusses the following case in D. 2,14,57 pr.:

Florentinus libro octavo institutionum
Qui in futurum usuras a debitore acceperat, tacite pactus videtur, ne intra id tempus sortem petat.

Florentinus, Institutes, book 8
"A person who accepts in advance interest from a debtor seems by implication to have agreed that he will not seek the capital within the period for which he accepted interest."

Following Roman law, these discussions took place as a result of formless agreements, the so-called *pacta*. In order to enter an agreement, more was required. One needed to use one of the accepted types of contracts. However, these could also come into being in a tacit way, with the exception of the *stipulatio*, a somewhat solemn oral agreement. Ulpian, for instance, discusses the tacit extension of a lease contract in D. 19,2,13,11.

21 Cf. § 863 I ABGB (Austrian Civil Code): "Man kann seinen Willen nicht nur ausdrücklich durch Worte und allgemein angenommene Zeichen; sondern auch stillschweigend durch solche Handlungen erklären, welche mit Überlegung aller Umstände keinen vernünftigen Grund, daran zu zweifeln, übrig lassen." ("It is possible to declare one's will not just explicitly by words and generally accepted signs, but also tacitly by acts which do not leave any sensible reason to doubt its existence, considering all circumstances.").

Ulpianus libro tricesimo altero ad edictum
Qui impleto tempore conductionis remansit in conductione [...] reconduxisse videbitur.
Ulpian, Edict, book 32
"When a man remains in the leasehold after the term of hire is over, he will be construed [...] as having rehired."

However, there was a problem that probably led the *Bundesgerichtshof* to accept the doctrine of the "sozialtypisches Verhalten" ("socially typical behaviour"). After all, before she parked her car, *Frau* Beavis had explicitly said that she did not agree to have her car guarded and was therefore not required to pay. Did this not amount to an impediment of concordance of intention, so that no agreement could be entered? Must not, instead, something be constructed that had the same legal results, i. e., a factual contractual relation? Here, too, the traditional doctrine of the tacit agreement of intention could lead to a simpler solution. She could appeal to two *adagia*, one originating from Roman law and the other from canon law. The *adagium* from Roman law reads *venire contra factum proprium nemini licet*, no one may set himself in contradiction to his own previous conduct, which expresses the doctrine called estoppel in English law.[22] This is based on Ulpian, who discusses the following case in D. 1,7,25 pr.

Ulpianus libro quinto opinionum
Post mortem filiae suae, quae ut mater familias quasi iure emancipata vixerat et testamento scriptis heredibus decessit, adversus factum suum, quasi non iure eam nec praesentibus testibus emancipasset, pater movere controversiam prohibetur.

Ulpian, Opinions, book 5
"After the death of a daughter, who had been living as a *mater familias* as if lawfully emancipated and who had appointed testamentary heirs before her death, her father is estopped from initiating proceedings which would give the lie to his own act by raising the allegation that he did not carry out a lawful emancipation or did not do so in the presence of witnesses."

Apparently, the father had attempted to remove her from his authority by emancipating her – as it was called – and he had acted as if this had been done legally for

22 Cf. e. g. *Erwin Riezler*, Venire contra factum proprium, Studien im römischen, englischen und deutschen Zivilrecht, Leipzig 1912, 13, and on estoppel 55 ff.; *Hans Josef Wieling*, Venire contra factum proprium und Verschulden gegen sich selbst, Archiv für die civilistische Praxis (AcP) 176 (1976) 334, and, more recently, *Lisa Isola*, Venire contra factum proprium, Herkunft und Grundlagen eines sprichwörtlichen Rechtsprinzips, Frankfurt a. M. 2017, 108.

as long as she was alive. If that had not been the case, the daughter would not have owned her own possessions and she would not have been able to dispose of her non-existent inheritance by testament. Everything that allegedly was the daughter's would then turn out to be owned by her father. This was no doubt the reason that in this case the father still had an interest in disputing the validity of the emancipation.

The *adagium* from canon law reads *protestatio facto contraria non valet*, the objection, or proviso, that contradicts the action, is invalid.[23] This *adagium* is based on a gloss on the Liber Sextus, the third part of the *Corpus Iuris Canonici*.[24] Someone makes a proviso, but acts in a way that is contrary to that proviso. This is without a doubt what someone does who drives into a car park where it is clearly signposted that payment is required and who subsequently parks, stating that she is not willing to pay. In the German literature, this *adagium* specifically is called upon to explain the *Hamburger Parkplatzfall* via the law of contract, without having to appeal to a factual contractual relation or socially typical behaviour.[25]

One of the critics of the *Bundesgerichtshof* ascertained that the Court tends to embrace new principles "zukunftsfroh" ("while cheerfully looking towards the future"), without any compelling reasons, and that a more cautious jurisprudence would save the Court from making later revocations. He remarks that it would be effective if a highest judge accepted a new doctrine of which it was hard to estimate all consequences, only if all the traditional solutions had been exhausted. It is in accordance with the peculiarity of law that is created by judges from case to case, to cautiously examine case histories, so that one can be persuasive when there is a real need to move into new directions, "so wie es der Ruhm der grossen römischen Praktiker war" ("for which the great Roman practitioners were famous").[26] Still the doctrine of socially typical behaviour or the factual contractual relationship haunts the German manuals and textbooks: the prevailing opinion rejects it, but it is still being debated at length.[27]

---

23 Cf. e. g. *Arndt Teichmann*, Die protestatio facto contraria, in: Festschrift für Karl Michaelis, ed. *Hans-Martin Pawlowski*, Göttingen 1972, 294.

24 Liber sextus Bonifacii 1,6,25 Glossa ad *Protestetur*. Cf. *Detlef Liebs*, Lateinische Rechtsregeln und Rechtssprichwörter, Munich 2007[7], P 125 (183).

25 Cf. on this critically e. g. *Karl Larenz/Manfred Wolf*, Allgemeiner Teil des Bürgerlichen Rechts, Munich 1997, § 30, Nr. 32; *Julius von Staudinger*, Staudingers Kommentar zum Bürgerlichen Gesetzbuch, Berlin 2017, ad § 133, Nr. 59 ff. (*Reinhard Singer*); Münchener Kommentar zum Bürgerlichen Gesetzbuch, Munich 2006, Vol 1,1, "vor § 116", Nr. 26 (*Ernst A. Kramer); Helmut Köhler*, Kritik der Regel "protestatio facto contraria non valet", JZ 36 (1981) 464.

26 *Franz Wieacker*, A note on the Hamburg car park case in: JZ 12 (1957) 62. Cf. *idem*, Willenserklärung und sozialtypisches Verhalten, in: Göttinger Festschrift für das Oberlandesgericht Celle, Göttingen 1961, 263.

27 Cf. e. g. *Martin J. Schermaier*, Historisch-kritischer Kommentar zum BGB, eds. *Mathias Schmoeckel* et al., Vol I, Tübingen 2003, "vor § 104", Nr. 6; *Dieter Medicus*, Allgemeiner Teil des BGB, Heidel-

Those who like theories like these, will certainly enjoy the doctrine propounded by the highly learned Bekker from Greifswald in 1857 about the purchase of a railway-ticket, a doctrine called the "*Personificationstheorie*".[28] The case was discussed by one of my predecessors on the chair of Roman law in Groningen: Wiardus Modderman.[29] I will quote him. Does the ticket give its buyer the right to enter the train?

> "Neen, dat is *te* eenvoudig; dat is geen juridieke constructie. Het kaartje geeft het recht van toegang, doch niet aan u, maar aan zich zelf. Subject van dat recht is het papier. Gij zijt ongeloovig? Hoor dan's mans eigene woorden: 'Das Papier selber ist das fragliche Rechtssubject, Gläubiger oder wenn man lieber will, statt des Rechtssubjects, loco creditoris, Träger der Forderung.' Komt gij dus door middel van uw kaartje naar binnen, dan kan dit alleen omdat gij dat papier representeert. Prof. Bekker spreke zelf: 'Jeder Inhaber erhält die Befugniss dies Recht, dass *nicht sein* Recht wird, gegen den Schuldner geltend zu machen. Der Inhaber wird, wenn man so sagen will, *Vertreter des Papiers*.' Eigenlijk zouden dus alleen de kaartjes ... met het spoor mogen reizen, maar omdat de directien zoo beleefd zijn, vertegenwoordiging toe te laten, zelfs zonder geregistreerde volmacht, kunt *gij* de plaatsen innemen die voor de kaartjes bestemd zijn. Laat ons dus nooit meer klagen over ... spoorwegdirectien, maar hare beleefdheid en vrijgevigheid dankbaar op prijs stellen!"[30]
>
> "No, that is *too* simple; that is not a juridical construction. The ticket does give the right to enter, but not to you: to itself. The subject of that right is the paper. Do you not believe so? Well, then listen to the man's own words: 'The paper itself is the subject in question of the right, creditor or, if one prefers, instead of the subject of the right, loco creditoris, bearer of the claim.' So if you enter with the help of your ticket, this is only possible because you represent the paper. Let Prof. Bekker speak for himself: 'Every keeper acquires the power to enforce this right, which does not become his right, against the debtor. The keeper becomes in other words the *representative of the paper*.' So only the tickets ... actually would be allowed to travel by train, but because the boards are as polite as to allow representation, even without a registered proxy, *you* are able to take the places meant for the tickets. So let us never again complain about ... the boards of railway companies, but appreciate their politeness and liberality in gratitude!"

---

berg 2010, Nr. 244 ff.; and, somewhat older, *Werner Flume*, Allgemeiner Teil des Bürgerlichen Rechts, II. Das Rechtsgeschäft, Berlin 1979³, 95 (§ 8); *Lambrecht* (fn. 16), passim, and *Dieter Medicus*, Bürgerliches Recht, Cologne 1996¹⁷, 132 (Nr. 189).

28 *Ernst Immanuel Bekker*, Die Geldpapiere, in: Jahrbuch des gemeinen deutschen Rechts, Vol 1, Leipzig 1857, 266; 361–462, espec. 292 f.

29 *Wiardus Modderman*, Practijk en Theorie der Rechtswetenschap, public lecture, Groningen 1875.

30 *Modderman* (fn. 29) 18.

VI. "All he Needed was a Watch"

Let us now go back to England and the Beavis case. This case was, as stated before, based on the principle that, by parking in the car park that was managed by ParkingEye, Beavis had entered into an agreement with them. For this reason, the signs said: "By parking within the car park, motorists agree to comply with the car park regulations." This made the provision about the amount that would have to be paid, in case the car was parked too long, a contractual clause. Since English law had until then been rather strict in regard to penalty clauses and only allowed clauses that contained an actual estimation of the damage to be suffered, the so-called *liquidated damages*, the British Parking Association, of which ParkingEye was a member, tried to include these types of clauses under the allowed category via a Parking regulation. Clause 19 of the BPA Code of Practice stipulates: "This charge must be based on the genuine pre-estimate of loss that you suffer", and "If your parking charge is based on a contractually agreed sum, that charge cannot be punitive or unreasonable."

However, the problem for ParkingEye was that it had already been established that they did not suffer any damages from Beavis' parking. On the contrary, the fines for overstaying were its source of income, because they did not charge a parking fee for the allowed parking time. Therefore, Beavis must have thought that his case would be an easy one to win, as long as he took the viewpoint that he had entered into an agreement with penalty clauses. A pure penalty clause, with no link to the actually suffered damage, had until then always been considered invalid, in accordance with the English precedents.

This judgment changed all that. The United Kingdom Supreme Court now holds that penalty clauses, unless extravagant, can have good commercial reasons, as in the case of Mr Beavis: "Mr Beavis was well aware of the two-hour limit, and could reasonably be expected to comply with it. All he needed was a watch", the author of the judgment Lord Sumption told him at the hearing of the case.

Mr Beavis, however, did not yield. He published a petition to the government on the internet and hoped to collect 100.000 signatures to force parliament to discuss his case. After six months, the count was 12.809 signatures and the petition was closed down.[31] Thus Mr Beavis will be able to remain angry and principled.

31 See: <https://petition.parliament.uk/petitions/111925> (11/5/2017).

Wataru Miyasaka, Tsukuba

Corpus ex distantibus in Roman Law

A Basis for Floating Lien in Japanese Law

I. Introduction*

1. A Collective Entity of Things in Japanese Civil Law

The Japanese Civil Code (JCC) adopts a policy of one real right over one thing as its principle. It is said that this principle has a double meaning. Firstly, two or more real rights whose contents are the same cannot be established with regard to one and the same object. Secondly, a property right can only comprise one single and independent object. Therefore, for a collective entity of things not one real right, but several rights exist whose number is identical to the number of objects. The Article 85 of JCC provides that "the term 'things' as used in this Code shall mean a tangible thing." Therefore, even if we imagined a collective entity of things and defined it as one "thing", this entity would be intangible and could therefore not be a "thing" under Article 85 JCC. In result, the JCC excludes a collective entity of objects from the concept of "Things" which are the reference for the existence of real rights. This limitation of Japanese property law complicates the integration of a floating lien into the JCC, although this kind of security has significant weight in Japanese business.

2. Floating Lien in Japanese Law

The floating lien is a type of mortgage in Japanese law. The mortgage is a type of a real security right. A debtor as a mortgagor does not transfer the possession of the object to his creditor but carries on making use of it, and transfers the ownership of it to the creditor for the mortgage. This process takes place in the following way: The debtor sells the object to the creditor, who promises to let the debtor repurchase the object when the debt is repaid. Then the creditor leases the object to the debtor. If the debtor does not fulfil his obligation to pay, the creditor can, as the owner of the object, avoid the formal enforcement procedure and can alternatively secure the payment. If the debtor's obligation is resolved,

* I am deeply grateful to all contributors to this anthology for their productive comments and suggestions to my paper during and after the conference at Fukuoka in 2016.

the ownership of the object returns to the debtor. There is no provision for the mortgage in JCC, but in the commercial practice the contract for the mortgage is used widely and traditionally, and, judicial precedents of the Japanese Supreme Court have established the law of the mortgage.[1] The floating lien makes a collective entity of movables the object of mortgage. The collective entity of movables is composed of changing components, like raw materials or merchandise stocks in a shop or a warehouse.

3. Problems with the Floating Lien in Japanese Law and Judgments of the Japanese Supreme Court

When we only look at the object as individual movables, not as a collective entity of things, some problems arise.[2] Firstly, we must establish each mortgage over each individual movable as often as it is carried into a shop or warehouse. When a mortgagor does not perform his obligation but rejects delivery of the individual movables to a mortgagee, the latter may take an action for recovery of them against the former based on his ownership. If, however, the mortgagee fails to establish the mortgage over a certain movable, he must identify the specific movable among huge stocks and eliminate it from the object of the action. Secondly, we must extinguish each mortgage over each individual movable as often as it is carried out of the shop or warehouse. If a mortgagor sold some mortgaged movables to a third party but did not extinguish the mortgage over them, the mortgagee may take an action for recovery of them against the third party on the basis of his ownership, because he is an owner within a scope of the purpose of security. The mortgagor, however, is prevented from making profit by trading raw materials or merchandise stock, and therefore the establishment of the mortgage does not have much meaning for the mortgagor.

In relation to the first point, the Japanese Supreme Court admitted on 15th February 1979[3] that "Things can be an object of the mortgage when the extent of the object is identified in a designation of its type, its location, and its quantitative range." In this judgment the Supreme Court seems to consider a collective entity of movables as an object of a real right. According to this position, a mortgage influences both the current legal status and the future fortune of movables since these are considered as being a part of a collective entity of objects. On the premise of this judgment and with regard to the second argument, the

1 *Hiroshi Oda*, Japanese Law, New York 2011[3], 177–179.

2 *Megumi Hara*, Syugobutsu to sekininzaisan (A collective entity of a lot of things and non-exempt property), Hogaku kyoshitsu 417 (2015) 10–15.

3 Saiko saibansyo minji hanreisyu (Japanese Supreme Court civil case reporters) 33–1–51.

Japanese Supreme Court declared on 20th July 2006[4] that a mortgagor can alienate individual movables mortgaged to a third party within the range of normal management of business. If, however, the alienation is out of range of normal management of business and the individual movables are withdrawn from the collective entity, for example, by carrying a movable out of its storage location, the mortgage has no effect on the movables withdrawn and as a result; the third party acquires ownership of them.

4. Influences of the Term "Things" in French Code Civil and German Civil Code upon Drafting Process of JCC

The correspondence between these judgments, however, indicates that the term "things" of JCC has not satisfied the demand for floating lien in practice. It must be stated that the Japanese civil and commercial law is lacking terms of utilization of movables for the creation of credit in difference to the introduction of *gage sur les stocks sans dépossession* into the French *Code de Commerce* revised in 2006. It can be considered that the concept of "bien" ("object") of the French *Code Civil*, which includes not only tangible things but also intangible things and has its origin in the Roman law, contributes to the recent amendment in France.[5] However, historically, it would have been possible for JCC to adopt a similar concept of "thing" to that of the French *Code Civil*.

The concept of "thing" under the Article 85 of JCC derives from the article 778[6] of the first draft of the German Civil Code (*Bürgerliches Gesetzbuch*). It is said that the drafters of the JCC excluded the Article 6 of the Property Part in the old JCC, which would have provided that "in the term 'things' both tangible and intangible things were included" and was mainly drafted by Gustave Emile Boissonade.[7] In fact, Boissonade drafted this article with the concept of "bien" of the French *Code Civil* in mind. While the bill of the old JCC, including the above-mentioned Article 6 was approved at the Imperial Diet, a controversy arose between the supporters, who mainly consisted of scholars trained in French style, and the opponents, who received legal education according to

4 Saiko saibansyo minji hanreisyu 60–6–2499.

5 *Mika Yokoyama*, France ho niokeru syoyu (*propriété*) gainen. Zaisan to syoyu nikansuru jyorontekikosatsu (The concept of propriété in French law. Introductory study about property and ownership), Hokkaido Journal of New Global Law and Policy 12 (2011) 257–297.

6 "Sachen im Sinne des Gesetzes sind nur körperliche Gegenstände."

7 *Naoki Kanayama*, Mutaibutsu no syoyu to senyu. Minpo 85 jyo, 163 jyo, 205 jyo ron (Ownership and possession of intangible things. Article 85, 163, and 205 of Japanese Civil Code), in: Zai no tayouka to minpogaku (Diversification of Property and Civil Law Theory), eds. *Katsumi Yoshida et al.*, Syojihomu 2014, 620–647.

the English style. The opponents criticised the above-mentioned Article 6 stating that it was curious that ownership over ownership could exist since rights were included in intangible objects and that a typical example of the rights over things was ownership.[8]

When the drafting of a new Civil Code started, the drafts of the German Civil Code were the main reference. An article of the German drafts, which provided the term "Things" as only tangible objects, was accepted by the Japanese drafters who decided to adopt the principle of German Civil Code as a "sharp distinction between real rights and rights of obligations".[9] Therefore, being an intangible thing, a collective entity of objects was also excluded from the concept of "thing" in the JCC without much discussion.

During the course of the codification of the German Civil Code and in the Pandectistic jurisprudence as its foundation, the question arose whether a collective entity of a plurality of things could be considered as being a "thing" under the Code or not.[10] In this respect, naturally, *universitas rerum* in Roman law was examined and interpreted.[11] Article 778 of the first draft of the German Civil Code can be considered as a result of this discussion among Pandectists.[12] Despite this intensive debate in the German tradition, there has been – even up until now – no thorough examination of these historical foundations of the concept of "things" in Japanese law. Therefore, this article tries to examine the concept of *universitas rerum* which may be the origin of the concept of "bien" in the French *Code Civil*. The main idea is, that *universitas rerum* constituted a real security right over a plurality of objects in Roman law, even without possession.

---

8 *Kanayama* (fn. 7) 622–623.

9 *Kanayama* (fn. 7) 623–626.

10 *Erich A. Daubermann*, Die Sachgesamtheit als Gegenstand des klassischen römischen Rechts. Vornehmlich unter dem Blickwinkel von Veränderungen in ihrer Zusammensetzung, Frankfurt a. M. et al. 1993; *Martin Josef Schermaier*, ZRG RA 112 (1995) 602–612, 604.

11 *Johann Christian Hasse*, über universitas juris und rerum. Und über Universal- und Singular-Succession, Archiv für die civilistische Praxis 5 (1822) 1–65; *Leopold August Warnkönig*, über den Begriff und die juristische Wichtigkeit der sogenannten *universitas rerum*, Archiv für die civilistische Praxis 11 (1828) 169–204; *Carl Georg von Wächter*, über Sachgesammtheiten (*rerum universitates*) überhaupt und in besonderer Beziehung zum Pfandrechte. Erörterungen aus dem Römischen, Deutschen und Württembergischen Privatrechte (Nr. 1), Stuttgart 1845; *Heinrich Dernburg*, Das Pfandrecht nach den Grundsätzen des heutigen römischen Rechts, Vol 1, Leipzig 1860, esp. 454–461; *Heinrich Robert Göppert*, über einheitliche, zusammengesetzte und Gesamtsachen nach römischen Recht, Halle 1871.

12 *Taro Suizu*, Yuutaibutsu kitei nikansuru kisotekikosatsu I (Grundsätzliche Betrachtungen zur Vorschrift der körperlichen Sache I. Über § 1 TE-SachenR), Hogaku Kenkyu (Journal of Law, Politics and Sociology) 82 (2009) 211–274.

5. On *universitas rerum* in Roman law, Objects and the Scope of this Study

According to the theory of Roman law, *universitas rerum* is classified as either *corpus ex contingentibus* which denotes individual things being bound together physically and forming a single entity or *corpus ex distantibus* which denotes individual things not bound together physically but built as a unity.[13]

> D. 41,3,30 pr. Pomp. 30 Sab.
> Rerum mixtura facta an usucapionem cuiusque praecedentem interrumpit, quaeritur. tria autem genera sunt corporum, unum, quod continetur uno spiritu et Graece ἡνωμένον vocatur, ut homo tignum lapis et similia: alterum, quod ex contingentibus, hoc est pluribus inter se cohaerentibus constat, quod συνημμένον vocatur, ut aedificium navis armarium: tertium, quod ex distantibus constat, ut corpora plura non soluta, sed uni nomini subiecta, veluti populus legio grex. primum genus usucapione quaestionem non habet, secundum et tertium habet.
> "The question has been posed whether the mixing-up of things breaks the erstwhile *usucapio* of each element. Now there are three kinds of things: One is that suffused by a single spirit, which the Greeks call unitary, a slave, for instance, a beam of wood, a stone, and the like; another is that compounded of cohering individual elements, which is described as constructed, a house, say, a ship, or a cupboard; the third is that which is composed of individual entities, subsumed under one designation, such as a nation, a legion, or a flock. That the first kind should be open to *usucapio* presents no problem, but the other two do."

This article aims at examining the *corpus ex distantibus* because its concern is the collective entity of movables which is composed of components which are coming and going. The texts of Justinian's Digest[14] related to *grex*, a herd of cattle, and *merces in horreo* or *taberna*, merchandises stored in a warehouse or a shop can help in this respect, since they describe *grex* as *corpus ex distantibus* and *merces in horreo* is treated in the same way with regard to real security.

Before entering into the analysis, we should note that in Roman law *fiducia cum creditore* was a form of real security without possession of the object as well. The object of *fiducia cum creditore* was a *res mancipi* which could only be transferred via *mancipatio*. A debtor alienated a *res mancipi* to his creditor for the

13 *Max Kaser/Rolf Knütel/Sebastian Lohsse*, Römisches Privatrecht. Ein Studienbuch, Munich 2017[21], 119.

14 The English translations of the Digest have been taken from The Digest of Justinian, *ed. Alan Watson*, Philadelphia 1998.

mancipatio for real security. That way, the creditor acquired ownership over the object by civil law, although the creditor was bound by *pactum fiduciae*, a kind of special terms and conditions for the *fiducia*, and was not allowed to make use of the object or to alienate it against these terms and conditions.[15] In this respect, the *fiducia cum creditore* was similar to the mortgage of our time. And as we will see later, oxen, horses, mules, and donkeys were four-footed animals which formed a *grex* and these animals could be the object of the *fiducia cum creditore* because they were included in the category of *res mancipi*. This article, however, will limit itself to the legal treatment of *fiducia cum creditore*. On the one hand, a *grex* could also consist of animals that were not *res mancipi*; on the other hand, things which were called *merces* were almost without exception *res nec mancipi*. It must be noted in addition, classical texts on which the *fiducia* might have been recorded are said to be the object of interpolation by Justinian, which adds the difficulty of transmission.

II. The Legal Concept of *grex*

1. Settlement of the Pasturage and *grex* of Livestock in the History of Roman Economic Development[16]

Pasturage in Rome acquired an economic significance only after the second Punic War and its importance remained until the late imperial period. Roman people dominating the entire Italian peninsula from 3rd to 2nd century BC introduced the pasturage into the vast area of southern Italy, which was especially deteriorated by the continuing war and had only been recently acquired by Rome. Wealthy Romans took an interest in it. According to the authors of *De agri cultura*, pasturage was a more of a profit-earning business than grain production, and a *grex* could be easily maintained at modest costs. With the rising standard of living of the Roman people, their demand for production related to pasturage was increasing. This ensured a sufficient sales market for significant earnings and encouraged an increase in the number of animals making up a *grex*.[17]

For a *grex*, its adequate scale and the definite organisation were imperative. A large *grex* made it difficult to move from one rangeland to another every summer and winter; it was problematic to keep the animals safe from bandits and other animals throughout the journey as well as to ensure food for them both at the

15 *Kaser/Knütel/Lohsse* (fn. 13) 181–182.

16 *Jürgen Hammerstein*, Die Herde im römischen Recht. Grex als rechtliche Sachgesamtheit und Wirtschaftseinheit, Göttingen 1975.

17 *Hammerstein* (fn. 16) 22.

rangeland and in transit.[18] On the other hand, if the number of the animals in a *grex* was too small, it was difficult to recover the cost for herdsmen and pastoral dogs coming along with the *grex*. In addition, the application to magistrates was required for pasturing at *ager publicus*, and *leges*[19] provided that the rent was free up to a certain number of heads and, if it exceeded the legal limit, payment was obliged. Another fee was charged only at the transition through *ager publicus*.[20] Therefore it was necessary to keep the number of a *grex* constant.

To functionally constitute a *grex*, the best construction was required by age, a suitable proportion between males and females, and that of the number. Thanks to this, it was possible to reduce the rate of a plague outbreak, to increase productivity of young animals, and to enhance the value of the *grex*. Therefore, *dilectus*, "selection", took place every autumn. Unserviceable, especially the infertile or aged animals were eliminated and supplemented with younger animals.[21] The supplementation encouraged an image of *grex* which, even if the compositional units are renewed one by one, exists as an organisational band.[22] For those reasons, it was recommended that, if possible, people should acquire the ready-made *grex* rather than purchase individual animals from various *greges* accordingly and create it from a clean slate.[23] Therefore, the value of *grex* was not equivalent to the sum of the price of individual animals composing the *grex*. The organisation of *grex* and the grouping according to its function produced an added value.[24]

2. Roman Jurists' Views about the Legal Treatment of *grex*

A *grex* could be formed with sheep, goats, horses, mules, and asses which are four-footed cattle.[25] There are four typical situations in which the legal treatment of *grex* as *corpus ex distantibus* can be found: (a) usufruct, (b) *rei vindicatio*, (c) *possessio* and *usucapio*, and (d) the establishment of a real security right over *grex*.

18 *Hammerstein* (fn. 16) 37–38.

19 *Lex Licinia Sextia agraria* in 367 BC or *lex agraria* in 111 BC. See *Adolf Berger*, Encyclopedic Dictionary of Roman Law, Philadelphia 1953, 547, 556.

20 *Hammerstein* (fn. 16) 47.

21 *Hammerstein* (fn. 16) 54.

22 *Hammerstein* (fn. 16) 59.

23 *Hammerstein* (fn. 16) 42.

24 *Hammerstein* (fn. 16) 63.

25 D. 9,2,2,2 Gai. 7 ed. prov., D. 32,65,4 Marcian. 7 inst.

a) Usufruct of *grex*

The *grex* itself or the usufruct of a *grex* can be left as a legacy as attested by Ulpian and Pomponius:

D. 30,21 Ulp. 15 Sab.
Grege legato et quae postea accedunt ad legatarium pertinent.
"If a herd has been bequeathed, any subsequent accessions belong to the legatee".

D. 30,22 Pomp. 5 Sab.
Si grege legato aliqua pecora vivo testatore mortua essent in eorumque locum aliqua essent substituta, eundem gregem videri: et si deminutum ex eo grege pecus esset et vel unus bos superesset, eum vindicari posse, quamvis grex desisset esse: quemadmodum insula legata, si combusta esset, area possit vindicari.
"If a herd has been bequeathed and some herd animals die in the testator's lifetime and are replaced by others, it is taken to be the same herd. And if the livestock from this herd is diminished and only one ox survives, the legatee may vindicate it, although the herd has ceased to exist, just as when a tenement building has been bequeathed and is burned down the site may still be vindicated."

During the lifetime of the testator, the *grex* remains identical, even if some animals belonging to the *grex* die and the number decreases, or if the number increases because some specimen are added. Therefore, if a *grex* is bequeathed, the legatee can vindicate it from the heirs. If the number of the cattle decreases so much, that only one survives, it cannot be regarded as *grex* anymore, but the legatee can nevertheless vindicate this last animal for himself.

When the usufruct of a *grex* is left as a legacy, the usufructuary can acquire natural fruits of the *grex*. The natural fruits of the *grex* include not only milk or coat, but also young animals.[26] If, however, the number of animals belonging to the *grex* decreases because some of them die or are of no use, the usufructuary is obliged to keep up the number of the flock out of the young which are born into it.[27] For the usufructuary must not interfere excessively with the form of the object given at the time of the establishment, and cannot alter its nature.[28] If the number of the *grex* is reduced to such an extent that it can no longer be regarded as a *grex*, the usufruct comes to an end:

26 D. 7,1,68,1 Ulp. 17 Sab.; D. 47,2,48,6 Ulp. 42 Sab.
27 D. 7,1,68,2 Ulp. 17 Sab.; D. 7,1,70,3–4 Ulp. 17 Sab.
28 *Kaser/Knütel/Lohsse* (fn. 13) 175.

D. 7,4,31 Pomp. 4 Q. Muc.
Cum gregis usus fructus legatus est et usque eo numerus pervenit gregis, ut grex non intellegatur, perit usus fructus.
"If the usufruct of a flock is left as a legacy and the numbers of the flock are reduced to such an extent that it can no longer be regarded as a flock, the usufruct comes to an end."

On the contrary, if the usufruct over each individual animal was left as a legacy, the usufructuary does not have to keep up that number.[29]

b) *Rei vindicatio* of *grex*

There was a conflict of opinion between Julian and Pomponius about whether *rei vindicatio* may be brought up in connection to a *grex*. Julian said only individual things may be vindicated[30], but he did not give clear arguments for his view:

D. 6,1,56 Iul. 78 dig.
Vindicatio non ut gregis, ita et peculii recepta est, sed res singulas is, cui legatum peculium est, petet.
"A *vindicatio* is not allowed for a *peculium* as it is for a flock, but a party to whom a peculium has been bequeathed may sue for the individual items in it."

On the other hand, Pomponius affirmed the *vindicatio* of a *grex* in the twenty-fifth book of his Readings:

D. 6,1,1,3 Ulp. 16 ed.
Per hanc autem actionem non solum singulae res vindicabuntur, sed posse etiam gregem vindicari Pomponius libro lectionum vicensimo quinto scribit. idem et de armento et de equitio ceterisque, quae gregatim habentur, dicendum est. sed enim gregem sufficiet ipsum nostrum esse, licet singula capita nostra non sint: grex enim, non singula corpora vindicabuntur.
"By this action, according to Pomponius in the twenty-fifth book of his Readings, it is not only individual things which may be vindicated; *vindicatio* may also be brought for a flock. The same must apply to a herd of cattle, a troop of horses, and other animals grouped together. It is sufficient if we own the flock itself, even if the animals may not belong to us; for what is vindicated is the flock, not the individual beasts."

---

29 D. 7,1,70,3 Ulp. 17 Sab.

30 *Glossa ad* D. 6,1,56 understands that Julian denied not *vindicatio gregis* but *vindicatio peculii* only. Modern translations of the *Digesta* in each language seem to follow the understanding.

The disagreement is not expressed very clearly, but according to Ulpian, the point of controversy was, whether an owner of a *grex* may vindicate it if somebody else's animal is part of it. Ulpian answered this question as above: "it is sufficient if we own the *grex* itself, even if particular animals may not belong to us; for what is vindicated is the *grex*, not the individual beasts." Paul held the same view, and in this case, he even accepted another *vindicatio* for the person who owned the animal mixed in the *grex* against the owner of the *grex*:

D. 6,1,2 Paul. 21 ed.
Sed si par numerus duorum interfuerit, neuter solidum gregem, sed ne partem dimidiam totius eius vindicabit. sed si maiorem numerum alter habeat, ut detracto alieno nihilo minus gregem vindicaturus sit, in restitutionem non veniunt aliena capita.
"If two parties each own an equal number of animals, neither may vindicate the whole flock, nor even half of the whole. But if one of the two has the greater number, so that, when animals belonging to others are subtracted, what he vindicates is none the less the flock, then beasts belonging to others are not restored to him. "

D. 6,1,23,5 Paul. 21 ed.
Item quaecumque aliis iuncta sive adiecta accessionis loco cedunt, ea quamdiu cohaerent dominus vindicare non potest, sed ad exhibendum agere potest, ut separentur et tunc vindicentur: scilicet excepto eo, quod Cassius de ferruminatione scribit. dicit enim, si statuae suae ferruminatione iunctum bracchium sit, unitate maioris partis consumi et quod semel alienum factum sit, etiamsi inde abruptum sit, redire ad priorem dominum non posse. non idem in eo quod adplumbatum sit, quia ferruminatio per eandem materiam facit confusionem, plumbatura non idem efficit. ideoque in omnibus his casibus, in quibus neque ad exhibendum neque in rem locum habet, in factum actio necessaria est. at in his corporibus, quae ex distantibus corporibus essent, constat singulas partes retinere suam propriam speciem, ut singuli homines singulae oves: ideoque posse me gregem vindicare, quamvis aries tuus sit immixtus, sed et te arietem vindicare posse. quod non idem in cohaerentibus corporibus eveniret: nam si statuae meae bracchium alienae statuae addideris, non posse dici bracchium tuum esse, quia tota statua uno spiritu continetur.
"Where a thing has been joined or attached to another thing and so merges with that other by way of accession, the first thing cannot be vindicated by its owner, so long as the two are stuck together. He can, however, sue by the action for production to have it detached and then vindicate it. This is the subject to the exception mentioned by Cassius in regard to welding. He says that if an arm of a statue has been joined to the rest of the statue by welding, it is merged in the unified whole of the larger part, and once it has become another's property cannot, even though later broken off, revert to its former owner. It is not the same with what has been soldered with lead, because

welding effects fusion of two things made of the same material, whereas soldering does not have that effect. And so, in all these cases in which there are grounds neither for an action for production nor for an action *in rem*, an *actio in factum* is necessary. But in case of things which consist of a number of individual objects, it is accepted that all of them retain their separate identities, as, say, individual men or individual sheep. Thus I can vindicate a flock of sheep, even though your ram is mixed in with them, and you can vindicate the ram. The situation is different where the parts of the whole are stuck together; for if you fix an arm from someone else's statue on to my statue, it cannot be said that the arm is yours, because the complete statue constitutes a single whole."

It appears that in the first part of the fragment D. 6,1,2 Paul. 21 ed. *vindicatio gregis* is denied. But this interpretation would be incorrect[31]. It must be noted above all, that *vindicabit* is a future tense. This future tense describes a situation in which the parties will be put after they will excise their *vindicatio* and which will reflect the legal situation as to their real rights. In other words, it is a situation that, because of the *vindicatio*, neither the whole *grex* will belong to only one party nor will both parties acquire a half number of the total amount of animals in the *grex*. In addition to these conditions, if a third party is considered in a situation where "two parties each own an equal number of animals", the substantive legal relation in this case is the following: In terms of a *grex*, "two parties each own an equal number of animals" and the third party owns less or more than the number owned by the other two parties.

With these assumptions, the fragment can be interpreted as follows: First of all, if either party of two who own an equal number of animals brings an action of *vindicatio gregis* against the other who possesses the whole *grex*, the plaintiff can win the case about the whole *grex*. After that, the defendant, however, can bring a *vindicatio* with regard to the number of animals which belong to him and win the case. In another case after that, the third party above can use the *vindicatio* on the number of animals which belong to him and win the case. Consequently, their legal situation is put into existence by this series of *vindicationes*.

This implies, that if either one of the two parties, of which one has the greater number than the other uses a *vindicatio gregis* against the other, the plaintiff can win the case about the whole *grex*. After that, however, if both the defendant and the third party invoke a *vindicatio* with regard to the number of animals which belong to them, they can win the case. Therefore, their real rights can be realised by these *vindicationes* in this case as well. If this is right, Paul's fragment

31 According to *Glossa ad* D. 6,1,2 Paul. 21 ed., Iohannes Bassianus held that two parties who each own an equal number of animals in a *grex* may not vindicate the *grex*, but Hugolinus expressed an objection.

cannot be interpreted as denying the *vindicatio gregis*, but rather as accepting the *vindicatio gregis*.

In order to understand the fragment, a procedural view must be taken that considers the realisation of the relative real rights via the *vindicatio*. This implies that if it is clear for all parties how many animals belong to each party, *vindicatio* of individual animals is sufficient and the *vindicatio gregis* is unnecessary. There may be rare cases, however, where such a situation might be expected. In addition, the *vindicatio gregis* seems to have an important function for avoiding the danger of losing a lawsuit because of *pluris petitio* as is told in *Gai Institutiones* 4,17.[32]

In addition, Ulpian reports an opinion of Marcellus:

> D. 6,1,3 pr. Ulp. 16 ed.
> Marcellus libro quarto digestorum scribit: qui gregem habebat capitum trecentorum, amissis centum redemit totidem capita aliena ab eo, qui dominium eorum habebat vel aliena ab eo, qui bona fide ea possidebat: et haec utique gregis, inquit, vindicatione continebuntur. sed et si ea sola supersint capita, quae redempta sunt, adhuc eum posse gregem vindicare.
> "Marcellus, in the fourth book of his Digest, writes: 'One who had a flock of three hundred head lost a hundred of them and then bought the same number of other beasts from their owner or from a possessor in good faith.' These animals also, he observes, will be included in a *vindicatio* of "the flock". Even if the only survivors are those which he has bought as replacements, he can still vindicate "the flock".

Marcellus said that if the number of animals in a *grex* decreased and the owner of the *grex* additionally bought the same number of animals as those that have decreased, the animals bought are the object of *vindicatio*, because they are included in the *grex*, and that even if only the animals bought additionally survived and they switched places completely with the original animals, the owner can still vindicate the *grex*[33].

32 Nonetheless, it cannot be said that the *vindicatio* of a collective entity of things has no meaning for the modern law which is free of risk of *pluris petitio* as the dominant theorists of Pandectistic jurisprudence commencing with *Dernburg* argued. The meaning of *vindicatio gregis* is, as shown above, not only in hindrance of a lost lawsuit because of *pluris petitio*. *Dernburg* (fn. 11) 456 denied its meaning shown above as it is contradictory with the substantive right, but in the ancient Roman law, as no one denies, the substantive and procedural law was not divided.

33 *Glossa ordinaria* in the casus to this fragment says that the owner of the *grex* who bought the same number of animals from a *bona fide possessor* has the *actio Publiciana*. *Glossa ad Continebuntur* gives the argument that a person who brought *rei vindicatio* is regarded as having brought *actio Publiciana* at the same time, and cites D. 21,2,39,1 Iul. 57 dig. as proving example. Against

Finally, if an owner of a *grex* vindicated it and after that its number either increased or decreased, and then he tries to vindicate it once again, the defense of *res iudicata* will lie against him:

D. 44,2,21,1 Pomp. 31 Sab.
Si petiero gregem et vel aucto vel minuto numero gregis iterum eundem gregem petam, obstabit mihi exceptio. sed et si speciale corpus ex grege petam, si adfuit in eo grege, puto obstaturam exceptionem.
"If I shall have claimed a flock and the number of the flock either increased or decreased and I were again to claim the said flock, the defense [of *res iudicata*] will avail against me. But if I claim an individual head of cattle of the flock, I consider that the defense will prevail, if that head of cattle was part of the flock."

The reason is that, even if the number of animals belonging to the *grex* increases or decreases, or all the animals of which the *grex* is composed are replaced by new animals, the *grex* is the same as the former one, unless the number of the *grex* is reduced to such an extent that it can no longer be regarded as a *grex*.

c) *Possessio* and *usucapio* of *grex*

Although *rei vindicatio* may be pleaded for a *grex*, a *usucapio* of a *grex* is not allowed.

D. 41,3,30,2 Pomp. 30 Sab.
De tertio genere corporum videndum est. non autem grex universus sic capitur usu quomodo singulae res, nec sic quomodo cohaerentes. quid ergo est? etsi ea natura eius est, ut adiectionibus corporum maneat, non item tamen universi gregis ulla est usucapio, sed singulorum animalium sicuti possessio, ita et usucapio. nec si quid emptum immixtum fuerit gregi augendi eius gratia, idcirco possessionis causa mutabitur, ut, si reliquus grex dominii mei sit, haec quoque ovis, sed singulae suam causam habebunt, ita ut, si quae furtivae erunt, sint quidem ex grege, non tamen usucapiantur.

---

this, *Glossa ad Vindicare* raises the question if a *grex* can be usucapted under the *actio Publiciana*, but holds that it would be inconsistent with D. 41,3,30,2 Pomp. 30 Sab. because in this fragment *usucapio* of *grex* is denied (see below). It is difficult to agree with the argument that a person who brought *rei vindicatio* is regarded as having brought *actio Publiciana* at the same time. In D. 21,2,39,1 Iul. 57 dig., it is only stated that a person who brought *rei vindicatio* can still bring *actio Publiciana* separately. As it will be discussed below, the problem whether *usucapio* of *grex* is available must be distinguished from the possibility of the *vindicatio* of a *grex*. Therefore, it must be said that in this fragment *actio Publiciana* was not taken into consideration.

"We must now look to the third case. A flock or herd is not *usucapted* in the same way as individual things nor yet as those which are constructed or put together. What, then, is the position? Although the essence of a flock is such that it subsists through the accretion of animals, there is no *usucapio* of the flock as such; just as there is possession of individual animals, so also is there *usucapio* of them. Hence, if a purchased beast be incorporated with a view to augmenting the flock, the ground of its possession is not changed so that if the rest of the flock belongs to me, I own this beast also. But the individual animals have their own grounds of possession (acquisition: in Watson's translation), and so if any of the flock be stolen animals, they are still not *usucapted*."

According to Pomponius, the essence of a *grex* is such that it subsists through the accretion of individual animals. The *causa* of possession, however, is specific to the individual animals. If some animals are purchased and incorporated in a *grex*, the *causa* of their possession is not changed. Therefore, if the animals are purchased and incorporated in a *grex* have been stolen, their possession is still not acquired, because the defect of a stolen thing may not be cured by the incorporation.

d) The Establishment of a Real Security Right over a *grex*

It is possible to establish a real security right without possession over a *grex*:[34]

D. 20,1,13 pr. Marcian. form. hyp. sing.
Grege pignori obligato quae postea nascuntur tenentur: sed et si prioribus capitibus decedentibus totus grex fuerit renovatus, pignori tenebitur.
"If a flock is mortgaged, later born animals are included. Indeed, if the whole flock dies and is renewed, it remains subject to mortgage."

After the hypothec over the *grex* is established, later born animals are automatically included. If only the animals born into the *grex* have survived and if they have switched places completely with the animals which constituted it at the time of the establishment of the hypothec, the *grex* remains subject to the same right.

The Roman jurists' views cited until now lead to the following questions:

(a) Why can a *grex* be the same as the former one even after the number of it has decreased or increased?[35]

---

34 *Arnd Löffelmann*, Pfandrecht und Sicherungsübereignung an künftigen Sachen. Rechtsvergleich zwischen deutschem und römischem Recht, Cologne et al. 1996, 176–177.

35 D. 6,1,3 pr. Ulp. 16 ed.; D. 30,21 Ulp. 15 Sab.; D. 44,2,21,1 Pomp. 31 Sab.; D. 20,1,13 pr. Marcian. form. hyp. sing.

(b) Why can we not regard it as a *grex* when the number of cattle decreases so much that only one cattle survives?[36]
(c) Why is *usucapio* of a *grex* not allowed, although *rei vindicatio* may be brought up for a *grex*?[37]

3. Stoics' Ontology

In order to answer these questions, it is necessary to give an outline of the very influential Stoics' ontology. It has been widely accepted by the research on this topic[38] that, according to the texts of Pomponius (D. 41,3,30 pr.) and Paulus (D. 6,1,23,5) as described above, the Roman jurists' views about the legal treatment for *grex* were affected by the Stoics' ontology.[39]

a) Stoics' Monism

Stoics' monism is based on οὐσία which contains all entities in this world. This οὐσία is subdivided into the active part which consists of basic elements of fire and air, being said to be a warm breath, and the passive part which includes basic elements of water and soil.[40] This active part, called πνευματικὴ οὐσία, is a principle of action, the God in this world, which creates it and forms its order.[41] All entities come into existence from a mixture of these active and passive elements.[42] Depending on the composition of these active and passive elements, οἰκεία οὐσία, a fundamental character of every entity is determined.[43] This process is divided into different steps. At the most basic step the active elements as ἕξις are inherent throughout every entity. The ἕξις operates inside every entity

36 D. 7,4,31 Pomp. 4 Q. Muc.; D. 30,22 Pomp. 5 Sab.

37 D. 41,3,30,2 Pomp. 30 Sab.

38 *Warnkönig* (fn. 11) 170–171; *Göppert* (fn. 11) 7–70; *Martin Josef Schermaier*, Materia. Beiträge zur Frage der Naturphilosophie im klassischen römischen Recht, Vienna et al. 1992, 215–216; *Wojciech Dajczak*, Erwägungen des Pomponius zur Natur des *corpus* im dreißigsten Buch des Kommentars *ad Sabinum* (D. 41.3.30 pr.), RIDA 52 (2005) 117–130, esp. 122–125; *Andreas Groten*, Corpus und universitas. Römisches Körperschafts- und Gesellschaftsrecht zwischen griechischer Philosophie und römischer Politik, Tübingen 2015, 87.

39 *Göppert* (fn. 11) 10–13 quotes, for example, Plu., Moralia 142F–143A; S. E., M.7,102; 9,78; Sen., nat. 2,2; Sen., epist. 102,6; Ach. Tat., Intr. Arat. 14.

40 *Schermaier* (fn. 38) 81; *Groten* (fn. 38) 92.

41 *Göppert* (fn. 11) 20–21; *Schermaier* (fn. 38) 81–82; *Groten* (fn. 38) 92.

42 *Göppert* (fn. 11) 21; *Groten* (fn. 38) 93.

43 *Groten* (fn. 38) 95.

in order to keep and preserve it by its tension.[44] Moreover, the ἕξις ascends the entity to the higher steps and gives it φύσις, ψυχή, and λόγος.[45]

b) Stoics' "Categorical Theory"

In the Stoics' "Categorical theory", οἰκεία οὐσία is the first stage of the characters of τὸ ὄν, something that exists, and is called ὑποκείμενον, something that lies at the base. From the ὑποκείμενον, ποιότης, fundamental characters of τὸ ὄν come into existence. ποιότης indicates the effects of the active element, πνευματικὴ οὐσία which gives τὸ ὄν its form or shape.[46] The second stage of the characters of τὸ ὄν is τὸ ποιόν, the nature. The nature reveals ποιότης, fundamental characters of individual recognition object. The Stoics distinguish κοινῶς ποιόν, a universal nature which is common among every single object belonging to some species, from ἰδίως ποιόν, a peculiar nature which brings an identity of the individual object and its existence. ἰδίως ποιόν belongs peculiarly to every entity, and therefore enables recognition of it. Everything which has a recognisable nature is a *corpus*, and therefore exists.[47]

c) Different Types of *corpus* in Stoics' Theory

Individual *corpus*, ἡνωμένον, is penetrated by one ἕξις (*uno spiritu continetur*) and results from σύγχυσις, the mixture of the active and passive elements.[48] The σύγχυσις is one of the four various types of transformation, μεταβολαί, that Stoics defined. In the σύγχυσις, each of two different previously separated ποιότητες disappear and they are unified into the third, new ποιότης.[49] In contrast, συνημμένον is composed of several individual *corpora* which are neighbours to each other and are combined with main *corpus*. It comes into existence through a superficial contact, as a consequence of μῖξις παραθέσει, in which each *corpus* is adjacent.[50] In the μῖξις two different things occupy one and the same space and each one thing gets into the other, but they are not unified.[51] Therefore, συνημμένον lacks integrated ἕξις which only the individual *corpus* has. According to the Stoics' theory, however, συνημμένον has the integrated ποιόν. This

44 *Göppert* (fn. 11) 23–24; *Schermaier* (fn. 38) 83; *Groten* (fn. 38) 93–94.

45 *Göppert* (fn. 11) 24–25; *Groten* (fn. 38) 94.

46 *Göppert* (fn. 11) 26; *Groten* (fn. 38) 95.

47 *Göppert* (fn. 11) 26–27; *Groten* (fn. 38) 95–96.

48 As to the Stoa's mixture theory, see *Schermaier* (fn. 38) 177–180.

49 *Göppert* (fn. 11) 30, 33.

50 *Groten* (fn. 38) 101–102.

51 *Göppert* (fn. 11) 32–33.

integrated ποιὸν makes συνημμένον an object of integrated recognition and one *corpus*. In the case of συνημμένον the ποιὸν arises through καθ' ἁρμήν, direct and physical contact.[52] Furthermore, *corpus ex distantibus* is composed of *corpora* which are stand-alone, separated, and unattached to each other. This *corpus* is not recognised as the same single *corpus* as ἡνωμένον nor integrated one as συνημμένον, because it has no integrated ἕξις, nor direct and physical contact of *corpora* from which the integrated ποιὸν arises.[53] Notwithstanding, in the *corpus ex distantibus* a certain ποιόν, which is not recognised in the individual *corpus*, is seen as a collection of the *corpus*.[54]

The Stoics describe this ποιὸν with a choir, which is a familiar example to the ancient Greek culture[55]. Each individual singer cannot give to the audience a single impression of κατάταξις, an order, or a resonance which a choir can provide.[56] In this case the only decisive question is to know what is the concrete object of recognition from the specific point of view. For everything that its ποιὸν is recognisable, it comes into existence as *corpus* consequently. The singers of which the choir consists can be recognised, in their ἰδίως ποιόν, as every single singer, or as a choir which is composed of the singers, a bigger integrated entity than them.[57]

4. Answers to the Questions Based on the Stoics' Theory

This Stoics' theory gives answers to the questions raised above and grounds for the opinions of Roman jurists.

a) Why Can a *grex* be the same as the Former one even after the Number of it Decreases or Increases?

According to the Stoics' theory, *corpus* as a combination of several individual *corpora* can exist independently of its number or identity. For its ἰδίως ποιὸν continues independently of its οὐσία unless its usual character changes so essentially that it disappears.[58] In that case, what is the ἰδίως ποιὸν of a *grex*? The Stoics found an integrating tie in the internal, spiritual relationship among individual things. Impulse of crowding together leads animals to a *grex* and its

52 *Groten* (fn. 38) 103–104.
53 *Groten* (fn. 38) 102–104.
54 *Groten* (fn. 38) 104.
55 S. E., M. 7,102; 9,78; Ach. Tat., Intr. Arat. 14 raises a choir as example.
56 *Groten* (fn. 38) 104–105.
57 *Groten* (fn. 38) 106–108.
58 *Groten* (fn. 38) 131.

mutual sense brings about the integrated impulse, the common perception, and the cooperative behaviour. Therefore, each animal in a *grex* is no longer a single individual but a component of the whole *grex*.[59]

b) Why Can we not Regard it as a *grex* When the Number of the Cattle Decreases and only one Survives?

According to the Stoics' theory, the ἰδίως ποιὸν of a *grex* is the animals' impulse of crowding together and this ἰδίως ποιὸν depends on its usual fundamental ποιότης. Then, essential change in a collection of several individual *corpora* let the usual ποιότης cease to exist.[60] It is an essential change in it that the number of the animals in the *grex* decreases and only one survives. Therefore, the *grex* whose number becomes only one cannot be regarded as a *grex*.

c) Why is *usucapio* of a *grex* not Allowed, although *rei vindicatio* May be Brought for a *grex*?

According to Pomponius, it is because the object of *usucapio* must be that of *possessio* and only an individual animal as a single *corpus* can have a *causa possessionis*.[61] For example, *quod uno spiritu continetur* is an individual *corpus*, so it can be possessed and usucapted. Furthermore, συνημμένον, being composed of several individual *corpora* which are neighbours to each other, can be possessed and usucapted, if every several *corpora* remain as they were (*utrumque maneat integrum*), in other words, keep their condition as individual *corpus*.

A similar opinion is expressed by Labeo, a jurist of the 1st century AD:

> D. 41,3,30,1 Pomp. 30 Sab.
> Labeo libris epistularum ait, si is, cui ad tegularum vel columnarum usucapionem decem dies superessent, in aedificium eas coniecisset, nihilo minus eum usucapturum, si aedificium possedisset. quid ergo in his, quae non quidem implicantur rebus soli, sed mobilia permanent, ut in anulo gemma? in quo verum est et aurum et gemmam possideri et usucapi, cum utrumque maneat integrum.
> "Labeo says in his Letters, that if a man who needs ten days to complete *usucapio* of tiles or columns should incorporate them into a building, he will usucape all the same, if he possesses the building. What, then, of things which do not become embedded in

59 *Göppert* (fn. 11) 49–52; *Hammerstein* (fn. 16) 18.
60 *Groten* (fn. 38) 131.
61 D. 41,3,30,2 Pomp. 30 Sab.

the soil but remain removable, say, jewels in a ring? In such a case, it is true that since each remains intact, both the gold and the jewel can each be possessed and usucapted."

Labeo distinguishes by stating that tiles or columns can be possessed and usucapted if they keep their condition as individual *corpus*, but if these are incorporated into a building which is possessed over a sufficient period of time for *usucapio*, only the building can be usucapted even if tiles or columns have not been usucapted yet. So, why can only a single *corpus* have *causa possessionis*? Why can *quod ex distantibus constat*, which is a collection of individual *corpora* and *corpus* itself, not have *causa possessionis*? According to the Stoics' theory, whether we see *quod ex distantibus constat* as *corpus* itself or as a collection of individual *corpora* is only a matter of different points of view.[62] Therefore, it is possible to see that *quod ex distantibus constat* itself has *causa possessionis* and can be possessed and usucapted. In that case, however, it might be that one *causa possessionis* of *quod ex distantibus constat* itself and another *causa possessionis* of individual *corpus* which constitutes *quod ex distantibus constat* are contradictory to each other. For example, if, after a whole *grex* is bequeathed, an animal is purchased and incorporated into the *grex* (*quid emptum immixtum fuerit*), it is impossible that *causa possessionis* of the animal purchased later is both *pro legato* and *pro emptore*.[63] It is certain that the same thing can be possessed on the ground of several different *causae possessionis*.[64] For example, if I obtain an object which was possessed *pro emptore* by the deceased, I can possess it *pro emptore* and *pro herede*.[65] In that case, however, I possess the whole property *pro herede*. In contrast, in the former case, the legatee is not bequeathed the animal purchased later. So, the legatee, on the one hand, possesses the bequeathed whole *grex pro legato* and, on the other hand, the animal purchased later *pro emptore*.[66] It is impossible, however, to usucapt the animal purchased later under the title of *pro legato*, because the animal is not bequeathed and *causa possessionis* of the animal does not

62 *Groten* (fn. 38) 108, 126.

63 D. 41,3,30,2 Pomp. 30 Sab.

64 *Eric Pool*, Zur Bedeutung und Stellung der 'causa' im System klassischer Ersitzungsvoraussetzungen, in: Roman Law as Formative of Modern Legal Systems. Studies in honorem Wieslaw Litewski, Vol II, eds. *Janusz Sondel* et al., Krakow 2003, 37–60; *Wataru Miyasaka*, D. 23,3,67 Proc. 7 epist., Ein angemessener Lehrstoff in Bezug auf die Übertragung des Eigentums im römischen Recht, in: Aus der Werkstatt römischer Juristen. Vorträge der Europäisch-Ostasiatischen Tagung 2013 in Fukuoka, eds. *Ulrich Manthe et al.*, Berlin 2016, 253–275.

65 D. 41,2,3,4 Paul. 54 ed.

66 It is certain that, if the bequeathed property was possessed *pro emptore* by the legator, the legatee possesses it both *pro emptore* and *pro legato*, but this *causa possessionis* should be distinguished from that of the animal purchased later.

change from *pro emptore* to *pro legato*. In contrast, it is impossible to usucapt the bequeathed whole *grex* under the title of *pro emptore*, because the whole *grex* is not bought and *causa possessionis* does not change from *pro legato* to *pro emptore*. It is possible only to usucapt the animal under the title of *pro emptore*. Therefore, in the case of contradiction between *causa possessionis* of *quod ex distantibus constat* itself and another *causa possessionis* of individual *corpus* which constitutes *quod ex distantibus constat*, we should determine what is *causa possessionis* only in the individual *corpus*, not in *quod ex distantibus constat*.

III. On *Merces in horreo* or *in taberna*

In Justinian's Digest, in addition to the storage of merchandise, various uses of *horreum* in classical Roman times are described: Storage of food,[67] wine,[68] furniture,[69] documents,[70] or silver articles,[71] and earning revenue from lease.[72] Many of the texts in the Digest with regard to *horreum* ("about the storage") deal with the legacy and its object.

1. Collective Treatment of Merchandises in a Warehouse

Merchandises in a warehouse can collectively be the object of contracts or delivery without being taken away from there. When someone stipulates the wine, for instance, oil, or corn, which is in a warehouse, it is dealt with as a specified item under the *stipulatio*.[73] If a debtor is obliged to give the specified items such as "the weight of silver which I have in that warehouse", and the items are lost without fault on the debtor's part, nothing is due and therefore the creditor retains the risk.[74] By handing over the key of a storehouse in front of it, ownership and possession of the merchandise in the storehouse is transferred, and if the merchandise does not belong to the vendor, *usucapio* starts at once, since, according to Paul, it is regarded as delivered, if the parties agree on their transfer in the presence of the thing.[75]

67 D. 30,47,1 Ulp. 22 Sab.; D. 33,9,3,11 Ulp. 22 Sab.

68 D. 33,7,7 Scaev. 22 dig.; D. 30,47,1 Ulp. 22 Sab.; D. 33,7,12,29 Ulp. 20 Sab.; D. 33,7,12,39 Ulp. 20 Sab.

69 D. 33,7,20,8 Scaev. 3 resp.

70 D. 2,13,6 pr. Ulp. 4 ed.

71 D. 34,2,32,4 Paul. 2 Vit.; D. 35,2,30,4 Maec. 8 quaest. fideic.

72 D. 33,1,20,1 Scaev. 18 dig.; D. 10,4,5 pr. Ulp. 24 ed.; D. 19,2,56 Paul. off. praef. vig. sing.

73 D. 45,1,75,5 Ulp. 22 ed.

74 D. 35,2,30,4 Maec. 8 quaest. fideic.

75 D. 41,1,9,6 Gai. 2 cott.; D. 18,1,74 Pap. 1 def.; D. 41,2,1,21 Paul. 54 ed.

2. The Establishment of the Real Security Right without Possession over the *merces* in a Warehouse

A problem is whether it was possible to establish the real security right without possession over the *merces* in a warehouse. We cannot find any source in the Digest to tell us the answer clearly. The source which suggests the possibility, however, is the case of a marble dealer (a). In addition, evidence for this possibility has been transmitted in a non-legal text (b). The text suggests that an object of a real security right might be coming and going. Moreover, the case of the establishment of the real security right without possession over the *merces* coming and going cannot be found for a warehouse, but for *merces* being inside a shop (c).

a) Case of a Marble Dealer

> D. 20,4,21,1 Scaev. 27 dig.
> Negotiatori marmorum creditur sub pignore lapidum, quorum pretia venditores ex pecunia creditoris acceperant: idem debitor conductor horreorum caesaris fuit, ob quorum pensiones aliquot annis non solutas procurator exactioni praepositus ad lapidum venditionem officium suum extendit: quaesitum est, an iure pignoris eos creditor retinere possit. respondit secundum ea quae proponerentur posse.
> "A loan was made to a marble dealer subject to a pledge of the marble slabs, the sellers of which had been paid with the creditor's money. The debtor was also lessee of an imperial warehouse, rent for which had not been paid for several years. The imperial procurator claimed to sell the slabs in pursuance of his duty to exact payment. The question put was whether the creditor could retain them by way of pledge. Scaevola replied that according to the facts stated he could."

A marble dealer borrowed money and hypothecated the marble slabs. The money was used to pay the sellers. The debtor was also lessee of an imperial warehouse, and the rent had not been paid for several years. Therefore, the imperial *procurator* excused the slabs for retiring the unpaid rent. In this case, according to Scaevola, the creditor could retain them based on his hypothec. It may be noted incidentally that, with respect to acquiring the real security rights without possession, the legal position of each party depends on the chronology of the establishment of the respective rights. It is said that the one earlier in time has the better right (*prior tempore, potior iure*). This principle, however, is sometimes overruled and the later creditor prevails over the earlier:

D. 20,4,5 Ulp. 3 disp.
Interdum posterior potior est priori, ut puta si in rem istam conservandam impensum est quod sequens credidit: veluti si navis fuit obligata et ad armandam eam vel reficiendam ego credidero:
"Sometimes the later creditor prevails over the earlier, for instance, if the loan by the later was spent on preserving the mortgaged property. For example, a ship is mortgaged and I lend money to fit it out or repair it."

D. 20,4,6 Ulp. 73 ed.
Huius enim pecunia salvam fecit totius pignoris causam. quod poterit quis admittere et si in cibaria nautarum fuerit creditum, sine quibus navis salva pervenire non poterat.
1: Item si quis in merces sibi obligatas crediderit, vel ut salvae fiant vel ut naulum exsolvatur, potentior erit, licet posterior sit: nam et ipsum naulum potentius est.
2: Tantundem dicetur, et si merces horreorum vel areae vel vecturae iumentorum debetur: nam et hic potentior erit.
"The money preserved the object of the mortgage. Even if the loan was for provisions for the sailors, this view can be accepted, since without food the ship could not arrive safely.
1. So if someone lends money so that cargo secured in his favour may be saved or that freight may be paid on it, he will prevail, though his mortgage is later. Indeed, the freight itself has priority.
2. The same is held if the rent of a warehouse or site or freight for animal transport is owed. This too has priority."

If, for example, a transporter who leased a ship cargo borrowed money and hypothecated the freight to his creditor, and the money was paid as a rent from the transporter to the lessor of the ship, the creditor, even if there was another earlier creditor and he was the later one, could preferentially be satisfied from the freight. In this case, a lessee of a warehouse borrowed money and hypothecated the merchandise stored in it to his creditor. The money was paid as the rent from the lessee to the lessor of the warehouse. The creditor, even if he was the later one, could be satisfied from the merchandise if he prefers so. In this way, the third creditor can satisfy the claim of the lessor as the first creditor and succeed him thereby.

If a warehouse is leased, an implied agreement for the hypothec over goods brought in by the lessee is recognised for the lessor to secure the rent.[76] If the marble slabs were not stored in the imperial warehouse, the lessor's silent hypothec does not arise over them. If so, Scaevola remarks, the creditor could retain them preferentially. It is a possibility, however, that the marble dealer hy-

76 D. 20,2,3 Ulp. 73 ed.; D. 19,2,56 Paul. off. praef. vig. sing.

pothecated the slabs explicitly to the lessor of the warehouse. In this case, the lessor is the earlier creditor and the creditor who loaned money to the marble dealer is the later creditor. Or, if the marble slabs were stored in the imperial warehouse, the lessor's silent hypothec may arise over them. In this case, he is the earlier creditor and the creditor who loaned money to the marble dealer is the later. In these cases, the later creditor could not retain the slabs based on his hypothec, unless he satisfied the claim of the earlier. Why did Scaevola give priority to the creditor who loaned money to the marble dealer? It is likely that the marble dealer also explicitly hypothecated the slabs to their sellers therefore, they are the first creditors. Because of the payment of the price to the sellers, the third creditor who loaned money satisfies the claim of the sellers as the first creditors and succeeds them thereby. After all, the discussion between the Roman jurists shows that in Roman law a real security right could be established over the *merces* in a warehouse, even without possession.

b) Case of the Establishment of Real Security Right without Possession over Grain in a Warehouse

In general, grain is by its very nature a collective entity.[77] As made clear in many ancient texts, grain was transported and stored *en bloc*, and weighed and made into small portion as necessary. A very speaking example can be taken from the wax tablets that were excavated near Pompeii in 1959. They contain the documents from the archives of the family of the *Sulpicii* who were bankers and businesspersons at *Puteoli*. Among them, there are documents with a written record of a debt for a real security right over Alexandrian wheat, which was stored in a warehouse, and established the creditor's money claim. TP Sulp. 46 is a record of *locatio conductio* of a warehouse, which was written by a slave Nardus, whose master was Publius Annus Seleucus, the *horrearius* of the warehouse. TP Sulp. 79 is a record of an establishment of real security right, which was written by a *libertus* L. Marius Iucundus, whose *patronus* was Dida. According to these records, on 13th March 40, Seleucus leased the warehouse No. 26, which was a part of *horrea Barbatiana* located at the estate of Domitia Lepida, given to Gaius Sulpicius Faustus, for rent of one hundred *sestertii* per month. At the warehouse No. 26 the thirteen thousand *modii* of Alexandrian wheat were said to be stored, but these amounts are to be weighed by Seleucus and his slaves. Then, two days after, 15th March 40, Iucundus gave the thirteen thousand *modii* of Alexandrian wheat for security of his debts which amount to twenty thousand *sestertii* which he owed to Gaius Sulpicius Faustus. About this debt, TP Sulp. 53

77 Sen., nat. 2,2–3 (see also fn. 39) raises *frumentum*, wheat, as an example.

reports that Iucundus accepted the twenty thousand *sestertii* as *mutuum* from Faustus. Then, the consequence was laid down of what would happen, if Iucundus could not repay the twenty thousand *sestertii* by 15th May 40 or give satisfaction to Faustus in other manner. Faustus could sell the wheat, and, if the price exceeds the amount of the debts, Faustus should refund the surplus, and, if the price is less than the amount of the debts, Iucundus must repay the rest of his debts to Faustus or his heirs still, and finally, all risks with respect to the wheat were borne by Iucundus or his heirs.

The question therefore is: Did the amount of wheat stored in the warehouse undergo a change? This question and the sources have already been analysed in detail by many scholars.[78] But a small consideration can be added to their outcomes. There are two points which should be focused on. The first point is those thirteen thousand *modii* of Alexandrian wheat which were said to be stored in the warehouse No. 26 were not yet weighed. This means that the amount of wheat stored in this warehouse at that time could be more or less than thirteen thousand *modii*. In other words, the components of the object of this real security right could undergo a change, even after the establishment of the right over it. Therefore, it can be said that the wheat in the warehouse could be modified in its quantity. The second point is that Seleucus lent the warehouse No. 26 to Faustus, where the hypothec object was stored, even before the establishment of his right. Some scholars have argued, that with this *locatio conductio* Faustus acquired *possessio* of the wheat stored in the warehouse and prepared for risks such as declining in the value of the object of the real security right.[79] The term

---

78 *Jean Macqueron*, Deux contrats d'entrepôts du 1er siècle ap. J.C., T. Pomp. 7 et 44, in: Études offertes à Pierre Kayser, Aix-Marseille 1979, 200–212; *Giuseppe Camodeca*, Tabulae Pompeianae Sulpiciorum. TP Sulp. Edizione critica dell'archivio puteolano dei Sulpicii, Rome 1999; *Joseph Georg Wolf*, Der neue pompejanische Urkundenfund, ZRG RA 118 (2001) 73–132, esp. 113–116; *Gerd Krämer*, Das besitzlose Pfandrecht. Entwicklungen in der römischen Republik und im frühen Prinzipat, Cologne et al. 2007, 323–338; *Emmanuelle Chevreau*, La pratique du gage dans les Tabulae Pompeianae Sulpiciorum, in: Festschrift für Rolf Knütel zum 70. Geburtstag, eds. *Holger Altmeppen* et al., Heidelberg 2009, 183–196; *Hendrikus L. E. Verhagen*, Das Verfallpfand im frühklassischen römischen Recht, Dingliche Sicherheit im Archiv der Sulpizier, TR 79 (2011) 1–46; *Paul J. du Plessis*, Letting and Hiring in Roman Legal Thought. 27 BCE–284 CE, Leiden/Boston 2012, 173–189; *Eva Jakab*, Horrea, suretes et commerce maritime dans les archives des Sulpicii, in: Inter cives necnon peregrinos. Essays in honour of Boudewijn Sirks, eds. *Jan Hallebeek* et al., Göttingen 2014, 331–349; *Fabian Klinck*, Verpfändung und Speichermiete in den Tabulae Pompeianae Sulpiciorum, in: Facetten des römischen Pfandrechts, Studien zur Geschichte und Dogmatik des Privatrechts, ed. *Jan Dirk Harke*, Berlin 2015, 55–73.

79 *Camodeca* (fn. 78) 181–183 implies so by his direction of conferring another, quite similar case with this told us by TP Sulp. 45, 51 and 52, see also *Camodeca* (fn. 78) 121–124, 138–141. *Wolf* (fn. 78) 114–115; *du Plessis* (fn. 78) 178–179, 183–184 and 188–189; *Krämer* (fn. 78) 319 follows basically *Camodeca's* view.

possessio, however, and an avoidance of risks by acquiring *possessio* seems to need more particular explanation. It can be presumed that Faustus prepared for risks with the *locatio conductio horrei* at the cost of the rent, in the following two ways: Firstly, by entering the warehouse as a *conductor* and checking whether the wheat, as the object of the real security right, has altered in its quality by heat, dampness or by small animals and bugs.[80] These risks should be managed originally by the debtor who establishes the real security right, but it is possible that he neglects the management, especially if he becomes insolvent. Secondly, risks are managed by becoming *conductor* in order to prevent *locator* of seizing the object of the real security right in case the debtor as a *conductor* has not been paid his rent.[81]

A *locator's* real security right has priority over other creditors, if the *locatio conductio* including an agreement establishing the real security right has been concluded in advance.[82]

These assumptions lead to the suggestion that leaving the object of real security right without possession to the hands of the debtor involves a lot of risks. To avoid these risks, especially the disintegration of the good, it was useful for the creditor to become the *conductor*, because *locatio conductio horrei* provided the *conductor* with a kind of *possessio*. It was a type of a *possessio* for custody and administration of the object in *locatio conductio*. This custodial and administrative *possessio* was of help to administrate the object of the real security right locating the object of *locatio conductio*. But, for the following three reasons it is difficult

80 The warehouse in Ostia, for example, was equipped with facilities for such risks like *suspensurae* floors. *Gustav Hermansen*, Ostia. Aspects of Roman City Life, Edmonton 1981, 227–230.

81 See fn. 76.

82 D. 20,4,9 pr. Afr. 8 quaest.; *Klinck* (fn. 78) 68–70 says that an establishment of second-ranked real security right over an object of someone's first-ranked right at the same time was recognized only after Iulianus' time and raised D. 20,4,9,3 Afr. 8 quaest. and D. 20,1,15,2 Gai. form. hyp. sing. as examples. The former fragment tells us that such a second-ranked real security right can be confirmed only after a precedent right is solved and, at the time of solution, the object remains in bonis debitoris. According to the author, this understanding presupposes that the second ranked right does not become valid at the time of establishment. An expression in the fragment non … magis Maevii pignus convalescere placebat, however, shows that there was a minor, but different opinion. The opinion might admit the confirmation without any condition since before Iulianus. The latter fragment lets us know that, in practice at that time, a thing on which a real security right has already been established became the object of another real security right again in a way that the right was established on a surplus gained through selling the object by the first-ranked creditor or that it was done on the object itself anew after the first-ranked creditor has been satisfied, in order to avoid danger for a debtor pledging the one and same thing several times. The purpose of this practice, however, suggests that the matter which brings the danger has occurred in fact and such a pledge in itself has not been prohibited.

to assume that *locatio conductio* of the warehouse, where the object of the real security right was located, provided *possessio* to prevent Iucundus from selling and transferring the object without the creditor's permission: Firstly, the effect of *locatio conductio horrei* can only extend to the lent space in the warehouse, not directly to the object of the real security right located there. Until he exercises his right, a creditor with a real security right cannot seize the object directly. It cannot be expected that *actio quasi Serviana* had already been available in this period,[83] rather it has probably been developed later to solve these problems. Secondly, if the creditor as *conductor* tried to seal off the warehouse and prevent the debtor from selling and transferring the object of the real security right, this hindrance must be rejected by the *interdictum* based on the debtor's *possessio* of the object. Thirdly, it may be recognised by the parties that it is not a risk, but almost a certainty that Iucundus would try to sell and transfer the object of the real security right at his will. Fluctuation of the amount of wheat in the warehouse means that the wheat came in and out of the warehouse. The harvest season of wheat in Egypt was from April to early June.[84] The right time to journey across the Mediterranean was from early March to early September, but it took at least a month from *Alexandria* to *Puteoli* and a two-time round trip was the limit, because the north wind blew on the shipping route between *Alexandria* and *Puteoli* in this season.[85] However, the ship for transportation of grains is estimated to be able to carry a load of ten to fifty thousand *modii* (68 to 340 tons).[86] And the ships could be in a convoy.[87] If, additionally, we take into account the export rates of wheat from *Puteoli* to *Ostia* and its consumption inside the city of *Puteoli* and in the surrounding cities, it must be presumed that, after the middle of March at least, the amount of wheat stored in the warehouses for grains at *Puteoli*, including the warehouse No. 26 in this case, was never constant, but rather rose and fell. Such a coming and going seems to account for business by Iucundus who, in the beginning, (theoretically at least) deposited a bulk of wheat surpassing the amount of personal consumption by far. If Faustus acquired his *possessio* of the wheat by *locatio conductio horrei* and fully prevented Iucundus from changing the amount of the wheat, that would comprise a major obstacle to Iucundus' business and eventually generate a harmful effect to the debt repayment as well. It is more reasonable for Faustus, instead, to let Iucundus continue to run his business and therefore expect the repayment from the

83 *Kaser/Knütel/Lohsse* (fn. 13) 189.

84 *Geoffrey Rickman*, The Corn Supply of Ancient Rome, New York 1980, 121.

85 *Rickman* (fn. 84) 128–129, 131.

86 *Rickman* (fn. 84) 123.

87 *Rickman* (fn. 84) 129–130.

gaining. Furthermore, Faustus established an agreement with Iucundus about the short deadline of repayment only within two months and a foreclosure sale. These considerations seem to denote that there was no need for Faustus to acquire the possession of the wheat.

c) Case of the Establishment of a Real Security Right without Possession over Merchandises in a Shop

A case of *horreum* as in the archive of the Sulpicii has not been passed down by the Digest, but a case of *taberna*, which denotes "a shop", is passed down to us, even if the question of the real security right without possession having an effect on the goods when the contents of them change as well is left open:[88]

> D. 20,1,34 pr. Scaev. 27 dig.
> Cum tabernam debitor creditori pignori dederit, quaesitum est, utrum eo facto nihil egerit an tabernae appellatione merces, quae in ea erant, obligasse videatur? et si eas merces per tempora distraxerit et alias comparaverit easque in eam tabernam intulerit et decesserit, an omnia quae ibi deprehenduntur creditor hypothecaria actione petere possit, cum et mercium species mutatae sint et res aliae illatae? respondit: ea, quae mortis tempore debitoris in taberna inventa sunt, pignori obligata esse videntur.
> "When a debtor had pledged his shop to his creditor, he was asked whether he had accomplished nothing thereby, or if under the designation "shop" all the goods on the premises counted as pledged. And if in time these goods were sold and others bought and brought into the shop and then he dies, can the creditor sue with an action on the hypothec to take possession of all the property on the premises, although the kinds of goods have changed and the new property has been brought in? Scaevola responded: What is in the shop at the time of the debtor's death counts as pledged."

According to Scaevola, when a debtor had hypothecated his shop to his creditor, he would have by some time sold all the goods and bought others and brought them into the shop. When he dies, the creditor can bring an action on the hypothec and claim the goods which are in the shop at the time of the debtor's death. As a corollary of this, the creditor's real security right had an effect not only on the newly bought but also influenced the goods sold by the debtor's heir after his death as long as those are in the shop at the time of his death. This in-

88 *Fritz Sturm*, 2. Teil: Exegese von Scaevola (27 dig.) D. 20.1.34 pr., in *Hans Schlosser et al.*, Die rechtsgeschichtliche Exegese. Römisches Recht, deutsches Recht, Kirchenrecht, Munich 1993², 26–58; *Löffelmann* (fn. 34) 171–176; *Dietmar Schanbacher*, Vorausverpfändung und Erbfolge – Scaev. 27 dig. D. 20,1, 34 pr., in: *Harke* (fn. 78) 75–81.

dicated that the real security right without possession had an effect on the merchandises newly brought into the shop without the establishment of the right individually when components of the merchandises in a shop changed.

According to the preceding studies, especially Sturm's in-depth exegesis, the following three questions should be examined: (a) Why has it been argued by Scaevola whether the real security right over *taberna* had an effect on the merchandises having been located in the shop or not[89]; (b) What is the *merces* as the object of the real security right specifically in this fragment;[90] (b-1) Whether in the *merces* not only the stock of merchandises but also cash money or slaves as working staff are included; (b-2) Whether in the *merces* only the merchandises existing actually in the shop are included or, in addition to that, the goods sold and moved out by the debtor in the past and newly bought and brought into the shop as well;[91] (c) What is the ground of Scaevola's decision that the real security right had an effect on the merchandises which were in the shop at the time of the debtor's death.[92]

Sturm answers these questions as follows:

(a) Because it was argued whether *merces* were included in an objective meaning of the word *taberna* (not because the object of real security right could not be identified due to ambiguity of its meaning, nor because there is a discrepancy between the parties' declaration as *taberna* and their true intent as *merces*).
(b-1) In the *merces* only the stock of merchandises is included, because it is clear that the words in the fragment *omnia quae ibi deprehenduntur* or *ea, quae mortis tempore debitoris in taberna inventa sunt* substantially designate the *merces*.
(b-2) In the *merces* only the merchandises actually existing in the shop are included, because the *merces* in this fragment should not be understood as 'Sachgesamtheit' (*universitas rerum*) such as *grex*. The author raised three arguments: Firstly, the treatment of *grex* in Roman law such as *vindicatio gregis* or the establishment of real security right over *grex* was a special one ('Sonderrecht') deriving from the agricultural society in the archaic period and therefore it could not be extended to the treatment of *merces*. Secondly, the words in the fragment *omnia quae ibi deprehenduntur* or *ea, quae mortis tempore debitoris in taberna inventa sunt* indicate the goods actually existing in the shop. Finally, the fact that during the debtor's lifetime the goods newly bought and brought into the shop by him become the object of real security right and after his death the goods

89 *Sturm* (fn. 88) 34–37.
90 *Sturm* (fn. 88) 37–38.
91 *Sturm* (fn. 88) 38–42.
92 *Sturm* (fn. 88) 42–47.

sold and moved out by his heir remain in it can be explained in a different way from the one based on the understanding of *universitas rerum*: it is by a specific agreement between the creditor and the debtor that the extinguishment of real security right by the sale of the object and the establishment of it over the goods going to be bought by the debtor in the future are settled.
(c) Because by the debtor's death it becomes impossible to exercise the right to sell the object, which is given on condition that he buys the merchandises newly, and because his heir is not bound by the agreement. The author says the understanding of *merces* as *universitas rerum* cannot explain this question.

While the author's answers to (a) and (b-1) are understandable, it is difficult to accept the answers to (b-2) and (c). Concerning the answer to (b-2), against the author's three arguments counterarguments can be raised. Firstly, as an example of the special treatment of *grex* in Roman law, the author refers to a rule that *usucapio* of *grex* is impossible. The reason of this impossibility is, however, as shown above,[93] to avoid the contradiction between *causa possessionis* of *quod ex distantibus constat* itself and another *causa possessionis* of individual corpus which constitute *quod ex distantibus constat*. The need to avoid it is common with every *quod ex distantibus constat* and the rule can be extended to *merces* as such. Secondly, as the author says, if the word *merces* in this fragment indicates the goods actually existing in the shop, Scaevola would need not to add clauses with relative pronouns such as *quae ibi deprehenduntur or quae mortis tempore debitoris in taberna inventa sunt*. Finally, such a specific agreement does not contradict the understanding of the *merces* as *universitas rerum*. Adversely, in order to deal with the *merces* as the object of real security right without possession, the parties must make the agreement originally. Then, the contents of the agreement might become a custom in the establishment of the real security right without possession and be incorporated into the juristic concept of *universitas rerum*.[94] About the answers to (c), as shown above, it depends on the parties' agreement to deal with the *merces* as the object of real security right without possession, when the death of one party sets an end to the agreement and its effect is lost. Such a result might be incorporated into the juristic concept of *universitas rerum*.[95]

93 See II. 4. c).

94 As *Hendrikus L. E. Verhagen*, The evolution of pignus in classical Roman law. Ius honorarium and 'ius novum', TR 81 (2013) 51–79, 70 and 79 points out, such customs in the field of real security right have been developed through the merchants' practice and incorporated into law by *ius honorarium* or imperial law.

95 In his explanation of the matter *Dernburg* (fn. 11) 458–461 said that it was only a problem of the parties' intention whether the real security right has effect or not, and denied any possibility of the establishment of comprehensive right over the merchandises. And he argued that the reason the

Having said this, it is possible to assume that what holds true of a *taberna* is applied to *horreum* as well, because *taberna* or *tabernula*, which means "a small shop", and *horreum* are dealt with collaterally.[96] Therefore, it can be said that Roman jurists determined that, when components of the merchandises in a warehouse are changed after the establishment of a real security right without possession over them, the right had an effect on the merchandises newly brought into it.

IV. Conclusions

About the Roman law, this study has clarified the following points:

a) Apart from the individual movables, the *corpus ex distantibus* could be considered a movable. The term describes individual things not binding together physically but building a unity.
b) If the contents of *corpus ex distantibus* change, *rei vindicatio* can be pleaded. This is true, even if, among the *corpus ex distantibus*, individual things are included which are not owned by the person who vindicates. In this case, however, another *vindicatio* for the person who owns the individual things mixed in the *corpus ex distantibus* against the owner is possible.
c) *Corpus ex distantibus* can be the object of a usufruct, purchase and sale collectively.
d) It is possible to establish the real security right without possession over the *corpus ex distantibus*.

On the basis of these conclusions, it can be said that *corpus ex distantibus* had a similar character to the collective entity of movables authorised by the judgments of the Supreme Court in Japanese law. From this I assume that the two difficulties in the Japanese floating lien, which are pointed out at the introduction of this article, may be solved by a look to the Roman law. The consideration of the concept *universitas rerum* in Roman law not only serves as a protection of the mortgagor but also provides a theoretical base for Japanese civil and com-

real security right has no effect on the merchandises newly brought into the shop by the heir is that after the debtor's death his intention has an impact on his heir. If so, then about the merchandises sold by the heir after the debtor's death, the latter's intention that the real security right has effect on it cannot have an impact on his heir and it has no effect. This, however, conflicts with Scaevola's opinion. Therefore, I cannot accept *Dernburg's* view.

96 D. 33,7,7 Scaev. 22 dig.; D. 5,1,19,2 Ulp. 60 ed.

mercial law to meet the demand for the floating lien in practice. In addition, it shows a possibility to Japanese civil and commercial law to catch up with the current establishment of the utilisation of movables for the creation of credit. Furthermore, it tells us that, in order to construct a certain legal theory fundamentally, the understanding of the philosophy and social-economical history on which the legal theory is based is inevitable.

Takeshi Sasaki, Kyoto

Roman-Japanese Legacy with the Appointment of second Degree Successor

An Analysis of the second Petty Bench's Judgment (Japanese Supreme Court) on 18th March 1983

I. Introduction

The Japanese Civil Law contains several articles on the topic of bequest (*legatum*), but leaves out a definition of the legatee: therefore an heir can be named in the bequest of the same testament that states him as an heir.

In the Japanese practice of succession, the testator often leaves a will, according to which he makes someone (possibly even the heir) come into "my" inheritance. At the same time as the heir inherits from the testator he has a duty to execute the testament. Simultaneously, he would gain benefits from the estate. In other words, the legatee has a rightful claim to that will and cannot solely be obligated to execute it. It is to be noted that the inheritance tax upon the bequest for relatives in the first degree of kinship (or spouse) is twenty percent heavier than for other distant relatives.

In the Japanese Civil Law, only the single degree bequest exists. A testament which includes first and second degree bequests is questionable. In such case lawyers would argue that a testament with both first and second-degree beneficiary is only singularly valid (the second degree would be invalid) since the appointment of a second-degree inheritor limits the free disposition of the inheritance largely. This kind of bequest of the second degree is permitted in the article 2100 of the German Civil Code (*Bürgerliches Gesetzbuch*, BGB).[1] The difference to the Japanese law is noteworthy since the Japanese Civil Law has been largely modeled after the German Civil Law.

1 Article 2100 of the German Civil Code reads: "Subsequent heir. The testator may appoint an heir in such a way that the person only becomes an heir after another heir has first been heir (subsequent heir)." (translation according to <https://www.gesetze-im-internet.de/englisch_bgb/englisch_bgb.html#p7092> [13. August 2018]).

There are only two published cases in Japan that deal with the issue of a "bequest of the 2nd Degree": the first one is our case[2] and the second one was issued by the Okayama district court on 22nd February 2001, where the bequest was not recognised for the testator's wife but accepted for his child with the death of the testator's wife as the beginning of the initial term.

II. Summary of the Case

1. Preparing the Testament

Isaku Tsuge, a timber dealer in the prefecture of Nagasaki, had drawn up his will in holograph on 7th March 1974 (afterwards it was slightly corrected on 17th October 1976). His testament had eleven clauses. According to the seventh clause, a piece of land and a building in Babanomoto were bequeathed to his wife Asae (formerly Ms Takano), defendant of this case. However, the third subparagraph of the same (seventh) clause stated that the land and the building should be shared as a common property of the testator's eight relatives, after Asae's death; the eight relatives consist of his sister (Shizue, co-plaintiff of this case), his brothers (Hachiro, not involved in this case, Saburo and Hayata, co-plaintiffs), his nephew Goro Baba (general manager of the company Tsuge timber), his brother-in-law Kusuo Takano (brother of Asae), and his sisters-in-law Tamiko and Yoshiko Takano (sisters of Asae). It was remarked, that this testament was devoted to three beneficiaries, namely the testator's wife Asae, the testator's nephew Goro, who is the posthumous president of the company Tsuge timber, and the testator's brother Hayata. In the public documents, it is not shown in detail what kind of kinship exists between Isaku and Goro, but Goro is presumed to be a son of Isaku's (or Asae's) sister, whose last name, in that case, would be Baba.

We can suppose that the testator Isaku wanted to give Goro a decision-making power within the Tsuge family and the Takano family (see the family-tree attached). In this way, the running of the timber company was supposed to be stabilised before and after Asae's death. Since the land and the building bequeathed were venues used in the production of the timber-materials, Goro should have the final word about how to handle them. Two months after the correction of the testament, Isaku died on 24th December 1976 and his testament came into force. Half a year later, in mid-June 1977, his wife Asae had registered the land and the

2 The Judgment Document can be downloaded for free from the following website of Courts in Japan: <http://www.courts.go.jp> (02. June 2018).

building on account of her husband's single bequest (i.e. without any condition) in her own (individual) name at Nagasaki district legal affairs bureau.

2. In the Court

The plaintiffs, Shizue, Saburo and Hayata, claimed the confirmation of the bequest and that they are beneficiaries of Isaku's testament, so they demanded the registration of the land and of the building to be deleted with regard to Asae's single bequest. They considered Isaku's bequest in their favour to be a bequest with a condition so that the execution of the bequest was suspended until Asae's death. The co-plaintiffs made the secondary request of confirmation that if this is a conditioned bequest, then the testator's complicated will would be too obscure to be valid, so the testament itself and therefore the registration cannot be valid. On 29th November 1979, the first trial at the Nagasaki district court gave the judgment that Isaku's dual bequest would only be valid to its first half. Therefore the bequests for co-plaintiffs were considered to be invalid, and their claim should be rejected. In the decision, the reason why this dual bequest is not recognised was explained in the following way: firstly, the Japanese Civil Code (Art. 1002) specifically recognises the bequest with burden, but the dual bequest is not stated by law, so it has purposely been left out; secondly, if that dual bequest was admitted, the relationship between the first and the second degree beneficiaries would be unusual, so that their legal relationship would be very complicated. So the second half of the bequest, in other words, was considered to be a mere wish of the testator Isaku that could not be legally enforced in any way. That judgment was approved by the court of appeal at Fukuoka on 26th June 1980.

3. The Opinion of the Japanese Supreme Court

The co-plaintiffs made an appeal to the Japanese Supreme Court on the ground that the original court had not considered all eleven clauses of the testament, but had picked up only the first half of the seventh clause, so that the decision had been based insufficiently. On 18th March 1983, this assertion adopted, the Japanese Supreme Court issued the order for that case to be returned to the court of original jurisdiction in order to be re-examined in greater detail: the Supreme Court declared that the testament had not to be interpreted only by extracting some paragraph partially from a single clause, but by making specifications based on all of the clauses, the whole description of testament, and also the circumstances under which the testator had written that will, in order to search for his true motive and to define the true purpose of the will. As noted, the seventh clause of Isaku's testament consisted of three paragraphs: the first included the bequest for Asae (defendant), the second the maintenance of the land and the building for the timber company, and the third included the bequest for Shizue, Saburo, Hayata (plaintiffs) and the others after Asae's death. The other ten clauses dealt with the management of the timber company, the insurance of Asae's life and the bequest of other properties to Asae (testator's wife) and Goro (posthumous president of the company). In particular, the last eleventh clause stated that the bequeathed land and building were so difficult to liquidate, and therefore the secondary beneficiaries (Shizue et al.) should receive some rent from the company manager, probably Goro. The Japanese Supreme Court found four different possibilities to interpret this will:

(a) The second half of the dual bequest could not be legally binding and could only mean a kind of hope written in the testament, an interpretation that would be in line with the opinion of the court of appeal at Fukuoka.
(b) The bequest for Asae could mean that the beneficiary (Asae) had to transfer the bequeathed estate to the secondary beneficiaries in some way, for example by her own testament (bequest etc.).
(c) The bequest for the co-plaintiffs could be realised only in the case (or under the condition) that at Asae's death the bequeathed property would be hers.
(d) Asae would be forbidden to alienate that land and building, so her right in substance should be a usufruct (only to use and take fruit),[3] in other words, the bequest by Isaku in his own way was to be considered as a bequest that would begin with Asae's death (known as a bequest with instruction of initial term).

In order to make the court of appeal at Fukuoka examine Isaku's intention concerning these possibilities, the Japanese Supreme Court sent back the case to Fukuoka.

III. Review from the Viewpoint of a Japanese Romanist

As some Civil Law professors have already pointed out,[4] this kind of dual bequest (ordered by Isaku, the testator) always inflicts problems for the legal po-

3 As mentioned below (III), the Japanese Civil Code does not have any clause about usufruct, still less about the bequest of usufruct which Romans know. See *Pasquale Voci*, Diritto ereditario romano, Vol 2, Milan 1963², 311–312.

4 *Yukiko Urano*, Igon no kaisyaku, Jurist 225 (Feb. 2015) 168–169 with bibliography (Minpo Hanreihyakusen III, Family and Succession, eds. *Noriko Mizuno, Atushi Omura*).

sition of the first degree beneficiary: but it appears that the Japanese Supreme Court wanted to protect some benefits of the secondary beneficiaries (Shizue, Saburo and Hayata, co-plaintiffs).

In addition, under Japanese law, the testator can appoint an heir as a beneficiary of the bequest as well, if both are mentioned in this respect. But in this way, the heir-beneficiary should simultaneously have the obligation of executing the bequest (as an heir) as well as the right to obtain the bequeathed estate (as a beneficiary).[5] Romanists usually explain that the reason why Romans appointed the heir in the beginning of the testament was to clarify the duty of the heir.[6] This distinction between heir and beneficiary could solve our problem on dual bequest, which is mentioned above.

On the other hand, the Japanese Civil Code does not acknowledge the usufructuary right (although the former code did): this is a lifetime right to use and take benefit from some estate, especially useful for the widow.[7] Even if Isaku the testator really wanted to give this usufructuary right, the Japanese Supreme Court should issue a judgment that the usufruct is not prescribed by the law, and therefore must be invalid. But the Supreme Court itself has mentioned this possibility as being Isaku's intention. Japanese lawyers often admit some legal institution that has not yet been designated by statutes or courts, but whose admission could be proper for the actual Japanese society. In this respect, it would be better to investigate the roots of these notions in Roman law, for example, the bequest (*legatum*) and the legal concept of usufruct[8] in order to found the intro-

5 On the (in)transmissibility of usufruct to the heir see *Pasquale Voci*, Diritto ereditario romano, Vol 1, Milan 1967², 213–215.

6 Gai. 2,229; Ulp. reg. 24,15; D. 28,6,1,3 Mod. 2 pand.; *Voci* (fn. 3) 111 fn. 2; *Max Kaser*, Das römische Privatrecht, Vol 1, Munich 1971², 686 fn. 5; *Wolfgang Kunkel/Heinrich Honsell*, Römisches Recht, Berlin 1987⁴, 454 fn. 1; *Ulrike Babusiaux*, Wege zur Rechtsgeschichte: Römisches Erbrecht, Cologne 2015, 244–245.

7 *Kaser* (fn. 6) 448.

8 In order to secure the widow's life and at the same time the good succession for the small enterprises, Japanese practical lawyers and civilists insisted for a long time on the legalisation of the so-called "Bequest with 2nd Degree". After the reduction of the bequest tax and its equalisation to the inheritance tax in 2003, the Trust Act was reformed in 2006, 86 years after the enactment of the old law: according to article 91 of the new law, this kind of bequest is recognised by means of trust, but authorised its validity only for about 100 years, i. e. for the lifetime of the beneficiary who acquires the beneficial interest firstly after 30 years elapsed since the creation of the trust. The following translated text of law can be downloaded for free from the website of Japanese Law Translation Database System, managed by the Ministry of Justice (<http://www.japaneselawtranslation.go.jp/> [02. June 2018]): Trust Act, Article 91: A Trust with provisions that upon a Beneficiary's death a Beneficial Interest held by said Beneficiary is extinguished and another person acquires a new Beneficial Interest (including provisions that upon the death of the predecessor, another person

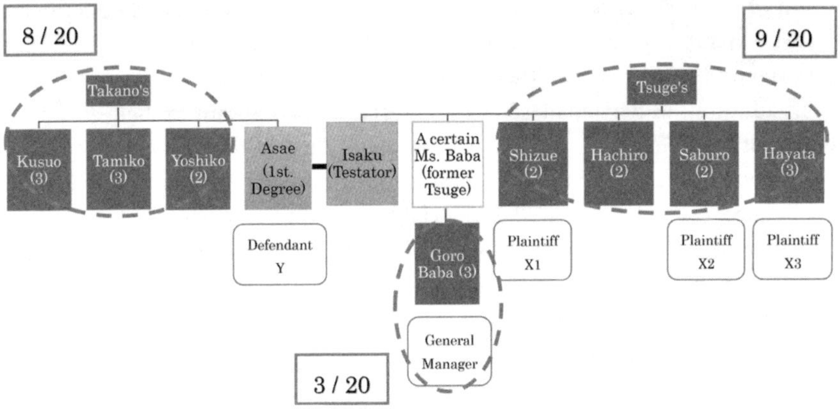

Family Tree of Tsuge's

duction of a new legal institution in Japanese law on a historical basis. Indeed on 6th July 2018, the Japanese Diet approved a revision of the right of residence for the living spouse (e. g. the widow) only in the field of law of succession (effective in a couple of years); according to the revision, the widow has two types of habitative right without alienating and profiting rights. She has a short-time right of residence (six months or until the end of the inheritance division) like French law (one year) on the one hand, and has a life-time residential right on the other hand. But the introduction of a new real right of usufruct (or *habitatio*) was denied avoiding the change of general rules of the Japanese Civil Code itself. Therefore these rights are considered as legal claim like rent but to be registered. Romanist can contribute some remarks concerning these new habitative rights by analysing the Roman situation of the widow with her *habitatio* gifted by her lamented husband's will.

acquires a Beneficial Interest as the Beneficiary) is valid, if any Beneficiary who is alive when 30 years have elapsed since the creation of the Trust acquires a Beneficial Interest pursuant to said provisions, until said Beneficiary dies or until the Beneficial Interest of said Beneficiary is extinguished.

PART THREE: MODERN DEBATES IN THE LIGHT OF ANCIENT LAW

Carlos Amunátegui Perelló, Santiago de Chile*

Again on the Middle Class in the Roman Republic

I. Introduction

The middle class has been an important topic for ancient economic history during the past last years. Different scholars have attempted to understand and quantify something that has been labelled as a Roman middle class or the middling sectors of Roman society. Among the most important, we should note Scheidel and Friesen's pioneering work,[1] where they attempted to fully quantify the middling sectors of the Roman Empire. Their calculations are based on models and assumptions on the population, economic size and consumption levels that might be expected in imperial times for the Roman population, comparing them with better-known levels for other pre-industrial societies. Although we cannot expect certainty, their estimates seem cogent with the archaeological and economic data that survives. With a somewhat different approach, other scholars have attempted to draw a cultural picture of the Roman middling social sectors of the Empire,[2] sometimes calling them middle classes, sometimes something else, like *plebs media*, in a language that sounds less anachronistic to modern scholarship. Anyhow, these studies rely on archaeological analysis of the houses in the best-preserved cities of the Roman world, like Pompeii, and make assumptions about the cultural background of non elite people who used to occupy them.

These studies represent two different approaches to Roman society, one economic, which attempts to quantify the importance of middling sectors of society, and another one cultural, which puts the weight on idiosyncratic aspects

---

* Roman law professor. Pontificia Universidad Católica de Chile. The present article is an amended version of an article published in RIDA: Carlos Amunátegui Perelló, The Decline of the Middle Class and the Fall of the Roman Republic, RIDA 61 (2015) 97–109. This article is part of the Fondecyt 1180022 Project.

1 *Walter Scheidel/Steven J. Friesen*, The Size of Economy and the Distribution of Income in the Roman Empire, JRS 99 (2009) 61–91, 82–84.

2 For instance, *Paul Zanker*, Pompeii. Public and Private Life, Cambridge 1998; *Paul Veyne*, «La plebe moyenne» sous le haut-empire romain, Annales 55 (2000) 1169–1199; *Emanuel Mayer*, The Ancient Middle Classes. Urban Life and Aesthetics in the Roman Empire 100 BC – 250 BC, Cambridge/London 2012.

that would define mental attitudes of non-elite towards work, social mobility, and art. It is important to distinguish these different conceptions of middling sectors beforehand, for according to one view a subject or social strata can be considered an elite, while according to another it might not. A typical example would be Trimalchio, the fictional character of Petronius' *Satyricon*, who has become a model of lots of money and no refinement. Although he is hugely rich, he conducts himself in a tasteless manner in order to ape the fashions and behaviours of the elite. Economically, he is part of the elite, although culturally he is not.

Another aspect of this dichotomy is social mobility. An economic perspective of middle classes does not usually take into account social mobility, which is a vastly important element of the cultural approach to the middle class. In a way, middle class can be defined as a segment of society, who aspires to upward social mobility, and consequentially, is one of the central aspects to it.[3] Anyhow, at least during the Early and Middle Republic, social mobility was extremely exceptional in Rome. The picture that the *fasti consulares* draw of the period seems to point to a stratified society, where only a handful of families share the major magistracies.[4] On the other hand, there is evidence of accelerated social mobility during the Late Republic,[5] when a commercial framework gave the chance to a small proportion of society (roughly between 6 and 12 percent of it)[6] to climb up the social ladder and become part of a new sub-elite segment of society, which some have labelled as middle class.[7] It seems this trend towards social mobility even accentuated during late antiquity, for the army and the bureaucracy seemed to open new ladders for upward mobility to some people who were brave or cultured enough to climb. In fact, Justin I, Justinian and Theodora are extreme examples of this mobility, for people with humble and even base social origins could eventually through talent occupy the pinnacle of power. In the early and middle antiquity we find nothing of the sort. During the fifth century BC, the well-known *serrata del patriziato*[8] seems to stand in the

---

3 *Mayer* (fn. 2) 24.

4 See *Andrew Drummond*, Rome in the Fifth Century I. The Social and Economic Framework, in: The Cambridge Ancient History, Vol 7.2, eds. *Frank William Walbank* et al., Cambridge 1989, 113–171, 163–171.

5 *John R. Patterson*, Landscapes and Cities. Rural Settlement and Civic Transformation in Early Imperial Italy, Oxford 2006, 184–263 and *Laurens Ernst Tacoma*, Fragile Hierarchies. The Urban Elites of Third Century Roman Egypt, Leiden 2006.

6 *Scheidel/Friesen* (fn. 1) 82–84.

7 *Mayer* (fn. 2) 24.

8 The expression *serrata del patriziato* was coined by De Sanctis at the beginning of the 20th century to illustrate the closure of the patricians as a social group in regard to the plebeians. According to

way of any social improvement of the plebs, while only in the Late Republic we start hearing of these *homines novi* who can cross the boundaries towards the elite, although their fathers or forefathers might have some little dark secrets, as Cicero or Augustus might show. Anyhow, a republican Theodora is somehow an impossible idea.

Our concept of middle-class departs from the cultural approaches, and for the purpose of this study is to establish a simple correlation between governance and wealth distribution. Although the concept of middle class is naturally exotic to Roman ideas, following Harris,[9] we could classify the Roman population according to a highly flexible criterion, which is ultimately taken from Aristotle.[10] We could distinguish between those who can live depending on alien labour – from slaves or other dependent people –, those who have enough property to secure their family's well-being through their own work in their land and those who are dependent workers, whether they are free or slaves.[11] In this sense, those who benefit from the land distribution policy of middle republican Rome become a kind of middle class.

All political systems alternate the use of force with the voluntary compliance of the governed to fulfil their goals. The proportion of violence that a system requires increases when its results are perceived as unfair, and decreases when citizens are participants of its successes. The wider the perception of unfairness, the larger the proportion the elite will have to invest in coercion to sustain the political order and, therefore, the system will have a smaller ability to expand and develop. In North's words: "The costs of maintenance of an existing order are inversely related to the perceived legitimacy of the existing system".[12] In other words, the governance of a society depends on the perceptions of the legitimacy of the governed.

The Middle Roman Republic was a remarkably stable political entity, which was able to develop into a participatory political regime with a high level of popular support and relatively low costs of maintenance. In this paper, we will

him, the frontiers between these social groups were not insurmountable until the second third of the fifth century BC. See *Gaetano De Sanctis*, Storia dei Romani, Vol 1, Turin 1907, 224.

9 *William V. Harris*, On the Applicability of the Concept of Class in Roman History, in: Forms of Control and Subordination in Antiquity, eds. *Toru Yuge* et al., Tokyo/Leiden 1988, 598–610, revised and reprinted in: Rome's Imperial Economy. Twelve Essays, ed. *William V. Harris*, Oxford/New York 2011, 15–26, 24.

10 Arist., Pol. 1289b.

11 Following a similar criterion, Knapp speaks of the ordinary man in Rome, defining him as the man that is socially below the senators and equestrians, but above the slave and day labourer. See *Robert Knapp*, Invisible Romans, Cambridge 2011, 5.

12 *Douglass North*, Structure and Change in Economic History, New York 1981, 53.

propose that the existence of an extended middle class was the key element that led to this remarkable stability and that its decline led to the crisis of the Late Republic.

II. Wealth Concentration and Middle Class in Republican Rome

Before treating the governance problems that affected antiquity, it is important to consider some key points regarding the creation and distribution of wealth that affect all pre-industrial societies. Firstly, it should be taken into account that in such societies, economic growth is negligible and, therefore, any increase in population will necessarily imply a new provision of dispossessed whose survival is uncertain.[13] Antiquity is a Malthusian world, where increases in productivity accomplished by technical innovation are soon absorbed by population increases that lead to new social crisis.[14] In such conditions, the most effective way to increase the GDP is to expand the mass of fixed capital through military conquest of the neighbouring territories.[15] This is the cause for the central role of war in antiquity, for it meant something equivalent to economic growth. Antiquity's military obsession was especially important for societies that had to deal with demographic growth or that held political systems that were involved in the effective amelioration of living conditions for the governed. That is why democracies in antiquity were invariably imperialistic, while aristocracies not necessarily.

Another element to consider is that antiquity's economic structure was not favourable for paid work. Although it existed,[16] its economic role was marginal, especially for the ubiquitous presence of slavery,[17] as for other strategies to

13 *William V. Harris*, Poverty and Destitution in the Roman Empire, in: *idem* (fn. 9) 27–54, 27.

14 On economic growth in Antiquity, the debate seems nowadays to be centred on the speed in which population growth can absorb the positive effects of economic growth. See *Walter Scheidel*, Physical Well-Being, in: The Cambridge Companion to the Roman Economy, Cambridge 2012, 321–333; *Richard Saller*, Framing the Debate over Growth in the Ancient Economy, in: The Ancient Economy. Evidence and Models, eds. *Walter Scheidel/Sitta von Reden*, New York 2010, 251–269; *Peter Temin*, The Roman Market Economy, New Jersey 2013, 195–239.

15 In Morley's words: "The importance of violence as a mode of accumulation and a cultural practice in antiquity can scarcely be exaggerated." *Neville Morley*, Trade in Classical Antiquity, Cambridge 2007, 505.

16 Recently the role of paid labour in Antiquity is under re-examination. The possibility of a real labour market has been put forward (*Harris* [fn. 13] 32). The most extreme position on the matter points to the existence of a large labour market fully operative during the Early Empire (*Temin* [fn. 14] 114–138).

17 Slavery seems to have been introduced during Etruscan monarchy, although we cannot be cer-

obtain subordinate labour typical of earlier antiquity.[18] Differently to modern world,[19] distribution of wealth and capital were equivalent. The irrelevance of economic growth and the dependence of income to capital implied that any governance crisis might quickly translate into propositions of agrarian reform, especially regarding newly conquered land.

1. Land Distribution and the Licinian-Sextian Laws

Following Roman historians, the eve of the Republic was rather shaky in social terms. Tradition reports a long struggle between two social groups, the patricians and the plebeians, whose origins are not clear.[20] This conflict would have

---

tain of it (*Gennaro Franciosi*, Res mancipi e res nec mancipi, Labeo 5 [1959] 370–390, 375; *idem*, Famiglia e persone in Roma antica, Torino 1992, 206; *Francesco De Martino*, Clienti e condizioni materiali in Roma arcaica, in: Diritto economia e società nel mondo romano, Naples 1997, 82–83; *idem*, Intorno all'origine della schiavitù a Roma in Diritto economia e società nel mondo romano, Naples 1997, 27–57).

18 Among them, we should mention the *clientela*, with its connected obligation of lending personal service to the *patronus*, *nexum*, a loan guaranteed with the physical person of the debtor, and the transfer of sons and daughters through *mancipium*.

19 In the modern world the distribution of income and capital are different. Generally speaking, capital tends to be much more concentrated than income, for the latter includes paid work (*Thomas Piketty*, Capital in the Twenty-First Century, Cambridge 2014, 39–71).

20 The theories about the origins of patricians and plebeians are discouragingly many. Some are based on a dualist hypothesis where there would be either an ethnical difference between them (*Vincenzo Arangio-Ruiz*, Storia del diritto romano, Naples 2006, 21) or at least regarding their citizenship (*Antonio Guarino*, Le origine quiritarie. Raccolta di Scritti romanistici, Naples 1973, 9–17). Others believe that the Patrician and Plebeian groups formed gradually during the Monarchy, either by the fulfilment of priestly duties (*Richard Mitchell*, The Definition of patres and plebs. An End to the Struggle of the Orders, in: Social Struggles in Archaic Rome. New Perspectives on the Conflict of the Orders, ed. *Kurt A. Raaflaub*, Oxford 2005, 128–167), by a process of wealth accumulation connected with the exercise of power in the Senate (*Louis Harmand*, Société et économie de la République romaine, Paris 1976, 32; *Drummond* (fn. 4) 172–242; *Arnaldo Momigliano*, The Origins of Rome, in: *Frank William Walbank* et al. (fn. 4) 52–112; *Arnaldo Momigliano*, The Rise of the Plebs in the Archaic Age of Rome, in: *Kurt A. Raaflaub* (fn. 20 above) 168–184; *André Magdelain*, De l'auctoritas patrum à l'auctoritas senatus, in: Jus imperium auctoritas. Études de droit romain, Paris 1990, 385–403; *Timothy J. Cornell*, The Beginnings of Rome and Italy from the Bronze Age to the Punic Wars (c. 1000–264 BC), London/New York 1995, 244–258; *Kurt A. Raaflaub*, From Protection and Defense to Offense and Participation. Stages in the Conflict of the Orders, in: *idem* (fn. 20 above) 185–222; *Gary Forsythe*, A Critical History of Early Rome, Berkeley/Los Angeles 2006, 162; *Christopher J. Smith*, The Roman Clan. The gens from Ancient Ideology to Modern Anthropology, Cambridge 2006, 305, or through the immigration of craftsmen of a predominantly urban environment (plebeians), confronted to an agrarian aristocracy (*Jean-Claude Richard*, Réflexions sur les "origines" de la plèbe, in: Bilancio critico su Roma arcaica fra monarchia e repubblica, Roma 1993,

developed for three key elements: legal knowledge, access to political power and the control of public land. Although the academic debate has literally been going on for centuries, we will only partially face the problem of land and its distribution as an element of our analysis.

Some scholars believe that the whole conflict is a mere invention of the analistic tradition, a kind of pseudo-historic anticipation of the real conflict for land control that took place during the second century BC.[21] Anyhow, there are enough elements in the tradition to discard this thesis partially or completely and to confirm the existence of a conflict over land control between these groups during the Early Republic.[22]

Apparently, the plebeian group did not have access to the newly conquered lands, which remained as public lands (*ager publicum*), theoretically open to the use of any citizen.[23] We do not know the exact reason for this exclusion, but in practice, it seems only the patricians had access to them[24] and they were the

---

27–41; *idem*, Patricians and Plebeians. The Origin of a Social Dichotomy, in: *Kurt A. Raaflaub* (fn. 20 above) 107–127), which eventually closed its ranks at the beginnings of the Republic. What we believe most likely is that the patricians were the members of the old gentilician clans, while the plebs were outsiders (*Francesco De Martino*, La gens, lo stato e le classi in Roma antica, in: *idem* (fn. 17, Diritto) 25–49; *idem*, Storia costituzionale romana, Naples 1973, 78; *Pietro Bonfante*, La gens e la familia, in: Scritti Giuridici. Famiglia e successione, Torino 1916, 1–17; *idem*, Teorie vecchie e nuove sulle formazione sociali primitive, in: Scritti Giuridici (fn. 20 above) 18–63; *Carlo Castello*, Studi sul diritto familiare e gentilizio romano, Roma 1942 (1972) 49; *Luigi Capogrossi Colognesi*, Diritto e potere nella storia di Roma, Naples 2007, 49–51).

21 *Richard Maschke*, Zur Theorie und Geschichte der römischen Agrargesetze, Naples 1906 (Reprint 1980), 14; *Emilio Gabba*, Motivazioni economiche nell'opposizione alla legge agraria di Tib. Sempronio Gracco, in: Polis and Imperium. Studies in Honour of Edward Togo Salmon, ed. *James Allan Stewart Evans*, Toronto 1974, 135.

22 *Feliciano Serrao*, Lotte per la terra e per la casa a Roma, in: Legge e società nella repubblica romana, ed. *idem*, Naples 1981, 67; *Drummond* (fn. 4) 237; *Saskia T. Roselaar*, Public Land in the Roman Republic. A Social and Economic History of Ager Publicus in Italy, 396–89 BC, Oxford/New York 2010, 28.

23 Sic. Flacc., grom. 101,9–13 and 102,9–13.

24 The patrician control of public land is quite straight-forward in the tradition. Nonius reports that the plebeians were excluded of the public land just because they were plebeians (Non. 149 M. 17: *Quicumque propter plebitatem agro publico eiecti sunt*). Although the reasons for this exclusion are unknown to us, we could theorize that their exclusion from the *gentes*, the original clans that composed the city, might lay behind it. Another possibility is that they simply lacked the social power to impose their control over public lands and that more powerful people (the rich patricians) could simply expel them by violence. Anyhow, during the monarchy, tradition reports many land distributions made by the kings to favour the poor (D. H. 2,62,2–3; 3,1,4–5; 2,29,6; 3,31,3; 3,9,8; 4,10,3; 4,13,1), but during the early Republic these distributions cease abruptly. By that time, the conquered land usually remains as *ager publicus*, safe from some rather exceptional cases in which colonies were established (Liv. 2,21,6; 2,31,4; 2,34,6; 3,1,5–6). The first massive land distribution

only ones that effectively occupied them. The struggle of the orders had at its core the plebeian demand for land distribution. The disruptive effects of agrarian reform laws are classically expressed in Livy's comment on the major public disorders caused by them.[25]

The conflict finally lowered its intensity only after 367 BC, after some 140 years of permanent hostility, with the *leges Liciniae-Sextiae*. These statutes, among other major reforms, limited the maximal amount of public land that any individual could occupy. From this moment onwards, each military victory was accompanied by a land distribution of the conquered territory, whether in the form of a direct assignation to the poor citizens or through the foundation of a citizen's colony.[26] Appian describes the process in the following paragraph:[27]

> Romans, while they conquered Italy's different regions, took part of their territory and established cities, or levied their own colonists to send them to the already existent ones.

It is interesting to corroborate the annalistic tradition with the information that archaeology offers. On the matter, from the fourth century BC, a true explosion of modest size settlements can be detected in Central Italy, which can be correlated with land division and its occupation by smallholders in a process directly linked with the *leges Liciniae-Sextiae*.[28]

This policy of land distribution of the newly conquered land to the poor is a key element to explain the high levels of governance and the military push that Rome enjoyed during the Middle Republic. The city was socially cohesive, for the common perception was that the benefits from public activity – mainly war –

---

during the Republic is not of agricultural land, but rather of urban space, through the *lex Icilia* of 456 BC, which distributed the Aventine. On the other hand, according to the tradition, the plebeian demands for the distribution of public land happen almost on a yearly basis, with more than ten bills rejected by the *patres* between 486 and 456 BC (*Luigi Capogrossi Colognesi*, La terra in Roma antica, Roma 1981, 6; *Annamaria Manzo*, La lex Licinia Sextia de modo agrorum, Naples 2001, 40–45; *Adelaide Russo*, Tiberio Gracco e la riforma agraria, in: La romanizzazione della Campania antica, Naples 2002, 161–193; *Smith* [fn. 20] 240 and *Roselaar* ([fn. 22] 26–29).

25 Liv. 2,41,3: "*lex agraria promulgata est, nunquam deinde usque ad hanc memoriam sine maximis motibus rerum agitata.*" ("When an agrarian law is promulgated, there is no memory that it has ever been done without major distress and agitation." The translation is my own.).

26 It is not known for certain how much land was usually taken from the defeated enemy. It is usually said that about a third of its territory was confiscated, although there were occasions in which this number could increase up to two thirds (*Roselaar* [fn. 22] 31–37).

27 App., BC 1,1,7. The translation is my own.

28 *Nicola Terrenato*, The Essential Countryside, in: Classical Archaeology, eds. *Susan E. Alcock/Robin Osborne*, Malden/Oxford 2012, 147–148.

were for the benefit of the common citizen, especially the poorer ones. War became a popular activity because it implied a source of economic benefits to the citizenry and supported the socio-economic stability of the city. Military success meant a massive input of fixed capital, an increase in the GDP and, therefore, economic growth. In Harris' words, Rome exported her poor to Italy and later to the provinces.[29] Nearly seventy thousand men (and their families) received land after the Samnite Wars alone.[30]

2. Middle Class during Hannibal's Wars

The benefits of war implied growth of the GDP. This growth was distributed among the citizenry directly through land distribution, which supported the creation of what could be called the Roman middle class. Naturally, we cannot directly quantify its importance in Roman social structure, for we do not have reliable statistics about poverty, wealth or even the number of slaves living in Rome at any point of history. Nevertheless, we do have one relatively trustworthy piece of information that could, at some point, help us to do a gross estimate of its extension. That is the number of active legions in Rome.

The republican army was recruited according to wealth. Only people who had some property could be levied, while the proletarians – the have-nots – until the Marian Reform were excluded. On the matter, we have very precise information thanks to Livy's account,[31] which might be anachronistic for Etruscan Rome, but seems trustworthy for middle republican society. Livy tells us that the census divided the army according to wealth into five classes. Those who were under the minimum wealth fell into the *infra classem* of the *proletarii* and were excluded from the army. It is likely that after the introduction of a salary for military service in 406 BC, legions were recruited indistinctly from the five wealthy classes,[32] granted that they were above the minimum level of proletarians.

During the Second Punic War, Rome was taken to the very limits of her military capacity, levying some years up to twenty-five legions. Each legion, ac-

---

29 *Harris* (fn. 9) 24.

30 *Timothy J. Cornell*, The Conquest of Italy, in: *Frank William Walbank* (fn. 4) 405.

31 Liv. 1,43. The text describes Servius Tullius' reform, which would introduce the *centuriae* as the basic units of military organisation. The numbers supplemented by Livy are rather unbelievable for monarchic Rome, for they would imply the existence of an army of almost 20 thousand men, for a city that did not have more than 50 thousand inhabitants. The most likely hypothesis is that such description is possibly based on the data established after the reform of 241 BC (*Cornell* [fn. 20] 180; *Smith* [(fn. 20] 174; *Forsythe* [fn. 20] 113).

32 According to Polybius, the minimum would be 400 drachmas during 216 BC (Plb. 6,19).

cording to Polybius,[33] would have at least four thousand two hundred men, although the figure could be higher and some legions would have up to six thousand men. If we take a median of five thousand men per legion, this would give us some 125 thousand men who could meet the minimum property standards to be part of the army. If we consider that adult male population in Ancient cities was usually around 25 percent of the total population,[34] this figure implies a total population with a middle living standard of about five hundred thousand men. Although the total population of Italy at the time should have been around three million inhabitants,[35] Roman population shortly after Hannibal's war was surveyed at 243.704 male citizens.[36] If we suppose that men were about half of the population something not necessarily true in a period of catastrophic military campaigns the total population of adult Roman citizens would be around 480 thousand people, to which we should add a number of boys and girls under 12 and 14 years respectively, that usually were not counted in the *census*. Following Saller's population figures,[37] with a life expectancy of about 25 years, the figure would imply about 50 percent of the total population (given that infant mortality between 0 and 10 years would reach almost half of the births), while if we take his upper figure of 32,5 years of life expectancy, adult population would be about 60 percent of the total. In short, the *census* figure implies a total population of 800 to 960 thousand Roman citizens, including children. Although the figures we are considering are far from exact and they simply give us an order of magnitude, they seem to tell us that between 52 and 62 percent of the Roman citizenry would have enough property to face every-day needs.[38]

This is a relatively high figure for what we could call Roman middle class. It is true that in this figure we are deliberately ignoring the situation both of slaves and resident foreigners, but the figure is anyhow impressive. Most Roman

33 Plb. 6,20,8.

34 *Kurt A. Raaflaub*, The Conflict of the Orders in Archaic Rome. A Comprehensive and Comparative Approach, in: *idem* (fn. 20) 22. For a complete study using higher and lower life expectancies: *Scheidel* (fn. 14) 40.

35 *Cornell* (fn. 30) 405.

36 Liv. 35,9,21,1. On the reliability of republican census figures: *Elio Lo Cascio*, Population and Demographic Studies, in: A Companion to the Archaeology of the Roman Republic, ed. *Jane Derose Evans*, Oxford 2013, 155–166.

37 *Richard P. Saller*, Patriarchy, Property and Death in the Roman Family, Cambridge 1994, 25.

38 Our figures are slightly more optimistic than Brunt's, that estimated the total number of *assidui* in about 50 percent of the population (*Peter Brunt,* Italian Manpower, London 1971, 64–66), but significantly lower than Rosenstein's, who estimates the total percentage of *proletarii* in about 10 percent of the population during Hannibal's War (*Nathan Rosenstein*, Rome at War, Chapel Hill/London 2004, 185–188).

citizens had enough wealth to live independently, working their own land and serving in the army during Hannibal's war.

Regarding the elite, we have no way to quantify it nor to measure the resources it accumulated, but it was always a rather small group. There were no more than three hundred senators and if we suppose a ten times larger group of *equites* and add up their families, the figure could not be more than twelve thousand people, about one percent of the total population. To sum up, and to return to Harris' categories, we could say that Roman population was divided into an elite that comprehended about 1 percent of the population, a middle class that accounted about 55–60 percent of the population and have-nots that were between 40–45 percent of the total. These figures sound awfully familiar and are not very different to the ones a modern democracy would put forward today.

Republican political system was based on a middle class that gave Rome its social ideal of a man that was also a soldier, a citizen and a farmer. This archetype was the model of republican civic life, an ideological incarnation of its virtues. Cincinnatus, who works his small farm, who was called to save the Republic and who returns the scarlet of dictatorship fifteen days after assuming the magistracy, represents the republican ideal. The common man, farmer, soldier, and citizen, assumes him as a model and can imagine himself a protector of the Republic.

Rome's conquest of Italy was backed by a harmonic political system, where its citizens were directly benefited by the prosperity gained. Support for the republican system was unanimous. With some excess, this political system has been described as Roman democracy.[39] It is beyond doubt that it was a participatory political system, where citizenry, through the *comitia* and the tribunes held power, and the common man not only had a voice in the decisions taken by the political apparatus but also benefited from the results. Its costs of maintenance were extremely low, to the point that Rome did not have a police to impose order nor a bureaucracy to administrate the system. To call it a democracy or not is a merely semantic problem.

3. The Decline of the Middle Classes in the Late Republic

Rome's social order declines quickly after Hannibal's war. The process has been described on several occasions and it can be related to different economic and social phenomena that the military successes of Roman polity implied. From

39 *Antonio Guarino*, Forma e materia della costituzione romana, in: Studi di diritto costituzionale romano, Naples 2008, 11–26.

our point of view, the most important one was the insertion of Rome in Mediterranean long-distance trade markets.[40]

Most of Roman smallholders were corn producers, although they usually cultivated vines and olives too, a typical feature of the Mediterranean *colotora promiscua*, which was in use in Central Italy at least since the seventh century BC.[41] It was aimed fundamentally to self-consumption, though the surpluses were usually traded to acquire a wide range of goods that they could not produce by themselves. Nevertheless, Roman conquests put into market vast quantities of superior quality grain, which entered gratis from Sicily – as a tribute – or at very low prices, from Egypt and Africa. This immediately expelled smallholders from grain markets, who simply could not compete. The result was the abandon of farms by many smallholders. Even in the immediate hinterland of Rome, where low transportation costs should help smallholders, farms were abandoned.[42]

The integration of Rome into the Mediterranean markets did not only have negative effects, but it also presented opportunities to the elite, which was in a position to benefit with the imperial expansion. The new markets opened vast opportunities for agribusiness, especially for the exportation of wine, oil, and honey. Nevertheless, most farmers could not benefit from these opportunities. Smallholders grew a crop optimised to satisfy their own corn needs. To alter this optimum and favour a new equilibrium to get surpluses of oil or wine for exportation would expose the farmer to famine.[43] Therefore, his possibilities to adapt to this new scenario were meagre. Even more, the farmer lacked the capital needed for the conversion.[44]

The wars conducted outside Italy brought a huge influx of liquid capital, which came from the monetization of the riches accumulated by the Hellenistic kings, whose vast reserves of silver were minted.[45] This influx reverted in the benefit of the Roman elite, who could acquire through purchase or simple violence the farms that smallholders were in the process of abandoning. With this capital,

40 This is what Harris calls the Hellenistic-Carthaginian system, which had been operating as a trade system from the East side to the West side of the Mediterranean basin during centuries (*William V. Harris*, The Late Republic, in: The Cambridge Economic History of the Greco-Roman World, eds. *Walter Scheidel* et al., Cambridge 2007, 513).

41 *Mario Torelli*, History. Land and People, in: Etruscan Life and Afterlife, ed. *Larissa Bonfante*, Detroit 1986, 52; *Forsythe* (fn. 20) 56.

42 *Rosenstein* (fn. 38) 7.

43 *Keith Roberts*, Origins of Business, Money and Markets, New York 2011, 119.

44 Nevertheless, some small farms were able to do it and produced surpluses for exportation (*Roselaar* [fn. 22] 155–156).

45 For a detailed account see: *Philip Kay*, Rome's Economic Revolution, Oxford 2014, 87–106.

they could create new productive units that were intended to produce surpluses for exportation and were majorly worked by slaves. These were the Roman villas. Appian puts some vivid colours to the situation:[46]

> The rich, hogging most of the undistributed land, with time became confident that they were not going to be dispossessed. Partly buying through persuasive methods, partly seizing through violence, they acquired the neighbouring properties and all the others that belonged to humble peasants, to cultivate *latifundia* …

A bit further he adds:[47]

> For these reasons the rich became maximally wealthy and the slaves abounded in the countryside, while famine and scarce population afflicted the Italian people, decimated by poverty, taxes and military service.

Besides the problems related to markets, war ceased to be of benefit for the general well-being of the citizenry. The devastating effects of the military occupation of Italy by Hannibal's troops for nearly twenty years have been held responsible for the decline of the Italian smallholder,[48] although they might not have had the importance traditionally attributed to them.[49] An element that might have deeper consequences is the development of long-distance conflicts of indefinite duration. Until Hannibal's war, military campaigns were a seasonal event that happened inside the Italian peninsula, relatively close to the citizen-soldiers home, so they could return to their properties in winter with the end of hostilities. War did not interfere with agricultural labour. On the other side, the military campaigns of the conquest of the Mediterranean basin required a permanent estrangement of the peasant from his land to develop operations in distant war scenarios. The conquest of Hispania implied the creation of a permanent occupation force, as also happened later with other provinces and ended up transforming the old Mediterranean into a new *mare nostrum*. This kind of war is incompatible with the farmer-soldier, and it ruined a large portion of the Roman middle class. Plutarch left us an interesting description:[50]

---

46 App., BC 1,1,7,18. The translation is my own.

47 App., BC 1,1,7,28. The translation is my own.

48 *Peter Brunt*, The Army and the Land in the Roman Revolution, in: Journal of Roman Studies 52 (1962) 69–86 and *idem*, Fall of the Roman Republic and Related Essays, Oxford 1988, 73.

49 *Rosenstein* (fn. 38) 26–62.

50 Plu., TG 8,3. The translation is my own.

> The dispossessed poor did not enrol in the army, nor could feed their children. Italy was at risk of becoming completely deserted of the free population and crowded with barbarian prisoners, for they worked the lands of the wealthy, excluding the citizens.

Although there were various attempts to implement agrarian reforms that could revert the disastrous results of Roman military expansion, none was able to reconstruct the old class of farmers that were the backbone of the republican system. The necessity of reforms was evident during the second half of the second century BC, when Gaius Laelius[51] made such a proposal, which he eventually had to retire, under senatorial opposition. More important were Tiberius' and Gaius Gracchus' reforms, which intended to rebuild the Roman smallholder class in order to increase the availability of recruits for the legions. They passed their laws even against the elite's violent answer. Anyhow, these bills were unable to revert the decline of the smallholders. The demand for an agrarian reform was at the very heart of every revolutionary movement and civil war that stormed the Republic during its last century.[52] Finally, when Augustus transformed the old Republic into the Principate, Rome's participatory government ceased to exist, as the demand for an agrarian reform.

The decline of smallholders caused the displacement of countryside population to Rome, which experienced a rapid increase in population, unparalleled until the early twentieth century's migratory movements. Rome increased its urban population from 200–300 thousand inhabitants, during the late third century, to a million, during the Late Republic. Rome became a city of *favelas*, where the poor lived in slums over its hills, always fearing pestilence and fire.

It is almost impossible to quantify the process and to put some numbers on the decline of Roman middle classes. Nevertheless, we can grasp the effects of such crisis in the lack of eligible men for military service. During the late second century, with a war burden significantly lower to the one experienced during Hannibal's war and a larger population, Rome was simply incapable of meeting the needs of the levy. Only with Marius' reform, which admitted the proletarians for the first time into the army,[53] the legions could be recruited. From then on, the army became the refuge of the poorest citizens, who saw in the legions a way out of their misery and in the personal success of their generals their only chance to ensure themselves some means of subsistence.

---

51 Plu., TG 8,4.

52 *Brunt* (fn. 48) 69–86.

53 Plu., Mar. 9.

During the second century BC Rome levied between 8 and 12 legions every year, that is to say, between forty and sixty thousand men.[54] Citizen population had grown up to almost four hundred thousand men, according to the census.[55] If we repeat the calculation previously made[56] for Hannibal's war, we would get to the conclusion that, before Marius' reform, Rome was not able to stand a military burden that implied the existence of 15–18 percent of what we earlier called middle class.

The result is eloquent. Although the numbers are not precise and are affected by various *caveat*, the order of magnitude is probably correct. This would corroborate what tradition tells us about the decline of Roman middle class, which diminishes from covering almost two-thirds of the population to less than a fifth. The governance crisis was inevitable, and the destruction of the republican political system unavoidable.

III. Conclusions

Our conclusions are, to some point, a confirmation of North's theory. The costs of maintaining the political system are inversely proportional to its legitimacy. The viability of a participatory political system is directly related to the benefits the population acquires from it. If the system tends to the creation of a large middle class, the system will consolidate. If it pauperises the middle class, it will inevitably implode and succumb before the ambitions of the destabilizing elements of society that will try to replace it, either by a system that effectively distributes wealth or by a different system that asserts its stability in a deeper use of coercion and social control.

In the Roman case, it was the Principate that rose from the ashes of the Republic, a non-participatory political system, which favoured commerce and social stability. The coercion level required to operate was higher than during the Republic, although much lower than during the later despotisms.

Nowadays, the rise of inequality in income distribution experienced in the United States and Western Europe is rather alarming. If it deepens, the partic-

54 See the table included in *Rosenstein* (fn. 38) 120–121.

55 The summary quotes 394.336 citizens in the census. See Liv. perioch. 63.

56 That is to say, taking the maximal number of the recruited (60 thousand), the number of *assidui* (that is, men over the property limit) would be about 240 thousand. If we add to the nearly 400 thousand men older than 14 years, the missing proportion of women and children we would arrive to a total population between 1.3 and 1.6 million citizens, depending on the life expectancy we choose. This would give a proportion of 18 to 15 percent of propertied citizens over the minimum census.

ipatory nature of their political regimes might jeopardise. The fall of what we have called Roman middle class occurred in a relatively short period of time, less than a century, although its effects were obvious earlier. Populism was the result of the destruction of these middle classes. The effects of populism are not new; even the Romans knew them well. These are the first symptoms of social and political decomposition.

Ulrike Babusiaux, Zurich

Coordination of Different Layers of Law in the Roman Empire and in the European Union

I. Introduction

The still predominant view characterises the Roman legal order as an uncoordinated mass of legal sources accumulated in the historical development but without clear hierarchy among them.[1] From this point of view, the Roman legal reasoning seems to differ profoundly from modern legal reasoning. Indeed, at least in the civil law countries since the age of codifications, private law has been organised in codes and statutes, whose application and interpretation are said to follow a strict methodological framework. However, the emergence of an autonomous European legal order that influences and competes with the national private law of the Member States has brought a change to this overly idyllic picture of legal positivism. The old question in Roman law of how to coordinate different legal sources without abstract hierarchy has, therefore, become an important topic in modern legal methodology as well. With this in mind, it is interesting to reconsider the question of coordination of legal sources in the Roman Empire and in contemporary private law influenced by the European Union.

The first part will try to explain the Roman legal order and the techniques known to the Roman jurists as to coordinate different legal sources (II), whereas the second part will give a brief introduction into the methodological implications of the European efforts of legal harmonisation for the application of private law in its Member States (III), before it turns to a comparison of the problems that have occurred in both historical examples, which will serve to verbalise a "message from antiquity" (IV).

---

1 See notably *Franz Wieacker*, Römische Rechtsgeschichte I, Munich 1988, 487–518; *Max Kaser/Rolf Knütel/Sebastian Lohsse*, Römisches Privatrecht, Munich 2014[20], § 2 Rn. 1; *Wolfgang Waldstein/Johannes Michael Rainer*, Römische Rechtsgeschichte, Munich 2014[11], § 22 Rn. 1–2. A summary in English can be found in *Salvatore Riccobono/Edward Nathan Source*, Outlines of the Evolution of Roman Law, University of Pennsylvania Law Review and American Law Register 74 (1925) 1–19.

II. Rome

The Roman legal order has been characterised as being composed of "layers of law" (Rechtsschichten).[2] This characterisation stems from the perspective of a positivistic lawyer who is used to codified law and includes two different aspects: The first assumption is that Roman law has been under constant development and is a product of a historical evolution; the second assertion implies that there is no visible structure to give precedence of one legal source over the other. From the vantage point of a continental European lawyer who is familiar with the Kelsenian pyramid of the legal system[3] Roman law seems, therefore, somehow 'unstructured'. The missing structure seems to imply a lack of methodology. Consequently, *Max Kaser* claimed that the Roman jurists did not have any rational methods for finding the legal solution to a case but that instead they proceeded according to their intuition.[4] This led to the assertion that the most important arguments in legal reasoning were the authority (*auctoritas*), meaning the personal standing of a jurist, and tradition, meaning the reasons, principles and 'figures of law' (Rechtsfiguren) that had been accepted by the generations of jurists before. Later on, *Kaser* added the influence of material principles, such as equity (*aequitas*) and justice (*iustitia*), and accepted the idea brought forward by *Franz Horak* that despite the somehow irrational formation of the legal opinion, there might have been an effort to explain the solution by reference to rational arguments afterwards.[5] Consequently, in his view, the process of legal reasoning in Roman law is not rational and remains a somehow 'intuitive process'. The most important corrections of this view – though never verbalised openly against *Kaser* – have been brought forward since the 1970s by *Dieter Nörr*. In his con-

---

2 For more on the history of this notion see *Ulrike Babusiaux*, Rechtsschichten, in: Handbuch des römischen Privatrechts, eds. *Ulrike Babusiaux et al.*, Tübingen (forthcoming).

3 For an introduction to this state-related view of law see *Nils Jansen/Ralf Michaels*, Private Law and the State. Comparative Perceptions and Historical Observations, RabelsZ 1 (2007) 345–397.

4 *Max Kaser*, Zur Methode der römischen Rechtsfindung, first in: Nachrichten der Akademie der Wissenschaften in Göttingen I, Göttingen 1962, 47–78, now in: Ausgewählte Schriften I, ed. *idem*, Naples 1976, 3–78; see also *Wolfgang Waldstein*, Evidenz und Intuition bei den Römischen Juristen, in: Gedächtnisschrift für Theo Mayer-Maly zum 80., eds. *Friedrich Harrer et al.*, New York 2011, 545–555. *Kaser's* statements must be understood with *Viehweg's* book in mind, on the role of topoi in juridical reasoning, see *Theodor Viehweg*, Topik und Jurisprudenz, Munich 1953. On this debate see *Ulrike Babusiaux*, Römische Rechtsrhetorik, in: Handbuch Juristische Rhetorik, ed. *Katharina von Schlieffen*, Berlin/New York 2019 (forthcoming).

5 *Franz Horak*, Rationes decidendi: Entscheidungsbegründungen bei den älteren römischen Juristen bis Labeo, Aalen 1969. This view is strongly influenced by the difference between context of discovery and context of justification (Entdeckungs- und Begründungszusammenhang) developed by *Hans Reichenbach* in 1938 and taken over by *Karl Popper*.

tributions, *Nörr* has shown the influence of the philosophical, philological and especially the rhetorical argumentation on the legal reasoning of Roman jurists. Namely, he proved that the Roman jurists had a theory for customary law, taken over from or parallel to the rhetorical schools;[6] furthermore, *Nörr* has explained that the reasoning with cases must be understood in the context of philosophical and rhetorical theory of proof by examples (*exemplum*);[7] and finally, his writings witness the profoundness of Roman legal argumentation ("Fallhöhe") that can only be understood in reference to other disciplines of Ancient knowledge, notably with regard to philosophical and rhetorical training.[8]

The evident problem when looking for methodological evidence in Roman legal writing is the nearly complete absence of direct proof within the transmitted texts. In fact, the works of Roman jurists contained in the Justinian legislation, especially in the Digest, seem only rarely to address methodological considerations; there are however some remarks and hints that might imply that at least the imperial Roman jurists used a more or less conscious methodology in their writings. As the most important bunch of Roman law texts is only available through the Justinian legislation, it cannot be decided, whether the Roman legal writing did not contain methodological explanations from their origin or whether the Justinian compilers deleted the methodological indications in their endeavour to create an own legal code. A possible means to resolve this dilemma is to analyse the legal texts contained in the Digest in the light of philosophical and rhetorical theory. In fact, since the Roman jurists, as part of the imperial elite, were trained in both fields, it might have been natural to them to use these teachings also in legal reasoning.[9] Especially in regard to the coordination of legal sources, it is reasonable to assume or accept that the Ancient rhetorical doctrine was of benefit to them as it offers a bundle of insights and tools on this topic. For this reason, the following analysis will present some teachings of the

6 The most important titles in this respect are *Dieter Nörr*, Zur Entstehung der gewohnheitsrechtlichen Theorie, first in: Festschrift für Wilhelm Felgentraeger, eds. *Max Kaser* et al., Göttingen 1969, 353–366; now in: Historia Iuris Antiqui I, eds. *Tiziana J. Chiusi et al.*, 645–658; and *Dieter Nörr*, Divisio und Partitio. Bemerkungen zur römischen Rechtsquellenlehre und zur antiken Wissenschaftstheorie, Berlin 1972.

7 *Dieter Nörr*, Zum Traditionalismus der römischen Juristen, first in: Festschrift für Werner Flume I, eds. *Horst Heinricht Jakobs* et al., Cologne 1978, 153–190, now in: Historia Iuris Antiqui II (fn. 6), 1119–1156; *Dieter Nörr*, exempla nihil per se valent. Bemerkungen zu Paul. 15 quaest. D. 46,3,98,8; Paul. 72 ed. D. 45,1,83,5, ZRG RA 126 (2009) 1–54.

8 A recent overview in *Ulrike Babusiaux*, Legal Writing and Legal Reasoning, in: The Oxford Handbook of Roman Law and Society, eds. *Clifford Ando et al.*, Oxford 2016, 176–187 with further references.

9 For a more thorough discussion of the problem see *Babusiaux* (fn. 4).

Ancient rhetoric on the coordination of legal sources and will then ask, whether these instructions could be helpful to deepen our understanding of juristic writings that deal with conflicting prescriptions of different legal layers. For this purpose, one example will be examined in more detail. In preparation of this, it is necessary to give a brief overview of the different layers of Roman law under the Principate.

1. The Different Layers of Roman Law under the Principate

The best overview of the Roman legal order can be gained through the only law book that has been passed on outside the Justinian codification. This work is called "*Institutiones*", which literally translates to "manual for beginners", and its author is a jurist named Gaius, whose writing has also been transmitted in Justinian's compilation.

a) *Ius civile* and *ius gentium*

Gaius starts his exposition with the famous words:

> Gai. 1,1
> Omnes populi, qui legibus et moribus reguntur, partim suo proprio, partim communi omnium hominum iure utuntur: Nam quod quisque populus ipse sibi ius constituit, id ipsius proprium est vocaturque ius civile, quasi ius proprium civitatis; [...]
> Translation by *de Zulueta*[10]:
> "Every people that is governed by statutes and customs observes partly its own peculiar law and partly the common law of all mankind. That law which a people establishes for itself is peculiar to it, and is called ius civile (civil law) as being the special law of that civitas (State), [...]"

The text is the very basis of (what is nowadays called) the "principle of personality", meaning that the application of rules is not linked to the territorial basis of the legislator but to the citizenship (or origin) of the person to whom the rule is applied.[11] This part of the law is called civil law (*ius civile*) deriving from

---

10 *Francis De Zulueta*, The Institutes of Gaius, Part I, Text with critical notes and translation, Oxford 1946, 2 f.

11 *Ludwig Mitteis* was fundamental, Reichsrecht und Volksrecht in den östlichen Provinzen des römischen Kaiserreichs. Mit Beiträgen zur Kenntnis des griechischen Rechts und der spätrömischen Rechtsentwicklung, Leipzig 1891; *idem/Ulrich Wilcken*, Grundzüge und Chrestomathie der Papyruskunde. Zweiter Band, erste Hälfte: Grundzüge, Stuttgart 1912, XII–XVIII.

the term *civitas* (city); the use of civil law is restricted to the citizens of the city (whose law is in question).[12] More specifically, it means that only Romans can make use of the Roman civil law, the *ius civile* or *ius Quiritium* but that Non-Romans are excluded from its application. But in Gaius' times (2nd century AD), Rome was already an Empire consisting of the city of Rome as a central power and several provinces, meaning foreign territories that had been occupied and taken under Roman control, which implied frequent legal contacts between Romans and Non-Romans.[13] This is why the jurist reminds his readers that there is another law not reserved solely for Romans but common to all men. This law is called *ius gentium*, the "law of the people".[14] It must be stressed that *ius gentium* is neither identical to modern public international law, nor to contemporary private international law. Rather, it covers a variety of rules that apply to all men regardless of their citizenship or their origin, which implies that rules of *ius gentium* can be used to overcome the division between people of different origins inherent to the concept of civil law.

Another important factor in this process of rapprochement between Romans and Non-Romans has been the layer of praetorian law.

b) *Ius praetorium*

Its definition is given by Papinian, a late 2nd century jurist, in his book on definitions:

> D. 1,1,7,1 Pap. 2 def.
> Ius praetorium est, quod praetores introduxerunt adiuvandi vel supplendi vel corrigendi iuris civilis gratia propter utilitatem publicam. Quod et honorarium dicitur ad honorem praetorum sic nominatum.
> Translation (*D. Neil MacCormick*, in: *Watson* I, 2)[15]:
> "Praetorian law (*ius praetorium*) is that which in the public interest the praetors have introduced in aid or supplementation or correction of the *ius civile*. This is also called honorary law (*ius honorarium*), being so named for the high office (*honos*) of the praetors."

12 On *ius civile* see *Max Kaser*, 'Ius honorarium' und 'ius civile', ZRG RA 101 (1984) 1–114.

13 On the legal contacts between Romans and Non-Romans in the provinces see recently *José Luis Alonso*, The Status of Peregrine Law in Egypt: Costumary Law and Legal Pluralism in the Roman Empire, JJP 43 (2013) 351–404.

14 On the bibliography of *ius gentium* see *Max Kaser*, Ius gentium, Cologne/Weimar/Vienna 1993.

15 *Alan Watson*, The Digest of Justinian Vol. I–IV, Philadelphia 1998.

The *praetor* or the *praetores*[16] were the judicial magistrates. Since the *leges Liciniae Sextae* (367 BC), they were in charge of the organisation of jurisdiction. The function was attributed annually and the *praetor* in charge published an edict at the beginning of the year that was meant to determine the claims, exceptions and commercial formulas he was willing to enforce.[17] The basis of these praetorian "promises" of legal enforcement and protection could be rules of different origin: they might stem from civil law or originate in *ius gentium* but they also could have been created by the *praetor* himself. These new rules are the very core of praetorian law and – as Papinian put it – they can "help, supplement or correct" the civil law.[18] A modern reader of the Papinian *bon mot* might be tempted to assume that praetorian law hence has precedence over civil law. But this assessment would not correspond with the Roman jurists' view; in fact, they did not reason in terms of precedence but held that both the rules of civil law and of the contradicting praetorian law were valid.[19] Since the civil law was nearly never formally abolished, it coexisted with the praetorian precepts, even if it was clear that certain civil rules would not be applied by the *praetor*.

A very clear example of this approach is the praetorian law of succession, the *bonorum possessio*. Just as the succession under civil law, the praetorian law is divided into testamentary and intestate succession. One example of a conflict between civil law and praetorian law can be taken from the intestate succession. Indeed, under civil law, only the children in the power of their father at the time of his death were the first legitimate heirs of their father, if he died without leaving a testament;[20] none of the children who had been emancipated were invited

16 There were at least two *praetores*: one for the city of Rome, the urban *praetor*; one for the non-citizen, the *praetor peregrinus*. Further information (in English) on these magistrates can be found in *Olivia F. Robinson*, The Sources of Roman Law. Problems and Methods for Ancient Historians, London/New York 1997, 5–8, 15 f. with further references.

17 On the praetorian function see *Max Kaser*, Zum 'ius honorarium', first in: Estudios jurídicos en homenaje al prof. Ursicino Alvarez Suárez, Madrid 1978, 231–249, now in: Römische Rechtsquellen und angewandte Juristenmethode, ed. idem, Vienna/Cologne/Graz 1986, 84–111.

18 Papinian's bon mot has been widely commented upon, see *Kaser* (fn. 12) 72 with Note 336; *idem* (fn. 17) 97–102; it has served for an interpretation of the function of good faith under § 242 BGB, see *Franz Wieacker*, Zur rechtstheoretischen Präzisierung des Paragraphen 242 BGB, Tübingen 1959.

19 A general explanation of the two layers can be found in *Kaser* (fn. 17) 94 f. with more references.

20 See Inst. 3,1 pr.–2: pr. *Intestatus decedit qui aut omnino testamentum non fecit, aut non iure fecit, aut id quod fecerat ruptum irritumve factum est, aut nemo ex eo heres extitit.* 1 *Intestatorum autem hereditates ex lege duodecim tabularum primum ad suos heredes pertinent.* 2 *Sui autem heredes existimantur, ut et supra diximus, qui in potestate morientis fuerunt: veluti filius filia, nepos neptisve ex filio, pronepos proneptisve ex nepote filio nato prognatus prognatave. nec interest, utrum naturales sunt liberi an adoptivi.* And the translation by *Joseph Anthony Charles Thomas*, The Institutes of

to take their father's share since according to civil law, the share was defined as a consequence of paternal power during his lifetime.[21] Yet, the *praetor* granted the possession of the share (*bonorum possessio ab intestato)* to emancipated children as well, although they were not entitled to be heirs under civil law. The Roman jurists welcomed this praetorian measure saying that the *praetor* established equality among all children of the deceased.[22] However, the emancipated child was not treated as an heir of civil law, as the *praetores* still required him to acquire ownership by adverse possession (*usucapio*).[23]

This example shows that the modern characterisation of civil and praetorian law as "layers of law" is only a first step to the understanding of the Roman legal system and cannot explain the functioning of the two stratas. Notably, even if the civil law and the praetorian law coexisted formally, they did not apply equally in every case. With regard to *bonorum possession ab intestato,* the civil law was overruled, whenever the *praetor* granted the respective share of inheritance to an emancipated child, but – as Gaius explains – even if the *praetor* could give the permission to take over the possession of the inheritance, he could not appoint

---

Justinian, Amsterdam 1975, 163: "A person dies intestate who did not make a will at all or did not make it in accordance with law or, again, if the will he made be broken or invalidated or if he has no surviving heir under it. 1 Under the law of the XII Tables, the inheritances of intestates go first to their direct heirs. 2 Direct heirs are those who, as we have said earlier, were in the power of the deceased; for instance, a son or daughter, grandchild of either sex by a son, as also a great-grandchild of either sex begotten by a grandson. And it does not matter whether such issue be natural or adoptive." See also D. 28,2,11 Paul. 2 Sab., on which see *Andreas Wacke*, Erbrechtliche Sukzession als Persönlichkeitsfortsetzung, ZRG RA 123 (2006) 197–247; *Martin Avenarius*, Continuatio dominii. Die vorklassische Mitberechtigung der künftigen Hauserben und der Vonselbsterwerb im klassischen Recht, in: Fides Humanitas Ius. Studi Luigi Labruna I, eds. *Luigi Labruna et al.*, Naples 2007, 231–252.

21 Gai. 3,19: *Statim enim emancipati liberi nullum ius in hereditatem parentis ex ea lege habent, cum desierint sui heredes esse.* (*Zulueta* [fn. 10] 157: "Thus to begin with, emancipated children have no rights under the statute to their ancestor's inheritance they have ceased to be *sui heredes*").

22 Gai. 3,25–26: 25 *Sed haec iuris iniquitates edicto praetoris emendatae sunt. 26 Nam liberos omnes, qui legitimo iure deficiuntur, vocat ad hereditatem, proinde ac si in potestate parentis mortis tempore fuissent, sive soli sint, sive etiam sui heredes, id est, qui in potestate patris fuerunt, concurrant.* (*Zulueta* [Fn. 10] 159: 25 "But these injustices of the law have been amended by the *praetor's* Edict. 26 For he calls to the inheritance all children deficient in statutory title exactly as though they had been in the ancestor's *potestas* at the time of his death, whether they stand alone or whether *sui heredes*, that is persons who were in the father's *potestas*, come in with them.").

23 On the relationship between *bonorum possessio* and *usucapio* see *Alfonso Castro Sáenz*, Aproximación a la *usucapio pro herede*, RIDA 45 (1998) 143–208, esp. 194–197. A brief overview in English can be found in *Georges M. Bush*, The Primitive Character and Origin of the *Bonorum Possessio*, Michigan Law Review 25 (1927) 508–522.

heirs.[24] At least in this respect, the civil law remained in force and determined that only children in the power of their father would be his natural heirs. In short, the application of the two stratas of law depended on the circumstances of the particular case and could hence vary from each individual decision to another. This characteristic of Roman private law can be referred to as casuistic reasoning.

The casuistic nature of Roman legal thinking is also relevant for the third layer of Roman private law, which is the "imperial law". The term resumes a variety of enactments of the Roman emperor. In regard to its content, this legal strata covers both civil and praetorian law but may involve new arguments and solutions due to the imperial purpose and the emperor's intentions. In accordance to this double-sided content, the imperial law can also be divided in two categories concerning its formal manifestation: in fact, the emperor may use existing forms of legislation in his own name, e. g. proclaiming an edict in the same manner as the *praetor*, or he may invent new forms of legal announcement including legally relevant conducts with no form at all.

c) Imperial law

The informal and far-ranging character of the imperial law is clearly expressed in a famous statement by Ulpian, the most cited jurist in the Digest, who was contemporary to the Severan emperor Caracalla[25]:

> D. 1,4,1 pr.–1 Ulp. 1 inst.
> pr. Quod principi placuit, legis habet vigorem: utpote cum lege regia, quae de imperio eius lata est, populus ei et in eum omne suum imperium et potestatem conferat.
> 1 Quodcumque igitur imperator per epistulam et subscriptionem statuit vel cognoscens decrevit vel de plano interlocutus est vel edicto praecepit, legem esse constat. Haec sunt quas volgo constitutiones appellamus.

---

24 Gai. 3,32: *Quos autem praetor vocat ad hereditatem, hi heredes ipso quidem iure non fiunt; nam praetor heredes facere non potest; (…). Sed cum eis praetor dat bonorum possessionem, loco heredum constituuntur.* (*Zulueta* [fn. 10] 159: "But those whom the *praetor* calls to an inheritance do not become heirs at civil law. (…) But when the *praetor* grants them *bonorum possessio*, they are established in the position of heirs.").

25 Antoninus Caracalla (211–217 AD) is known as the emperor who attributed Roman citizenship to all inhabitants of the Empire in his famous *constitutio Antoniniana* from 212 AD. On Ulpian's life and work see *Detlef Liebs*, § 424. Domitius Ulpianus, in: Die Literatur des Umbruchs. Von der römischen zur christlichen Literatur 117 bis 284 n. Chr., ed. *Klaus Sallmann*, Munich 1997 (= Handbuch der Lateinischen Literatur der Antike IV, eds. *Reinhart Herzog et al.*), 175–187; for an account in English see *Tony Honoré*, Ulpian. Pioneer of Human Rights, Oxford 2002[2].

Translation (*D. Neil MacCormick*, in: *Watson* [fn. 15] I, 14):
"pr. A decision given by the emperor has the force of a statute. This is because the populace commits to him and into him its own entire authority and power, doing this by the lex regia which is passed anent his authority.
1 Therefore, whatever the emperor has determined by a letter over his signature or has decreed on judicial investigation or has pronounced in an interlocutory matter or has prescribed by an edict is undoubtedly a law. These are what we commonly call constitutiones (enactments)."

According to Ulpian the emperor sets "law" whenever he makes a decision. That the jurist intents to comprise all imperial decisions in this assumption is made clear by the three examples that cover three different areas of imperial enactments. The first example, the emperor's written answers to requests (*rescripta*), refers to legal information given by the imperial chancellery to individuals or to legal entities that have approached the emperor for his help and advice.[26] These imperial replies serve as basis for the magistrates entrusted with the case and can be used as precedents in other affairs.[27] The second example, the *decreta*, mean the emperor's judgments that settle cases in first instance or in appeal. In fact, the imperial legal view taken in one affair will serve as argument for other cases since it will be regarded as the latest expression of legal knowledge.[28] The most striking example however, is Ulpian's third mentioning of formless incidental decisions, the so-called *interlocutiones*.[29] It seems that this term covers a variety of situations of unwritten legal utterances by the emperor, e. g. a provisional notification that a case will be postponed or a legal opinion expressed by the emperor without reference to a special case or affair. Despite their seemingly volatile nature, these decisions are to be treated as law as well, an idea that Ulpian expresses by equating them with a Roman statute (*lex*). Without putting too much into Ulpian's description, there seems to be an evident tension between statute (*lex*) of general application and a *interlocutio* that is uttered by

26 On *rescripta* see *Dieter Nörr*, Zur Reskriptenpraxis in der hohen Prinzipatszeit, first in ZRG RA 98 (1981) 1–46, now in: Historia Iuris Antiqui II (fn. 6) 1323–1368; on the epigraphic material see *Tor Hauken*, Petition and Response. An Epigraphic Study of Petitions to Roman Emperors, Bergen 1998, 181–249.

27 On the use of *rescripta* as precedents see notably *Ranon Katzoff*, Precedents in the Courts of Roman Egypt, ZRG RA 89 (1972) 256–292.

28 On *decreta* see *Maria Grazia Rizzi*, Imperator cognoscens decrevit: profili e contenuti dell'attività giudiziaria imperiale in età classica, Milan 2012.

29 On *interlocutio* see *Dieter Nörr*, Zu einem fast vergessenen Konstitutionentyp: Interloqui de plano, first in: Studi in onore di Cesare Sanfilippo III, Milan 1983, 519–543, now in: Historia Iuris Antiqui III (fn. 6) 1501–1525.

the emperor on a special occasion without long-lasting intention. If the jurist considers that they are equally legally binding, this can only mean that all imperial enactments must be taken into account for a case in which they might be relevant. That is to say that the emperor's statements form the basis of any casuistic legal reasoning, just as the civil and praetorian law. Ulpian's justification for this far-reaching relevance of the emperor's behaviour in legal matters lies in the political structure of the Principate. In fact, the jurist asserts that the emperor has gotten his authority and power from the people via a formal enactment, the law (*lex*).[30] As the people could enact laws, consequentially this right is also bestowed upon the emperor.

One prominent example of the legal imperial power can be attributed to the time of the first Roman emperor, Augustus (31 BC–14 AD). His legislative measure is only known through a report contained in Justinian's "*Institutiones*".

d) The Enforcement of *fideicommissa* since the Augustan Age

Justinian's report shows how informal requests by the deceased, the so-called *fideicommissa*, were enforced via an imperial enactment of Octavianus, the first emperor.

> Inst. 2,23 pr.–1
>
> pr. Nunc transeamus ad fideicommissa. et prius de hereditatibus fideicommissariis videamus.
>
> 1 Sciendum itaque est, omnia fideicommissa primis temporibus infirma esse quia nemo invitus cogebatur praestare id de quo rogatus erat: quibus enim non poterant hereditates vel legata relinquere, si relinquebant, fidei committebant eorum qui capere ex testamento poterant: et ideo fideicommissa appellata sunt, quia nullo vinculo iuris, sed tantum pudore eorum qui rogabantur, continebantur. postea primus divus Augustus semel iterumque gratia personarum motus, vel quia per ipsius salutem rogatus quis diceretur, aut ob insignem quorundam perfidiam iussit consulibus auctoritatem suam interponere. quod, quia iustum videbatur et populare erat, paulatim conversum est in adsiduam iurisdictionem: tantusque favor eorum factus est, ut paulatim etiam praetor proprius crearetur, qui fideicommissis ius diceret, quem fideicommissarium appellabant.

30 The best-known example of such a *lex* is the *lex de imperio Vespasiani*, on which see *Dario Mantovani*, Les clauses 'sans précédents' de la 'lex de imperio Vespasiani'. Une interprétation juridique, Cahiers du Centre Gustave Glotz 16 (2005) 24–43 with further references.

Translation (J. A. C. Thomas [fn. 20] 153 f.)

"pr. Let us now pass to trusts, and in the first place we shall treat of trust estates.

1. It should first be known that, originally, all will trusts were without validity, for no one was obliged, against his will, to make over what he was asked to make over; for, in respect of those to whom estates and legacies could not be left, testators would commit their estate as for the honour of those who were eligible to take by will. Hence they were called fideicommissa – committed to honour (fides) – because those so charged were under no legal constraint but only that of their own sense of decency. But thereafter the divine Augustus was the first more than once to direct the consuls to interpose their authority, being moved by consideration for the persons concerned, or because someone was said to have been so charged in the name of the Emperor's safety or on account of the gross betrayal of their trust by some. And since this appeared just and was popular, consular intervention was gradually converted into a regular jurisdiction: and so popular did these charges become that, in due course, a special praetor was created, with jurisdiction over will trusts, called the fideicommissary praetor."

Justinian explains that there had been a long tradition to fulfil the informal requests of the decedent, even if they were not legally binding; indeed, it seems to have been a moral duty to comply with the last wish of a decedent. These wishes were called *fideicommissa*, meaning "left to the general *fides,* the trustworthiness", or in today's terms: "trusts".[31] Since the trustees did not always satisfy the requests properly, Augustus is said to have ordered the consuls (as the highest magistrates) to compel the person to fulfil the plea of the decedent, hence to hand over ownership or to pay an amount to the favoured person.[32] These orders occurred, either because Augustus wanted to favour the person in need or because the decedent had asked the charged person "for the safety of the emperor". Other cases were induced because of the evident perfidy of the person in charge, meaning that the noncompliance was grossly unfaithful and trustless. All these decisions served as precedents and in the end the emperor's call to action lead to the creation of a new jurisdiction of the consuls that became a special type of procedure of imperial law (*cognitio extra ordinem*)[33]. Because of the growing popularity of trusts, emperors later created a special praetorian office. This *praetor fideicommissarius*, who – as distinguished from the ordinary *praetor*

31 On the Roman law of trusts see *David Johnston*, The Roman Law of Trusts, Oxford 1988.

32 On the role of the consuls see notably *Venanzia Giodice-Sabatelli*, La tutela giuridica dei fedecommessi fra Augusto e Vespasiano, Bari 1993, 65–84.

33 The term of *cognitio extra ordinem* covers a variety of changes in procedure that came along during the Principate. For a recent account (in English) see *Thomas Rüfner*, Imperial Cognitio Process (fn. 8) 257–269.

applying the civil and the praetorian law – was not an autonomous magistrate but an imperial officer.[34]

Despite the apparently incidental introduction of trusts, the admission of their enforcement must be seen as a legal revolution. In fact, according to civil and to praetorian law, the last will of the decedent was only binding if it had been established according to the strict formal specifications of Roman testamentary law. These implied the accomplishment of the ritual of the *mancipatio*, the establishment of a written document sealed by seven witnesses and the use of compulsory wording for every single testamentary arrangement (institution of heir, grant of a bequest, arrangement of a tutor, liberation of slaves etc.).[35] Infringement of these rules meant nullity of the will and occurrence of intestate succession.[36] In contrast, the establishment of a trust had no formal requirements: A trust could be constituted without any document; it could be done in simple writing or even speaking; no compulsory wording was dictated.

Despite the evident contradictions between the existing testamentary law and the new law of trusts, Augustus did not abolish the civil or praetorian law of succession, nor did his successors. Indeed, the new law of *fideicommissa* was not put in lieu of the two existing layers of law but was put above them. Yet, already the mere coexistence of the new and the old layers changed legal reasoning in most cases in reference to testamentary dispositions. Although Romans, loyal to their tradition, would still establish their testament according to the traditional law, after the Augustan reform, the testator could in principle also set out informal wills, whose success (as "trust") was guaranteed by the imperial administration. Therefore, it comes without surprise that the question arose whether an informal or invalid testament could be safeguarded as a *fideicommissum*. Even more, it seems that the testators were advised to use a clause safeguarding any testament that would have been void according to civil and praetorian law, as a *fideicommissum*[37]. It must therefore be underlined that the Roman jurists were

34 On the administrative role of the *praetor fideicommissarius* see *Max Kaser/Karl Hackl*, Römisches Zivilprozessrecht, Munich 1996², § 68.II.1, 452 with further references.

35 On the form of the Roman testament of civil law see the overview by *Thomas Rüfner*, Testamentary Formalities in Roman Law, in: Comparative Succession Law I (Testamentary Formalities), eds. *Kenneth G. C. Reid et al.*, Oxford 2011, 1–26.

36 Dying intestate however, was not only a legal problem but also a social and moral shame; we can therefore assume that it was to be avoided by every means. On this problem see notably *David Daube*, The Preponderance of Intestacy in Rome, Tulane Law Review 35 (1964/65) 253–262.

37 This problem is especially known for later informal amendments (*codicilli*), on which see D. 29,7,1 Ulp. 4 disp.: *Saepissime rescriptum et constitutum est eum, qui testamentum facere opinatus est nec voluit quasi codicillos id valere, videri nec codicillos fecisse: ideoque quod in illo testamento scriptum*

very well aware of the different requirements in the *ius civile* and *ius praetorium* on the one hand, and the imperial law on the other hand. But neither did they coin a general principle in order to overcome these differences nor did they see a general conflict between these requirements.[38] In fact, they seem to stick to a case by case view, in which the different layers had to be harmonised according to the individual circumstances.

In order to determine the criteria that the jurists applied in their casuistic approach, texts that show a collision of different legal layers (and rules) seem to be especially convenient. In the next section, one example of such a collision will be dealt with and some of the "tools" and methods used by the jurists in such a case will be examined.

2. One Example of Coordination in the Roman Law of Succession

The especially striking example concerns the revocation of testaments. The rules of the civil law are formal and clear:

a) Gai. 2,144

Posteriore quoque testamento, quod iure factum est, superius rumpitur; nec interest, an extiterit aliquis ex eo heres an non extiterit: hoc enim solum spectatur, an existere potuerit: ideoque si quis ex posteriore testamento, quod iure factum est, aut noluerit heres esse aut vivo testatore aut post mortem eius, antequam hereditatem adiret, decesserit aut per cretionem exclusus fuerit [...]: nam et prius testamentum non valet ruptum a posteriore, et posterius aeque nullas vires habet, cum ex eo nemo heres extiterit.

Translation (*Zulueta* [fn. 10], 107):

"An earlier will is also broken by a subsequent validly made will. It makes no difference whether an heir qualifies under the second will or not, the sole question being whether

est, licet quasi in codicillis poterit valere, tamen non debetur (Translation *W. M. Gordon*, in: *Watson*, [fn. 15] II, 445: "It has very often been stated in rescripts and constitutiones that a person who thought that he was making a will and did not intend it to be valid as a codicil is not regarded as having made a codicil either; and, therefore, what has been written in that will, although it could be valid in a codicil, nevertheless is not due."); D. 28,6,41,3 Pap. 6 resp. (...) *quae ita locum habebunt, si patris testamentum iure valuit: alioquin si non valuit, ea scriptura, quam testamentum esse voluit, codicillos non faciet, nisi hoc expressum est* (...). (Translation *W. M. Gordon*, in: *Watson* [fn. 15] II, 399f.: "(...) And this will apply if the father's will was legally valid; otherwise, if it was not valid that writing which he intended to be a will, will not make a codicil, unless this was expressly stated.")

38 However, the jurists seem to have applied the concept of *ius singulare* in order to preserve the formalities of the Roman will. For further references see *Ulrike Babusiaux*, Römisches Erbrecht, Cologne/Weimar/Vienna 2015, 191 f.

> one could have qualified. Therefore, if the person appointed by a subsequent validly executed will refuses to be heir, or if he dies either in the lifetime of the testator, or after his death but before entering on the inheritance, or if he is shut out by a *cretio* (clause requiring formal acceptance within a definite period), […] For the earlier will is invalid because broken by the second, and the second is of no effect because no one qualifies as heir under it."

According to Gaius, the revocation of a will under civil and praetorian law needs the establishment of a new will.[39] If the testator has made a new testament, this new one will revoke the existing one and only the second testament will be considered as legally binding. The rule is as easy as it is strict; the sole condition for the new one to supersede the old will is the validity of the latter. This view implies that there was no possibility under civil or the praetorian law to maintain two different wills of the same decedent via a conciliatory interpretation.[40] If the testator wanted to keep some of the old dispositions of the first will, he had to include them in the new will again. The reason for this strict all-or-nothing law was the formal character of the testament in the traditional layers of Roman private law.

However, since the fulfilment of formalities was no longer required under the imperial law, it changed the rules of revocation as well. The praetorian testament that gave priority to the document, whilst the civil testament combined the performance of an oral ritual and the written form, had already led to a gradual softening of the rules of civil law.[41] But the most important step was taken by the imperial enactments according to which somebody who had been instituted in a will, where the document had been destroyed by the testator without any formal revocation, was considered to be an heir according to civil law but considered ignoble to take the inheritance under the imperial law.[42]

One step further seems to have been taken by the Severan emperors at the beginning of the 3rd century. At least two transmitted fragments of juristic writing

---

39 This rule was very strict and implied that according to civil law even a destruction of the written document did not lead to the nullity of the testament, see *Sandro Serangeli*, Studi sulla revoca del testamento in diritto romano. Contributi allo studio delle forme testamentary I, Milan 1983, 7–30.

40 *Giuseppe Gandolfi*, Prius testamentum ruptum est, in: Studi in onore di Emilio Betti III, Milan 1962, 211–228.

41 On the oral and written form of the civil testament see *Mario Talamanca*, in: Mélanges en l'honneur de Carlo Augusto Cannata, ed. *Roland Ruedin*, Basel/Geneva/Munich 1999, 73–90 with further references.

42 This consequence has been regarded as interpolation of the Byzantine times but this suspicion is unfounded, see *Klaus-Peter Müller-Eiselt*, Divus Pius constituit. Kaiserliches Erbrecht, Berlin 1982, 184–198, 244–286.

seem to admit the combination of two subsequent testaments of the same testator and therefore witness a clear change of paradigm in comparison to the general principle of civil law. Both texts are cited by jurists of the mentioned epoch and it seems that the decision was regarded as exceptional and ground-breaking in both cases.[43] The most interesting evidence stems from a work published by the imperial jurist Iulius Paulus. This work titled *decreta* ("decrees") is a collection of imperial judgments and it is remarkable in more than one respect:[44] On the one hand, Paul's approach to the imperial decrees is special as it is not only presenting the emperor's decision but also refers to the preparatory discussions within the imperial council. On the other hand, Paul does not only give an account of the discussion but comments on the legal reasoning before the emperor and is often very critical with both his colleagues and the prince. This unique presentation of imperial legal reasoning can help to understand the jurists' techniques and self-definition in regard to the different layers of the Roman legal system.

b) The Case of Pactumeia Magna

D. 28,5,93 Paul. 1 imp. sent. cogn. prol. seu decr. 2

Pactumeius Androsthenes Pactumeiam Magnam filiam Pactumeii Magni ex asse heredem instituerat, eique patrem eius substituerat. Pactumeio Magno occiso et rumore perlato, quasi filia quoque eius mortua, mutavit testamentum Noviumque Rufum heredem instituit hac praefatione: «Quia heredes, quos volui habere mihi contingere non potui, Novius Rufus heres esto». Pactumeia Magna supplicavit imperatores nostros et cognitione suscepta, licet modus institutioni contineretur, quia falsus non solet obesse, tamen ex voluntate testantis putavit imperator ei subveniendum. Igitur pronuntiavit hereditatem ad Magnam pertinere, sed legata ex posterior testamento eam praestare debere, proinde atque si in posterioribus tabulis ipsa fuisset heres scripta.

Translation (*M. W. Gordon*, in: *Watson* [fn. 15] II, 392):

"Pactumeius Androsthenes had instituted Pactumeia Magna, the daughter of Pactumeius Magnus, as heir in respect of his whole inheritance and had substituted her father to her. When Pactumeius Magnus had been killed and a rumor had reached him that Pactumeius Magnus's daughter also was dead, he changed his will and instituted

43 The first one is D. 28,5,93 Paul. 1 imp. sent. cogn. prol. seu decr. 2; the second one is D. 36,1,30 Marcian. 4 inst. (the constitution is also cited in Inst. 2,17,3).

44 Paul's book has been transmitted in two different versions, the first one being intituled: *libri imperialium sententiarum in cognitionibus prolatarum* (books on the imperial judgments delivered in the cognitio extra ordinem), the second one is simply named: *libri decretorum* (books of judgments). These differences might be explained by the ephemeral nature of book-titles in Antiquity. For an overview on the bibliography on Paulus' work see *Liebs*, § 423. B.d (fn. 25) 172.

> that Novius Rufus as heir, prefacing the institution as follows: 'Because the heirs whom I wished that I might have I could not have, let Novius Rufus be heir. ' Pactumeia Magna petitioned our emperors and, having held a *cognitio,* although a limitation was placed on the institution, because an erroneous [limitation] does not usually form an obstacle [to an institution], the emperor took the view that, nevertheless, having regard to the testator's wishes, she should be helped. Therefore, he gave judgement that the inheritance belonged to Magna but that she must pay the legacies given in the later will, just as if she herself had been appointed heir in that later will. "

A certain Pactumeius Androsthenes had made two testaments.[45] In the first one, he had instituted a certain Pactumeia Magna, the daughter of Pactumeius Magnus and substituted her father to her. The motive of such a will might have been – this is also indicated by the names of the parties involved – that Pactumeius Androsthenes was the freed man of Pactumeius Magnus.[46] After having heard rumours of Pactumeius Magnus being killed,[47] Androsthenes changed his testament and instituted a certain Novius Rufus as heir. In his new testament, Androsthenes explicitly stated that this institution was a replacement solution since he could not have the heirs (Pactumeia Magna and Pactumeius Magnus) who he wished to have. After Androsthenes' death, it turned out that Pactumeia Magna was alive and she requested to be heard by the emperors Septimius Severus and Caracalla. The emperors indeed decided that she should get the inheritance but she would have to fulfil all the bequests that had been given in the second testament. This solution that makes use of a combination of the two subsequent testaments established by Pactumeius Androsthenes is in blatant contradiction to the civil law of testamentary revocation and must therefore be justified by the imperial jurists. In his report, Paulus alludes to the discussion that must have taken place in the emperors' council. He states that: "although a *modus* was placed on the institution, because a false assumption does not usually form an obstacle, nevertheless the emperor took the view that (...) she should be helped."[48]

This argumentation is twofold and seems to allude to an alternative justification of the exceptional outcome of the case: On the one hand, the emperor seems to reject the view that the introductory clause could be interpreted as a

---

45 For the last thorough analysis of the fragment see *Maria Grazia Rizzi*, Imperator cognoscens decrevit, Milan 2012, 349–365, with further references 349 fn. 256.

46 *Hans Josef Wieling*, Testamentsauslegung im römischen Recht, Munich 1972, 189 f.

47 Hist. Aug., Comm. 7,6–7. Pactumeius Magnus, a former prefect of Egypt (176/177 AD), was sentenced to death by imperial order of Commodus in 189 AD. For the prosopographic identification see *Arthur Stein*, s. v. Pactumeius Magnus Nr. 5, in: RE XVIII.1, Stuttgart 1942, coll. 2155 f.

48 This is my own translation that differs slightly from *Gordon's*.

condition of the revocation. This interpretation could have led to the result that the condition of the second testament was not materialised, so that the first will would still be valid and Pactumeia be regarded as heir.[49] On the other hand, the emperor's words seem to imply that the second testament was a modal institution, meaning that the *modus* imposed a certain conduct on the new heir.[50] Since in our sources, *modus* is mainly attributed to bequests (*legatum sub modo*) it is coherent that the emperor invokes a principle suited to the law of bequests in order to determine the legal effects of this addition. The principle in question is used to overcome a false designation of a bequeathed item and is referred to as *falsa demonstratio non nocet* ("a false designation does not harm").[51] By the time of Paul, this rule is understood in the sense that any false indication of a descriptive or justifying element to determine the bequeathed item does not hinder the validity of the bequest, if the item can be clearly identified.[52] A good illustration of this principle can be found in the commentary to the praetorian edict written by the 2nd century jurist Gaius (D. 35,1,17 pr.—1 Gai. 2 de legatis ed. praet.). He cites three different cases: In the first and easiest situation, the testator has used a wrong designation concerning the item left to the legatee, e.g. referring to a different origin of the item. If the origin indicated by the testator is wrong but if the item can however be clearly identified, the bequest is valid.[53] The same rule applies, whenever the testator has used additional attributes to describe the bequeathed item, e.g. the professional skills of a slave as "cook", when it turns out that the slave in question was a "sewer". Again, if the identity of the slave can be determined with certainty in regard to other characteristics, the slave meant by

---

49 The basis of this interpretation is the adversative conjunction of *licet modus institutioni contineretur.*

50 On the definition of modus see *Settimio Di Salvo*, Il legato modale in diritto romano. Elaborazioni dommatiche e realtà sociali, Naples 1973, 3–22.

51 In this point my interpretation differs from *Rizzi's* (fn. 45) 353 who states that the emperors violate the principle.

52 On the principle see *Hans Josef Wieling*, Falsa demonstratio, condicio pro non scripta, condicio pro impleta im römischen Testament, ZRG RA 87 (1970) 197–245, whose conjecture that Gaius' cases are exposed without knowledge is not convincing (206).

53 D. 35,1,17 pr. Gai. 2 de legatis ed. praet.: *Demonstratio falsa est, veluti si ita scriptum sit: 'servum Stichum, quem de Titio emi', 'fundum Tusculanum, qui mihi a Seio donatus est'. nam si constat, de quo homine, de quo fundo senserit testator, ad rem non pertinet, si is, quem emisse significavit, donatus esset, aut quem donatum sibi esse significaverat, emerit.* (Translation *J. A. C. Thomas*, in: *Watson*, 184: "It is a false particularization if, for instance, there be written 'the slave Stichus whom I bought from Titius', 'the Tusculan estate which was given to me by Titius. ' For, so long as it is clear which slave or estate the testator has in mind, it is irrelevant that he received as a gift what he says he bought or that he bought what he says was a gift.")

the testator will be bequeathed.[54] The last, and for our context the most relevant interpretatory step was taken, when the Roman jurists decided that the principle of *falsa demonstratio non nocet* should also be applied to a wrong cause, meaning a false justification or explanation of the bequest. The examples cited by Gaius are the following:

> D. 35,1,17,2 Gai. 2 de legatis ed. praet.
> Quod autem iuris est in falsa demonstratione, hoc vel magis est in falsa causa, veluti ita "Titio fundum do, quia negotia mea curavit", item "fundum Titius filius meus praecipito, quia frater eius ipse ex arca tot aureos sumpsit": licet enim frater huius pecuniam ex arca non sumpsit, utile legatum est.
> Translation (*J. A.C. Thomas*, in: *Watson* [fn. 15] III, 184):
> "The law in respect of false particularization applies the more to a false explanation, for example, 'I give the estate to Titius because he looked after my affairs" or "let my son Titius take the estate as a preferred gift because his brother abstracted so many gold pieces from the chest'; the legacy is valid, even though the brother did not take the money from the chest."

According to Gaius the bequest "I give Titius an estate, because he took care of my affairs" or the bequest "my son Titius shall get an estate in advance since his brother took so many gold coins out of my ark" are valid, even if the facts that the testator assumed about Titius are completely wrong. In other words: relevance is not given to the testator's motives to grant a bequest but to the effective attribution of the bequest in the testator's will. Despite the testator's false estimation, the heir will be held to comply with the bequest. If this reasoning was applied to the modal institution in the second will, one could therefore conclude that the emperor's argument "*quia falsus non solet obesse*" meant to maintain the validity of the institution in the second testament. This would imply that despite the wrong assumption of Pactumeia Magna's death (*falsa causa*), the modal institution of the second heir still had to be regarded as valid.[55] At first sight,

---

54 D. 35,1,17,1 Gai. 2 de legatis ed. praet.: *Igitur et si ita servus legatus sit: 'Stichum cocum', 'Stichum sutorem Titio lego', licet neque cocus neque sutor sit, ad legatarium pertinebit, si de eo sensisse testatorem conveniat: nam et si in persona legatarii designanda aliquid erratum fuerit, constat autem, cui legare voluerit, perinde valet legatum ac si nullus error interveniret.* (Translation *J. A. C. Thomas*, in: *Watson* [fn. 15] III, 184: "Hence, even if a legacy be made in the terms, 'I leave my cook, Stichus', or 'my cobbler, Stichus, to Titius', he will belong to the legatee, although not a cook or a cobbler, so long as it is established that this is the man whom the testator has in mind. Again, if there be some error in designating the person of the legatee but it is clear to whom the testator wishes to make his legacy, the legacy will be valid as though no error had occurred.")

55 A slightly different understanding of the rule for falsa causa can be found in D. 35,1,72,6 Pap. 18

this assessment is negative for Pactumeia Magna but it still opens the way for another assumption that leads to the contrary and positive outcome for her in the emperor's argumentation. In fact, even if the *modus* does not affect the validity of the second institution, it proves without doubt that the testator wished to have another heir than the one he instituted in the second testament, and moreover that this divergent wish is an integral part of this second testament. Therefore, just as a legatee under a *modus*, the heir of the second testament will have to adapt his conduct to the testator's wishes, i. e. render the inheritance to the woman instituted in the first and now revoked testament.

This somewhat entangled argumentation leads to the result that Pactumeia Magna is not heir in the sense of civil law but that the heir of the second will nevertheless has to pass the inheritance to her because of the testator's wish expressed in the modal institution. Whether this interpretation of the *modus* must be understood as the application of the imperial law of trusts or whether this is a sort of contamination of the civil law by the imperial law that stresses the testator's intention is not relevant in this respect.[56] In any case, it seems that the overcoming of civil law principles is encouraged by the existence of a non-formal parallel legal order, the *fideicommissa*, and that in case of a discrepancy between both layers of private law, the imperial law will prevail.

---

quaest.: *Falsam causam legato non obesse verius est, quia ratio legandi legato non cohaeret: sed plerumque doli exceptio locum habebit, si probetur alias legaturus non fuisse.* (Translation J. A. C. Thomas, in: Watson [fn. 15] III, 194: "The truer view is that an incorrect motivation is no impediment to a legacy because the reason for a bequest is no part of the bequest; still the defense of bad faith will generally be applicable if it be established that the testator would not otherwise have made the legacy.") on which see *Ulrike Babusiaux*, Papinians Quaestiones. Zur rhetorischen Methode eines spätklassischen Juristen, Munich 2011, 103–113 with further references.

56 It seems to be tempting however to construct the solution according to the law of *fideicommissa*: Since the testator declared that she would have been heir, if she was alive, she can obtain the inheritance via a *fideicommissum*. This shows that the introductory declaration contained in the second testament is interpreted in the sense of a trust in her favour; moreover, this interpretation does not openly contradict the solution obtained via the application of civil and praetorian law. In fact, also the imperial council holds that the second will is the only one to be valid; however, the heir of the second testament will not be allowed to keep the inheritance since the decedent declared that Pactumeia Magna should be heir if she lived. And this declaration is thought to be a trust. Hence, the heir of the second will be obliged to hand over the succession to her. With this argument, there is no need to contradict civil nor praetorian law; they are kept but the solution of the case is framed according to the imperial law. This interpretation also explains the second part of the emperor's decision, i. e. to burden Pactumeia Magna with the bequests distributed in the second testament. In fact, these bequests, whether they are established according to civil law principles or imperial law, can themselves be interpreted as *fideicommissa*. Therefore, the whole second will is reinterpreted as a trust: the main trust, the inheritance, is attributed to Pactumeia Magna, who has to fulfil the accessory trusts, the bequests.

Even if Paul's account of the imperial judgment shows that this decision was considered an extreme example of getting over the rules of civil and praetorian law, it is also evident that the jurist's collection of imperial decrees was meant to make them and their argumentation available for inferior judges, lawyers in courts and parties in other cases.[57] Therefore, despite the extraordinary circumstances of the case, it is plausible to consider that the legal argument, developed by the imperial court, could be used in other cases. If the legal foundations of the argumentation can be developed by a comparison to other material of the Digest – *modus*, *falsa demonstratio*, trust – the methodological tools behind this argumentation are rather difficult to grasp.

Following *Dieter Nörr*'s suggestions, one could be inclined to analyse the emperor's decision in the light of the rhetorical theory, especially the Ancient rhetorical doctrine of *status*. This doctrine tries to systematise the typical arguments that may be raised by the opponents of a particular issue (*status* or in Greek *stasis*).[58] The origin of these issues may be diverse and may refer to establishment of the facts (*genus rationale*) or to the interpretation and application of the laws (*genus legale*).[59] The question in Pactumeia Magna's case would refer to the applicable law and the coordination of civil law principles with the imperial law on trust. More specifically, this question would raise the issue of contradicting rules, which is dealt with by the so-called *status legum contrariarum*, i. e. the point of issue of contradicting laws. The most comprehensive description of this tool (in the hands of the rhetoricians) is provided in a manual from the second century AD, the *institutio oratoria* written by Quintilian, the most contemporary to the Roman jurists of the Principate.[60]

57 On this function of Paul's book see *Cesare Sanfilippo*, Pauli decretorum libri tres, Milan 1938, 178; on the larger judicial context see *Nicola Palazzolo*, Potere imperiale ed organi giurisdizionali nel II secolo d. C. L'efficacia processuale dei rescritti imperiali da Adriano ai Severi, Milan 1974, 66.

58 For a thorough dealing of the theory see *Lucia Calboli Montefusco*, La dottrina degli 'status' nella retorica greca e romana, Hildesheim/Zurich/New York 1986; for more recent bibliography see *Hellmut Geißner*, s. v. Statuslehre, in: Historisches Wörterbuch der Rhetorik VIII, ed. *Gert Ueding*, Darmstadt 2007, 1327–1350 (Antiquity) with references c. 1366 f.

59 The classification differs between different Ancient rhetorical writers; on Cicero's view see *Antoine C. Braet*, Variationen zur Statuslehre von Hermagoras bei Cicero, Rhetorica: A Journal of the History of Rhetoric 7 (1989) 239–259.

60 For a schematic overview on Quintilian's classification see *Geißner* (fn. 58) 1346; on Quintilian's teaching on *status* see also *Erling B. Holtsmark*, Quintilian on Status. A Progymnasma, Hermes 96 (1968) 356–368.

c) The status legum contrariarum

Quint., inst. 7,7,1–6

1 Proximum est de legibus contrariis dicere, quia inter omnes artium scriptores constitit in antinomia duos esse scripti et voluntatis status: neque inmerito, quia, cum lex legi obstat, utrimque contra scriptum dicitur et quaestio est de voluntate; in utraque id ambigitur, an utique illa lege sit utendum.

2 Omnibus autem manifestum est numquam esse legem legi contrariam iure ipso, quia, si diversum ius esset, alterum altero abrogaretur, sed eas casu collidi et eventu. Colliduntur autem aut pares inter se, ut si optio tyrannicidae et viri fortis comparentur, utrique data quod velit petendi potestate: hic meritorum temporis praemii conlatio est:

3 Aut secum ipsae, ut duorum fortium, duorum tyrannicidarum, duarum raptarum, in quibus non potest esse alia quaestio quam temporis, utra prior sit, aut qualitatis, utra iustior sit petitio.

4 Diversae quoque leges confligunt aut similes aut inpares. Similium aliae quibus etiam citra adversam legem contradici possit, ut in hac controversia: "Magistratus ab arce ne discedat. Vir fortis vel alia nulla obstante quaeri potest an quidquid optarit accipere debeat, et in magistratus multa dicentur quibus scriptum expugnetur, si incendium in arce fuerit, si in hostis decurrendum.

5 Aliae contra quas nihil opponi potest nisi lex altera: "Tyrannicidae imago in gymnasio ponatur. Mulieris imago in gymnasio ne ponatur. Mulier tyrannum occidit". Nam neque mulieris imago ullo alio casu poni potest nec tyrannicidae ullo alio casu summoveri.

6 Inpares sunt cum alteri multa quae opponi possunt, alteri nihil nisi quod in lite est, ut cum vir fortis inpunitatem desertoris petit. Nam contra legem viri fortis, ut supra ostendi, multa dicuntur, adversus desertores scripta non potest nisi optione subverti.

Translation (*D.A. Russell*, in: *Loeb* 271 ff.):

"1 We have next to discuss contrary laws. All the writers of textbooks have agreed that in antinomia (conflict of laws) there are two issues of letter and spirit. This is a justifiable view, because, when one law stands in the way of another, both parties speak against the letter, and the question between them is about the spirit: the doubt with regard to both laws is whether this is the law that must be applied.

2 It is clear to everyone that one law can never be contrary to another in juristic principles, because if there were distinct principles one law would be cancelled out by the other; collisions between laws are thus due to chance and the way things turn out.

3 Equal laws conflict either one with another, as when we set the choice of the tyrannicide against the choice of the war hero, both being given the power to ask for any-

thing they wish; in this case the comparison is between their services, the occasion, and the reward; or internally, as when we have two war heroes, two tyrannicides, or two victims of rape, in which the only question can be one of time (which request was first?) or quality (which was more just?).

4 Diverse laws also conflict. These may be similar or <unequally matched. First, similar laws.> Some may be contradicted even without an opposing law, as in the following controversia: "A magistrate must not leave the citadel, a war hero <may choose what reward he wishes. A magistrate who had been a war hero left the citadel. He chooses as his reward exemption from the other law"; here, even as regards the war-hero law>, and even if there is no opposing law, the question whether he ought to be given whatever he asks may be raised; and as regards the law about the magistrate, many points can be made to impugn the letter: suppose there is a fire on the citadel, or a sally has to be made against the enemy.

5 <Some again> cannot be opposed except by another law: 'A statue of a tyrannicide shall be set up in the gymnasium. <No statue of a woman shall be set up in the gymnasium.> A woman has killed a tyrant. ' For there are no other circumstances in which a woman's statue can be put up and no other circumstances in which a tyrannicide's can be removed.

6 Laws are unequally matched when there are many possible objections to one but no to the other, except for the matter in dispute: for example when the war hero asks pardon for a deserter as his reward. Here, as I have shown, many things can be said against the war hero law but the letter of the law against deserters can only be subverted by the exercise of the choice."

Quintilian gives an overview of the problem of conflicting laws in rhetorical theory. Since there are different understandings of the concept in Greek and Latin rhetorical writing, he first provides a definition of the contradictory nature of law (αντινομία).[61] In stating that the status of contrary laws must be regarded as a reduplication of the status of wording and intention (*status verbi et voluntatis*) (1), he follows the prevailing view of most Ancient rhetorical writers. This *status* refers to problems of interpretation that may arise for the application of every law. These interpretatory questions can be roughly and schematically characterised as a conflict between the letter of the law (*verba*) and the legislator's intention (*voluntas*). In this view, an inconsistency between two laws can be investigated, established or overcome via the interpretation of each law in question by examination of its wording and its scope. One can for example think of a contradiction between the text of two laws that might prove to be irrelevant, if it can be established that they have been written with the same intention. But

61 For an account of Ancient rhetorical writing see *Calboli Montefusco* (fn. 58) 166–178.

the interpretatory approach does not resolve the problem of contrary laws since Quintilian shows that collision is not a matter of pure normative discrepancies (2). In fact, he holds that laws rarely contradict each other in general or by the legislator's intention but that collisions between laws occur by chance and accident (*casu collidi et eventu*). In this view, the conflict between two laws is a matter of the case itself and is linked to the occurrence of a special situation which is covered by both laws. It must be noted already at this point that if this perception was shared by the Roman jurists, it could explain why they did not reason – like modern continental European lawyers – by referring to a hierarchal structure of the different sources (see p. 132 above) but that they stuck to a casuistic approach to resolve inconsistencies between the different layers of Roman private law. In this view, casuistic would not mean "intuitive" (see p. 132 above) but could rely on the rhetorical structures that Quintilian presents in the following sections of his manual (3–6). In fact, he classifies different instances of collisions of laws and shows how to resolve them. It is worth considering them in more detail:

According to Quintilian's exposition, the main division is to be drawn between the conflict of equal laws (*leges pares,* 3) and the conflict of diverse laws (*diversae leges,* 4–6). For the first group, the rhetorician further distinguishes between the conflict of equal laws against one another (*inter se*) and the conflict in the application of one and the same law to different people (*secum ipsae*); in the first case, there are conflicting rules for the same person ("someone who killed a tyrant and who is a war hero at the same time"); in the second case, there are different people asking for the application of the same law although it cannot be applied by default to all of them ("as when there can only be one person favoured by the law on tyrannicide or the law for a war hero"). The examples cited by the rhetorical teacher show that *leges pares* are laws with the same (or very similar) legal consequences, whereas diverse laws, the second group, concern the conflict of laws that prescribe opposing legal consequences. Hence, the concept of *diversae leges* is the one that comes the closest to the modern idea of conflicting legal prescriptions.

It is therefore of utmost interest to learn that the conflict of diverse laws is further to be subdivided in the conflict of similar laws (*leges similes,* 4–5) and unequal laws (*leges impares,* 6). According to Quintilian, with regard to the first subdivision, a divergence between similar laws may occur on the one hand, if the parties invoke the law for a special purpose that contradicts other legal prescriptions (4); on the other hand, the divergence of similar laws can also be observed, whenever laws have different scopes but apply to one and the same case (or person, 5). In these situations, it seems to depend on the argumentation and the circumstances of the individual case which law or which part of the similar laws prevails. The conflict of unequal laws as the second subdivision is characterised by a situation, where the two conflicting laws do not have the same weight and power; in these cases, it seems to be clear that the more powerful law will apply and supersede the other (6).

The following scheme tries to summarise Quintilian's teaching:

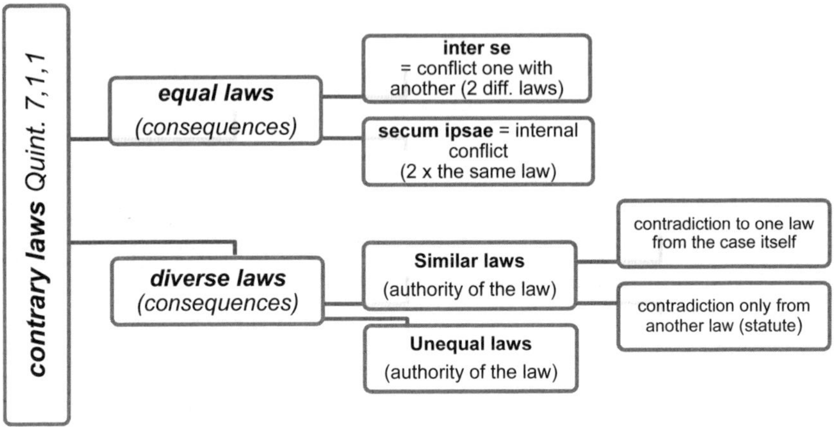

Scheme

d) Criteria to Determine the Authority of a Law

Quintilian's teaching on conflicting laws seems to leave one crucial point unsolved: How to determine the authority of a law in comparison to another one? The orator does not deal with this problem in this section but seems to presuppose the value of each law, when he explains the issue of similar laws in comparison to unequal laws. The best account of the criteria that may be used to establish the authority of the laws in questions can be found in Cicero's textbook "*de inventione*" that deals with the preparation of the rhetorician's argumentation. As Quintilian's own work draws on Cicero's example, it seems to be appropriate to use Cicero's presentation to shed some light on Quintilian's assumptions. Since Cicero's exposition in inv. 2,144–147 is very complex his view will be summarised for the scope of this contribution.

The passage of "*de inventione*" also deals with *leges contrariae* and – just as Quintilian – Cicero explains the problem of diverse law via an example (inv. 2,144),[62]

62 Cic. inv. 2,144: *Ex contrariis autem legibus controversia nascitur, cum inter se duae videntur leges*

where two laws applying to the same person provide for a reward and the death penalty for the same conduct. In order to determine, which of both laws to apply on the person in question, Cicero does not use a general classification like Quintilian (similar laws – unequal laws) but enters directly in the estimation process that serves to establish which law to give priority (inv. 2,145–147).

The first and most important criterion for this comparison is the scope of the law or in Cicero's words: "it is necessary to compare the laws, by considering which law has reference to more important that is to say more honourable and more necessary matters" (*oportet contendere considerando, utra lex ad maiores, hoc est ad utiliores, ad honestiores ac magis necessarias res pertineat,* Cic. inv. 2,145).[63] The authority of the law is then to be determined with regard to

---

aut plures discrepare, hoc modo: lex: "qui tyrannum occiderit, olympionicarum praemia capito et quam volet sibi rem a magistratu deposcito et magistratus ei concedito". Et altera lex: "tyranno occiso quinque eius proximos cognatione magistratus necato". Alexandrum, qui apud Pheraeos in Thessalia tyrannidem occuparat, uxor sua, cui Thebe nomen fuit, noctu, cum simul cubaret, occidit. Haec filium suum, quem ex tyranno habebat, sibi in praemii loco deposcit. Sunt qui ex lege occidi puerum dicant oportere. Res in iudicio est. In hoc genere utramque in partem idem loci atque eadem praecepta convenient, ideo quod uterque suam legem confirmare, contrariam infirmare debebit. Translation (*Harry Mortimer Hubell*, in: Loeb 313): "But from contrary laws a controversy arises, when two or more laws appear to be at variance with one another. In this manner:–There is a law, 'That he who has slain a tyrant shall receive the reward of men who conquer at Olympia; and shall also ask whatever he pleases of the magistrate, and the magistrate shall grant it to him.' There is also another law—'When a tyrant is slain, the magistrate shall also put to death his five nearest relations.' Alexander, who was the tyrant of Pherae, a city in Thessaly, was slain by his own wife, whose name was Thebe, at night, when he was in bed with her; she, as a reward, demands the liberty of her son whom she had by the tyrant. Some say that according to this law that son ought to be put to death. The matter is referred to a court of justice. Now in a case of this kind the same topics and the same rules will suit each side of the question; because each party is bound to establish his own law, and to invalidate the one contrary to it."

63 Cic. inv. 2,145: *Primum igitur leges oportet contendere considerando, utra lex ad maiores, hoc est ad utiliores, ad honestiores ac magis necessarias res pertineat; ex quo conficitur, ut, si leges duae aut si plures erunt,[aut] quotquot erunt, conservari non possint, quia discrepent inter se, sed ea maxime conservanda putetur, quae ad maximas res pertinere videatur; deinde, utra lex posterius lata sit; nam postrema quaeque gravissima est; deinde, utra lex iubeat aliquid, utra permittat; nam id, quod imperatur, necessarium, illud, quod permittitur, voluntarium est; deinde, in utra lege, si non optemperatum sit, poena adiciatur aut in utra maior poena statuatur.* Translation (*H. M. Hubell*, in: Loeb 313): "First of all, therefore, it is necessary to compare the laws, by considering which law has reference to more important that is to say, to more honourable and more necessary matters. From which it results that if two or more, or ever so many laws cannot all be maintained, because they are at variance with one another that one ought to be considered the most desirable to be maintained, which appears to have reference to the most important matters. Then comes the question also, which law was passed last; for the newest law is the most important. And also, which law enjoins anything, and which merely allows it; for that which is enjoined is necessary that which is allowed

further criteria. In Cicero's enumeration this is the time of the promulgation of the law, meaning that the more recent law will be of higher importance, the mandatory or prohibitory nature of the legal command, implying that a law that orders will be of higher relevance than a law that grants an allowance. Finally the necessary or simply optional character of the legal enactment that can be derived from the sanctions for the infringement of the law is its exceptional or general character and the urgency of the legal command.[64] Further arguments refer to the wording of both laws that might be more or less certain or evident in interpretation (Cic. inv. 2,147).[65]

---

is optional. Also one must consider by which law a penalty is appointed for the violation of it; or which has the heaviest penalty attached to it."

64 Cic. inv. 2,146: *nam maxime conservanda est ea, quae diligentissime sancta est; deinde, utra lex iubeat, utra vetet: nam saepe ea, quae vetat, quasi exceptione quadam corrigere videatur illam, quae iubet; deinde, utra lex de genere omni, utra de parte quadam; utra communiter in plures, utra in aliquam certam rem scripta videatur; nam quae in partem aliquam et quae in certam quandam rem scripta est, propius ad causam accedere videtur et ad iudicium magis pertinere; deinde, ex lege utrum statim fieri necesse sit, utrum habeat aliquam moram et sustentationem; nam id, quod statim faciendum sit, perfici prius oportet.* Translation (*Hubell*, in: Loeb 316): "For that law must be the most carefully maintained which is sanctioned by the most severe penalties. Again, one must inquire which law enjoins, and which forbids anything; for it often happens that the law which forbids something appears to be a kind of exception as it were to amend the law which commands something. Then, too, it is right to consider which law comprehends the entire class of subjects to which it refers, and which embraces only a part of the question; which may be applied generally to many classes of questions, and which appears to have been framed to apply to some special subject. For that, which has been drawn up with reference to some particular division of a subject, or for some special purpose, appears to come nearer to the subject under discussion, and to have more immediate connexion with the present action. Then arises the question, which is the thing which according to the law must be done immediately; which will admit of some delay or slackness in the execution. For it is right that that should be done first which must be done immediately."

65 Cic. inv. 2,147: *deinde operam dare, ut sua lex ipso scripto videatur niti, contraria autem aut per ambiguum aut per ratiocinationem aut per definitionem induci, <cum> sanctius et firmius id videatur esse, quod apertius scriptum sit; deinde suae legis ad scriptum ipsum sententiam quoque adiungere, contrariam legem item ad aliam sententiam transducere, ut, si fieri poterit, ne discrepare quidem videantur inter se; postremo facere, si causa facultatem dabit, ut nostra ratione utraque lex conservari videatur, adversariorum ratione altera sit necessario neglegenda. Locos autem communes et, quos ipsa causa det, videre oportebit et ex utilitatis et ex honestatis amplissimis partibus sumere demonstrantem per amplificationem, ad utram potius legem accedere oporteat.* Translation (*H. M. Hubell*, in: *Loeb* 316): "In the next place, it is well to take pains that the law one is advocating shall appear to depend on its own precise language; and that the law with a contrary sense should appear to be introduced with a doubtful interpretation, or by some ratiocination or definition, in order that that law which is expressed in plain language may appear to be the more solemn and efficient. After that it will be well to add the meaning of the law which is on one's own side according to the strict letter of it; and also to explain the opposite law so as to make it appear to have another meaning, in order that, if possible, they may not seem to be inconsistent with one another. And, last of

The brief overview of Cicero's arguments show that – just like Quintilian – Cicero is not presenting a general structure of the authority of legal sources but gives advice for the conflict of laws in a special case. The criteria explained by Cicero are meant to assist the advocates in their search of arguments.[66] Once again, there are no general rules and no hierarchical structures only the rational persuasion strategies that shall help to convince the audience and especially the court of the superiority of the law in favour of the orator's client.

Turning to the legal texts again, one has to admit that this rhetorical perception of legal conflicts does not seem to differ profoundly from the situation encountered in cases before the imperial court. In the Pactumeia Magna's case related by Paul (supra II.2b), the plaintiff must have tried to prove the authority of the imperial law in order to overcome the restrictive civil law principles since it was impossible to get the inheritance on the basis of civil law. One can imagine that she would have presented her rational arguments as to efficiently claim her case as well as appealed to the emperor's grace in general.[67] These arguments could have been developed and presented by an orator or by any other representative that would be admitted within the imperial council. Epigraphical evidence even indicates that the imperial legal counsellors themselves in some cases played the role of the party representatives and exposed the opposing views in front of the emperor.[68] In any case, the emperor's decision in Pactumeia Magna's case must have been explained and motivated in a understandable way – as has been

---

all, it will be a good thing, if the cause shall afford any opportunity for so doing, to take care that on our principles both the laws may seem to be upheld but that on the principle contended for by our adversaries one of them must be put aside. It will be well also to consider all the common topics and those which the cause itself furnishes, and to take them from the most highly esteemed divisions of the subjects of expediency and honour, showing by means of amplification which law it is most desirable to adhere to."

66 On the role of topics for the invention of arguments see *Lucia Calboli Montefusco*, Logica, retorica e giurisprudenza, in: Per la storia del pensiero giuridico romano. Dall'età dei pontefici alla scuola di Servio. Atti del seminario di San Marino, 7–9 gennaio 1993, ed. *Dario Mantovani*, Turin 1996, 209–228; *Gualtieri Calboli*, Die Topik in Jurisprudenz und Rhetorik, in: Topik und Rhetorik. Ein interdisziplinäres Symposion, eds. *Thomas Schirren et al.*, Tübingen 2000, 555–565.

67 The wording *supplicavit* could be interpreted in this sense, see *Rizzi* (fn. 45) 351 with further references.

68 This is shown in the inscription of Dmeir from the age of Caracalla (SEG XVII 759), on which see *Pierre Roussel/Fernand de Visscher*, Inscriptions du temple de Dmeir, Syria 23 (1942) 173–300; *Wolfgang Kunkel*, Der Prozeß der Gohariener vor Caracalla, in: Kleine Schriften, ed. *idem*, Weimar 1974, 254–266; a picture is available on <https://medihal.archives-ouvertes.fr/medihal-00489132/image> (04. Dec. 2017); for the latest interpretation see *Veronika Wankerl*, Appello ad principem, Munich 2009, 193–226.

developed above –, Paul's protocol indeed gives some legal arguments that must have been raised and discussed.

Thus, the question arises whether this legal reasoning contains also rhetorically valid arguments with regard to the issue of conflicting civil and imperial laws. In other words, Paul's argumentation has to be considered with regard to Cicero's criteria on the authority of laws in Cic. inv. 2,144–147.

e) Criteria of Legal Authority in Pactumeia Magna's Case

From the perspective of Ancient rhetorics, Pactumeia Magna' s case constitutes an issue of diverse law, meaning conflicting legal consequences applying to the same case. In fact, according to civil law Novius Rufus was the (only) heir to Pactumeius Androsthenes, whereas under the rule of imperial law it was possible to interpret the *modus* of the second testament as a trust in favour of Pactumeia Magna. The main argument used by the emperor to make a choice between the two laws was the testator's volition (*voluntas*): "the emperor took the view that, nevertheless, having regard to the testator's wishes, she should be helped" (*tamen ex voluntate testantis putavit imperator ei subveniendum*). As explained above, the emperor did not choose the easiest way to reason his decision since he refused a) to interpret the introductory clause as a condition for the second will, b) to consider the institution as invalid because of the testator's false assumption. In the light of rhetorical theory, these two arguments that seem to have been raised during the proceedings could be seen as an attempt to diminish the conflict between civil and imperial law. The emperor, however, seems to have refused to remove the conflict by ways of interpretation. Rather, his statement seems to stress the inconsistency of the principles of civil law with the imperial decree.

If this assumption proves to be correct, the sole argument of the testator's wishes suffices to prove the superior legal authority of the imperial law and hence reduces the conflict to a question of unequal laws (*leges impares*). The imperial interpretation of Androsthenes Pactumeius' will as connected to *fideicommissa* would therefore be justified by the superior inner value of the imperial private law. In fact, relying on Cicero's criteria, this argument would refer to the purpose of the imperial rule and would therefore show that only the emperor's interpretation is consistent with the most important issue in testamentary law, the testator's will. If civil law does not obtain results in correspondence with this general testamentary aim, it is evident that the imperial jurists cannot follow the civil law but have to give preponderance to the imperial law that respects the testator's intentions. It remains undefined, whether this insight can also help to understand other rulings of the imperial council; however, it would help to explain the predominance of imperial law in the long run.

To sum it up, the traditional view of intuitive legal reasoning in Roman law must be challenged since it can be shown that behind the seemingly apodictic case-solution of Roman emperors and jurists a vast armoury of very meticulous argumentation seems to be seminal. This inner structure of the Roman legal thought can be further explained by considering that the doctrine of Ancient rhetoric was part of the general education of the elite in Roman time. It was therefore accessible to legal writers, imperial counsellors and the Roman emperors as well. With this result, the traditional view of a somewhat "unstructured" legal reasoning in the Roman Empire cannot be maintained. It is much more likely that the fine lines of argumentation inherent to the sources have not yet been grasped.

Having said this, a further deepening of our understanding of the complexity of Roman legal reasoning could give helpful insights to modern challenges of legal methodology in Europe that are linked to the efforts of European harmonisation in legal matters.

III. Europe

Under the impression of the First and the Second World War, Europe has made important efforts to grow together.[69] The very beginning of this still ongoing process was the Treaty of Rome (TEC) that created the European Economic Community (EEC)[70] and was signed by Belgium, France, Italy, Luxembourg, the Netherlands and West Germany in 1957. The intention was to bring peace to Europe via economic cooperation. In 1973, the Community included Denmark, Ireland and the United Kingdom.[71] In 1981, Greece joined; in 1986 Portugal and Spain. Since the formal establishment of the European Union in the Maastricht Treaty ("Treaty establishing the European Union" [TEU]), signed in

69 The following sketch of the European harmonisation process is deliberately limited to essential information and does not constitute a thorough discussion of methodological problems. For further bibliography on the topic see The Oxford Handbook of European Union Law, eds. *Anthony Arnull et al.*, Oxford 2015, esp. Part II.

70 Previous treaties were the Treaty establishing the European Coal and Steel Community (ECSC) in 1952 and the plan for a European Defence Community and a European Political Community that failed in 1954.

71 In March 2017, the UK notified its intention to break off the European Union. On the legal implications of this so-called "Brexit" see <http://www.europarl.europa.eu/RegData/etudes/STUD/2017/607328/IPOL_STU(2017) 607328_EN.pdf> (01. Dec. 2017).

1993, the EU has been enlarged by further countries, namely Cyprus, the Czech Republic, Estonia, Hungary, Latvia, Lithuania, Malta, Poland, Slovakia and Slovenia.[72] Due to the growth of the community, a structural revision was put into force in the Treaty of Lisbon ("Treaty on the Functioning of the European Union" [TFEU]) in 2009.[73]

Without entering in details, the very peculiar structure of the EU law, especially the evolving nature of its organisation, must be kept in mind. It stems from the fact that the EU has been founded as an international organisation and has constituted a confederation of its Member States; but due to the emphasis on economic convergence and the creation of own organs, it has obtained attributes of a federation. The most particular feature is the existence of an own legal system, the EU law,[74] initialised by the Treaties but now mainly created by its institutions. As the legislative power of the EU institutions have not replaced the national legislation, the legal systems of all Member States nowadays present a compound of pure national, EU inspired domestic law[75] and pure EU law. If conflicts arise about the compliance of a Member State to EU law, the Commission can send a formal notice and ask the Member State to comply; in the final

72 On the accession process and its constitutional difficulties see *Anneli Albi*, EU Enlargement and the Constitutions of Central and Eastern Europe, Cambridge 2005.

73 For the text see <http://eur-lex.europa.eu/legal-content/EN/TXT/?uri=celex%3A12007L%2FTXT> (04. Dec. 2017); for an introduction to content and history see *C. Tomuschat*, Lisbon Treaty, in: Max Planck Encyclopedia of Public International Law, 2011, <http://opil.ouplaw.com/home/epil> (04. Dec. 2017).

74 In accordance to the Treaty of Maastricht, the correct denomination is EU law (= law of the European Union); however, the more general expression "European law" will be used here as a synonym.

75 EU inspired domestic law is due to the indirect legislation procedure via directive. According to Art. 288 TFEU (= formerly Art. 249 TEC) "a directive shall be binding, as to the result to be achieved, upon each Member State to which it is addressed but shall leave to the national authorities the choice of form and methods." The idea behind this means of legislation was to allow a further harmonisation of law in Europe while respecting the existing national differences in legal culture, e. g. between jurisdictions of civil and common law. Directives can be adopted in all matters for which the EU has competence; in practice the directive has been notably used for the harmonisation of law of the Member States. Especially for private law, directives have therefore been taken for the establishment of the common market and in the area of consumer protection law. The legislative procedure of a directive is two-fold: In the first place, the competent European institutions (formerly mainly the Commission, nowadays the Parliament) will decide upon the content of a directive; in the second place, it will then be up to the Member States to transpose the directive into their national law, normally meaning that they will pass a corresponding law. The content and the timely transposition of the EU directives in domestic law will be controlled by the EU institutions, mainly the Commission.

stage of this infringement procedure,[76] the Commission or another Member State can bring an action to the European Court of Justice (ECJ). If the Court finds that the Member State has not complied with the European regulation, it will be asked to take the necessary measures, i. e. to adapt the law or to adopt a new legislation in respect of the directive. The infringement procedure has been an important instrument in the hands of the Commission to monitor the implementation of the European directives in the Member States. But another procedure before the ECJ has been proven even more effective in establishing a coherent and uniform legal order within the Member States. This procedure is the preliminary ruling by the European Court of Justice introduced already in the Treaty of Rome. In the version of the Lisbon Treaty the relevant provision reads:

> Article 267 TFEU
> The Court of Justice of the European Union shall have jurisdiction to give preliminary rulings concerning:
> (a) The interpretation of the Treaties;
> (b) The validity and interpretation of acts of the institutions, bodies, offices or agencies of the Union;
> Where such a question is raised before any court or tribunal of a Member State, that court or tribunal may, if it considers that a decision on the question is necessary to enable it to give judgment, request the Court to give a ruling thereon.
> Where any such question is raised in a case pending before a court or tribunal of a Member State against whose decisions there is no judicial remedy under national law, that court or tribunal shall bring the matter before the Court. […]

The provision entitles the EJC to decide with binding effect on the interpretation of treaties and on the validity and interpretation of acts of the institutions, meaning also the validity of European legislation, i. e. decisions, directives and regulations. This competence is interlaced with the activity of the national courts that submit their interpretatory question of EU law to the ECJ. In this respect, the EU court and the national courts are meant to work together since it is the task of the national courts to apply European law and national law that stems from European directives but the interpretation of European law is left to the ECJ. This exclusive competence explains why the inferior national courts are free to refer to the ECJ, whenever a question of interpretation arises, whereas the

76 On the different stages see <https://ec.europa.eu/info/law/law-making-process/applying-eu-law/infringement-procedure_en> (01. Dec. 2017). The legal foundations are Art. 258–260 TFEU (= Art. 226–228 TEC).

court or tribunal of last resort has to present the matter to the ECJ. It is on this basis that the ECJ has established an autonomous European legal order[77] that constitutes the very difference of European law as a supranational legal order to an international treaty.

1. European Law as a New Legal Order within the Member States

The two main characteristics of European law that took shape in the judicature of the ECJ are the following: (1) European law has direct effect within the Member States; and (2) it has precedence over the domestic law of the Member States. Both concepts can be best explained by the relevant decisions of the ECJ that recognised these principles.

a) The Assertion of Direct Effect

The first decision in this respect is the Case 26/62 NV Algemene Transport- en Expeditie Onderneming van Gend & Loos v Netherlands Inland Revenue Administration, normally referred to as "Van Gend & Loos" from the year 1963.[78] In this case, the name-giving Dutch company had imported a chemical product from Germany, for which the Dutch authorities charged an import duty of 8% in application of a tariff ordinance of 1st March 1960. The claimants held that this ordinance violated Art. 12 of the TEC that had entered into force on the 1st January 1958 and that contained a stand-still clause for custom duties; the Dutch authorities, on the contrary, objected that the question raised was not one of interpretation and that the ECJ was not competent to decide on the prevalence of European law on Dutch law. The ECJ held:

> The objective of the EEC Treaty, which is to establish a Common Market, the functioning of which is of direct concern to interested parties in the Community, implies that this Treaty is more than an agreement which merely creates mutual obligations between the contracting states. This view is confirmed by the preamble to the Treaty which refers not only to governments but to peoples. It is also confirmed more specifically by the establishment of institutions endowed with sovereign rights, the exercise of which affects Member States and also their citizens. Furthermore, it must be noted

77 On the ECJ see *Anthony Arnull*, The European Union and Its Court of Justice, Oxford 2006², esp. 184–266 on the direct effect.

78 Available online: <http://eur-lex.europa.eu/legal-content/EN/TXT/?uri=CELEX:61962CJ0026> (04. Dec. 2017); on the case see *Franz C. Mayer*, Van Gend & Loos Case, in: Max Planck Encyclopedia of Public Law, Oxford 2013, available at <http://opil.ouplaw.com/home/epil> (04. Dec. 2017).

> that the nationals of the states brought together in the Community are called upon to cooperate in the functioning of this Community through the intermediary of the European Parliament and the Economic and Social Committee. In addition the task assigned to the Court of Justice under Article 177, the object of which is to secure uniform interpretation of the Treaty by national courts and tribunals, confirms that the states have acknowledged that Community law has an authority which can be invoked by their nationals before those courts and tribunals. The conclusion to be drawn from this is that the Community constitutes a new legal order of international law for the benefit of which the states have limited their sovereign rights, albeit within limited fields, and the subjects of which comprise not only Member States but also their nationals. Independently of the legislation of Member States, Community law therefore not only imposes obligations on individuals but is also intended to confer upon them rights which become part of their legal heritage.

This acknowledgement of direct effect of the European Treaty without further action on the part of the Dutch state, was based on three major arguments, the first being the creation of independent powers of the EEC whose acting could have direct effect on the individuals in the Member State. The second argument referred to the contracting parties' intentions to limit their sovereign rights within the application of the Treaty. The third argument was framed with regard to Art. 177 TEC (= Art. 267 TFEU) and invoked the role of the ECJ that had been created as a supranational instance to secure the uniform interpretation of Treaty. This proper judicial protection was held to be an argument for the direct effect on individuals since they would use the arguments of European law within their law suits.[79]

The importance of the individual claimant for the triumphant progress of European law can be shown by the second landmark decision that was issued only one year later, the Costa v E. N. E. L. case 6/64 from 1964.[80]

---

79 Direct effet and direct applicability are to be distinguished, see *Jan A. Winter*, Direct Applicability and Direct Effect – two Distinct and Different Concepts in Community Law, Common Market Law Review 9 (1972) 425–438. On the further development see *Dorota Leczykiewicz*, Effectiveness of EU Law Before National Courts. Direct Effect, Effective Judicial Protection and State Liability, in: The Oxford Handbook of European Union Law (fn. 69) 212–248 with further references.

80 <http://eur-lex.europa.eu/legal-content/EN/TXT/?qid=1512469402603&uri=CELEX:61964CJ0006> (04. Dec. 2017); on the case see *Meinhard Hilf*, Costa v. E. N. E. L. Case, in: Max Planck Encyclopedia of Public International Law, 2007, available at <http://opil.ouplaw.com/home/epil> (04. Dec. 2017).

b) The Precedence of European Law

The case opposed an Italian citizen (Mr Costa) and the national electricity company of Italy (E. N. E. L.). In fact, the Italian government had decided to nationalise the electricity industry by creating the "Ente Nazionale per l'Energia Elettrica" (E. N. E. L.). The law was passed in 1962, i. e. after the coming into force of the EEC Treaty in 1958. Mr Costa found that the nationalisation infringed Art. 37 (2) TEC that imposed on the Member States to refrain from new monopolies of commercial character in order to assure equal conditions of supply or marketing of goods for individuals in the Member States. In order to bring the question in front of a court, Mr Costa refused to pay his electricity bill to E. N. E. L. and requested that the case be referred to the Italian constitutional court and to the ECJ for preliminary rulings. Whereas the Italian constitutional court decided that Italy was liable according to international law, the ECJ ruled that the Treaty had priority over the Italian law. The arguments were the following:

> As opposed to other international treaties, the Treaty instituting the E.E.C. has created its own order which was integrated with the national order of the Member States the moment the Treaty came into force; as such, it is binding upon them. In fact, by creating a Community of unlimited duration, having its own institutions, its own personality and its own capacity in law, apart from having international standing and more particularly, real powers resulting from a limitation of competence or a transfer of powers from the States to the Community, the Member States, albeit within limited spheres, have restricted their sovereign rights and created a body of law applicable both to their nationals and to themselves. The reception, within the laws of each Member State, of provisions having a Community source, and more particularly of the terms and of the spirit of the Treaty, has as a corollary the impossibility, for the Member State, to give preference to a unilateral and subsequent measure against a legal order accepted by them on a basis of reciprocity.

This interpretation of the Treaty was derived from several articles of the EEC, mainly Art. 189 TEC (= 249 TFEU) that states that the European organs "shall make regulations and issue directives, take decisions, make recommendations or deliver opinions." And that "a regulation shall have general application. It shall be binding in its entirety and directly applicable in all Member States." The EJC held that this provision meant that European law could not be contradicted by national law, even if the internal law was adopted after the European legislation.

The consequences of this approach to European law for the national courts were clearly expressed in an equally famous case, the so-called "Simmenthal II"-decision of 1978, Case 106/77.[81] The ECJ first recalls the principles found in former decisions:

> In accordance with the principle of the precedence of Community law, the relationship between provisions of the Treaty and directly applicable measures of the institutions on the one hand and the national law of the Member States on the other, is such that those provisions and measures not only by their entry into force render automatically inapplicable any conflicting provisions of current national law but in so far as they are an integral part of, and take precedence in, the legal order applicable in the territory of each of the Member States also preclude the valid adoption of new national legislative measures to the extent to which they would be incompatible with Community provisions.

The ECJ then explains the role of the national courts that "must accordingly set aside any provision of national law which may conflict with it, whether prior or subsequent to the Community rule." This obligation is a direct consequence of the principle of primacy of EU law over domestic law.[82]

In conclusion, the proposed brief analysis of the authority of EU law within the national legal order clearly reveals the double-sided nature of EU law: On the one hand, it has priority over the national rules and the national courts are requested to leave the national law aside, whenever it collides with existing EU law. Even if in the cases cited this was only the primary law, i. e. the treaties, the rule was later on also applied to what is called secondary EU law, i. e. regulation emitted by the European institutions.[83] On the other hand, the EU law does not take part in the hierarchy of the national law but constitutes in itself a distinct legal order. In other words: The primacy of European law does not affect the validity of a contradicting domestic rule but is reduced to the non-application of a provision.

2. The Different Layers of Law in Member States of the European Union

Even if one might be inclined to demonstrate restraint against a comparison between imperial Rome and a modern supranational order already on the sole

81 See Case 70/77 Amministrazione delle Finanze dello Stato v Simmenthal SpA; <http://eur-lex.europa.eu/legal-content/EN/TXT/?qid=1512469457667&uri=CELEX:61977CJ0070> (04. Dec. 2017).

82 See *Leczykiewicz* (fn. 79) 216–217.

83 On the precedence of European law see *Monica Claes*, The Primacy of EU Law in European and National Law, in: The Oxford Handbook of European Union Law (fn. 69) 178–211 with further references, who rightly distinguishes between the view of the ECJ and the national courts.

ground that the latter is bound to the rule of law, whereas the former is not, some similar features between the Roman order during the Empire and the role of European law within national legal systems are obvious.

The first similarity is the multiplication of legislators that tend to increase conflicts and misunderstandings between different laws. In fact, both in imperial Rome and in modern European law, the addition of a new legislative body without abolishing or overruling the existing one can be observed. For the Roman world, there is no clear separation between legislation and judicial output since the emperor is both the highest judge and the most powerful legislator, whereas within the European Union, judicial and legislative power are clearly separated due to the theory of the division of powers. Despite these evident differences, the question on how to coordinate legal sources stemming from two different legislative bodies can be and has been asked for both historical situations.

The second similarity between Roman imperial law and European law is the absence of a hierarchical structure in the Kelsenian sense: although most Member States of the European Union follow a kind of legal hierarchy within their national law and although European law has been given a hierarchical structure since the Treaty of Lisbon,[84] no hierarchical argument can be used to determine the relation between EU and domestic law.[85] As has been shown above (III.1b), even the ECJ does not argue in terms of a hierarchical primacy but only speaks of a prior application of the EU law with regard to contradicting national law. Similarly, the Roman imperial law did not abolish the existing republican rules but added itself on top of them without a clear hierarchical supremacy. However, as has been seen in the Pactumeia Magna case, to which other decisions could be added (above II.2.b–e), the imperial rule proved to be more powerful when it came to a conflict to the republican layers in application to a case.

The last interesting point of comparison between imperial Rome and modern Europe that can only be briefly mentioned consists in the legitimacy that the new legislators – the emperor on the one hand, the EU on the other hand – try to obtain via moral assessment or policy considerations. As shown for the Augustan reform of *fideicommissa*, the emperors aimed to overcome the formalistic

84 On the hierarchy within European law see *Deirdre Curtin/Tatevik Manucharyan*, Legal Acts and Hierarchy of Norms in EU Law, in: The Oxford Handbook of European Union Law (fn. 69) 103–125. A list of sources and their hierarchy can be found in *Jan Komárek*, Legal Reasoning in EU Law, in: ibidem, 28–51, 44.

85 The well-known term of "layers of law" for Roman law has been used for the description of administrative law in the European Union by *Matthias Ruffert*, Rechtsquellen und Rechtsschichten des Verwaltungsrechts, in: Grundlagen des Verwaltungsrechts I, eds. *Wolfgang Hoffmann-Riem et al.*, Munich 2012², 1163—1255.

traditional approach to the law of succession and to allow a freer interpretation of the decedent's will; according to the resonance within the population – Justinian mentions that the *fideicommissa* became "popular" –, this reform met with requirements of the time. Concerning the EU, a great amount of legislation in private law matters related to consumer protection, to the equality of the sexes and to worker protection also frequently occurs within preliminary rulings of the ECJ. One explanation for the amount of claims could be that traditional domestic policy rules are sometimes not consistent with the more forward-looking ideas of the European legislator, which leads to frictions between EU rules and national legislation.[86]

IV. Conclusion: The Message from Antiquity

It would be easy to object against the above mentioned comparison between Roman imperial law and EU legislation and to put forward fundamental differences between modern law-making and imperial adjudication. But such an endeavour would miss the point of the forgoing composition. As reminded above (see p. 9 f.), it is difficult to learn from history. Yet, just as the analysis of passed times is conditioned by our contemporary preconceptions, the analysis of historical problems, evolutions or legal structures can open up new aspects of contemporary problems, evolutions or legal structures. In this respect, the legal historian can find new aspects to old problems that are inspired by contemporary views as he or she can consider parallels in history for modern phenomena. In both cases, it is the personal experience of the historian that will lead to new and deeper understanding of the historical or the present problem. If there was a message from antiquity, it could therefore be framed as an invitation to consider Roman legal reasoning in order to overcome the short-sided or one-way view of a contemporary observer of his or her own time.

86 On the conflicts between EU law and national private law see *Hans Werner Micklitz*, Monistic Ideology versus Pluralistic Reality: Towards a Normative Design for European Private Law, in: Pluralism and European Private Law, ed. *Leone Niglia*, Oxford 2013, 29–51, espec. 42–44.

Mariko Igimi, Fukuoka

An Observation on Consumer Protection in Electronic Sale of Goods from the Perspective of Roman Law

I. Introduction – What is in Common?

It has been over three decades since the development of internet technology has brought significant changes in business and related fields of law. Set on a new stage of the internet, even a simple contract such as a sale of goods, attracted much attention of lawmakers, legal practitioners and writers.[1] The sale of goods on the internet is said to have several "new" features that require a "new" legal framework.

One of these features is that no shop in the real world is required for the online sale of goods. The virtual market can easily cross any borders including such as those between state territories and jurisdictions. The seller can be in one jurisdiction and the buyer in another. The distance between sellers and buyers is no longer an obstacle to conclude such a contract. At the same time, the lack of a "real" store prevents the buyers from direct or "real" access to the object that they are about to buy. They have no other choice but to believe the description of the goods offered by the seller. Moreover, the conclusion of the contract requires only several "clicks" and no "real" action such as transfer, payment, signature or a seal on papers. These tend to cause buyers, especially the consumers, anxiety about the outcome of the contract.[2] Are these, however, "new" issues?

Ancient Romans also experienced a significant change of the legal environment in terms of sales contracts. Consensual contract, under which only four types of contracts fall in Roman law, namely *locatio conductio*, mandate, partnership and sale, was new to the Romans.[3] Consensual contracts were legal

1 Cf. Judge Easterbrook's denial of "Cyberlaw" as legal subject in *Frank Easterbrook*, Cyberspace and the Law of the Horse, University of Chicago Legal Forum (1996) 207–216. It was also in 1996 that UNICITRAL issued Model Law on Electronic Commerce which influenced laws on e-commerce in many jurisdictions.

2 Examples about the enforcement of their rights, redress for the breach of contracts and for the defect of goods, etc.

3 Gai. 3,135. Cohen argues that the consensual contract was already introduced in the 4th century BC in Athens. However, his view hardly finds any followers. Cf. only *Edward Cohen*, Consensual

institutions developed under the category of *ius gentium*, a layer of Roman law, which could be applied to all peoples regardless of their citizenship.[4] Now, the sale could cross borders, the seller can be a citizen of one city-state and the buyer could belong to another. The distance between sellers and buyers was no longer an obstacle to conclude a contract, because a contract of sale could now be concluded merely by consensus. On the other hand, as sale in Rome was mainly the sale of specified things, the obligation of the seller was only to transfer the object in the current condition. Hidden defects of goods, in principle, did not affect the conformity of the seller's obligation. Buyers, however, often had no other choice but to believe the description of the goods, *dictum*,[5] offered by the sellers. This must have been a problem, when sales between strangers gradually became common, due to the expansion of the Roman territory.[6] Moreover, now that the conclusion of the contract requires only a consensus and no formal action, these must have caused buyers anxiety about the outcome of the contract.

This article focuses on legal issues arising from sale of goods online and tries to discuss them from the perspective of Roman law.[7]

II. Consumer Protection – Protection through Inequality[8]

Just as in classical "modern civil law", typically represented in the original French Civil Code, Roman law did not institutionalise consumer protection law. Consumer protection was hardly needed, because very few people had legal capacity of transaction in Rome. Today, all humans are equal and are equally capable of legal transactions, with only a few exceptions, such as the under age or those suffering mental illness. In Rome, however, only the head of the family, *pater familias*, and the family members selected by the *pater familias* were entitled to be involved in legal transactions. In principle, only the heads of the families were

Contracts at Athens; *Eva Jakab*, Antwort auf Edward Cohen, both in: SYMPOSION 2003. Vorträge zur griechischen und hellenistischen Rechtsgeschichte, ed. *Hans-Albrecht Rupprecht*, Vienna 2006, 73–83 and 85–91.

4 In English language, cf. only: *George Mousourakis*, Fundamentals of Roman Private Law, Heidelberg 2012, 29.

5 "*Dictum*" literally means (the things) "said".

6 In English language, cf. only *George Mousourakis*, Roman Law and the Origins of the Civil Law Tradition, Heidelberg 2015, 12.

7 Roman law which will be referred to in this article, would be the law of the 2nd century BC to Classical period (around the 3rd century AD) in Ancient Rome.

8 Cf. *Mariko Igimi*, TAMEN COACTUS VOLUI. Die Römer und die Privatautonomie. in: Privatautonomie. Aufgaben und Grenzen, ed. *Marco Haase*, Baden-Baden 2015, 151–159.

sui iuris with legal competence and all the other family members were under *alieni iuris*, i. e., under the power of their male ascendants, such as their fathers, grandfathers, etc. Beside heads of the families, some *filii familias* and slaves were also capable of legal transactions if they were equipped with *peculium*. *Peculium* is the asset, which is given by the *pater familias* to individual members of his family. Although *peculium* belonged to the head of the family theoretically, they could even engage in business independently, within their own *peculium*. Therefore, it could be seen that giving *peculium* to family members is a good way to enrich the assets of the *pater familias* himself, as long as the members are successful in their businesses. The *pater familias* could sue debtors of family members directly and prevent loss. On the other hand, when the creditors of the family members sue the *pater familias* to claim the payment, he could first deduct the amount owed to himself by the family members, and his liability was limited to the amount of the remaining *peculium*. Although the *patres familias* were thus legally protected, we could perhaps well assume that the *peculium* would only be given to the family members who can be trusted to bring profit to the *pater familias*, who might observe the behaviour of the members within his family, begin with a small sum to check the proficiency of a selected family member, and then give him a larger amount, if he was successfully managing the asset. This also must have served as a training process for the future *pater familias*. Well trained in the harsh society of Rome, the *patres familias*, in ideal cases, were probably experienced enough and autonomous already by the time they became *sui iuris*. They were so well prepared to accept the consequences of what they once decided, that basically there was little need for protection.

If, however, the *patres familias* could not live long enough to train the family members, leaving young children behind as *sui iuris*, protection was desirable. Boys at the age of 14, and girls at the age of 12, obtained full legal capacity that they had to survive in the bitter legal world of Rome. In the next text, Ulpian[9] seems to indicate a sign of consumer protection.

D. 18,1,11 pr. Ulp. 28 Sab.[10]
Alioquin quid dicemus, si caecus emptor fuit vel si in materia erratur vel in minus perito discernendarum materiarum? In corpus eos consensisse dicemus? Et quemadmodum consensit, qui non vidit?

---

9 Domitius Ulpianus was a Roman Jurist in the late classical period in the 3rd century AD. His works are the most quoted in the Digests.

10 All translations of the Digests are cited from The Digest of Justinian, ed. *Alan Watson*, Vols. I–IV (1985).

> "Now, what if the purchaser were blind or a mistake over the material were made by a purchaser unskilled in distinguishing materials? Do we say that the parties are agreed on the thing? How can a man agree who cannot see it?"

This text has to be understood in the context of *dissensus* on the material of sales objects, which were sold as silver but were mixed with lead, etc.[11] It seems the traditional view among Roman jurists was to disregard *materia* and to concentrate on *corpus* and *substantia* of the object.[12] Ulpian, however, was concerned about the blind or unskilled purchasers. He says, "Now, what if the purchaser were blind or a mistake over the material were made by a purchaser unskilled in distinguishing materials? Do we say that the parties have agreed on the thing? How can a man agree who cannot see it?" and leaves the question unsolved. The remedy of *in integrum restitutio* that was given to young people under 25 years by the praetor[13] might be one of the answers in Rome, but it remains a question until the present day, how we could equalise the capability, information, power, etc. of the contracting parties.

III. Consensual Contract – "New" in Rome

If the Romans could not be protected as "consumers," how did they cope with newly introduced consensual contracts?

> D. 18,1,1,2 Paul. 33 ed.
> Est autem emptio iuris gentium, et ideo consensu peragitur et inter absentes contrahi potest et per nuntium et per litteras.

11 This text can be, and often is, understood in the context of error which was merely a variation of failed consensus in Rome. Prior to this text, D. 18,1,9 pr. Ulp. 28 Sab. emphasizes the essentiality of agreement for consensual contract: It is obvious that agreement is the essence in sale and purchase; the purchase is not valid if there is disagreement (dissentiunt) over the contract itself, the price, or any other element of sale. Following this statement, he continues to discuss what should be agreed in order to meet consensus on the sales object. There would not be a consensus, thus nor the sales contract, if there is no agreement on the actual thing (*corpus*) itself (D. 18,1,9 pr. Ulp. 28 Sab.), whereas a mistake on name of the object would not affect the consensus, as long as *corpus* is agreed (D. 18,1,9,1 Ulp. 28 Sab.). Further texts dealing with errors, such as D. 18,1,9,2 Ulp. 28 Sab.; D. 18,1,10 Paul 5 Sab. and D. 18,1,11,1 Ulp. 28 Sab. define what elements of the sales object should exactly be agreed on, in order to establish a consensus which is essential for the sales contract.

12 Cf. Marcellus in D. 18,1,9,2 Ulp. 28 Sab. or perhaps Paulus in D. 18,1,10 Paul. 5 Sab.

13 *Mousorakis* (fn. 4) 115.

> "A sale is a contract of the law of nations and so is concluded by simple agreement; it can thus be contracted by parties not present together, through messengers, or by correspondences."

In this text, firstly, Paul[14] states that the consensual sale is *ius gentium*. As the principle of *lex personalis* was prevailing in the ancient world, the applicable law was determined according to the city-state, which the applied parties belonged to. Therefore, Roman civil law, *ius civile*, could only be applied to Roman citizens. However, due to the expansion of Roman territory and the increase of inter-city-state transactions, a need for a law, which covers the entire territory of "multi-national" Rome was desired. *Ius gentium*, or the law of peoples, which applied to all free men, regardless of their citizenship, was an answer to this issue. In this sense, the consensual sale was designed to function in "cross border" situations and had an "international" character.

Paul also writes that a sale can be contracted "by the parties not present together", which indicates that the presence of parties had been essential for the transaction until the introduction of a consensual sale. The traditional transaction that functioned as a sale is assumed to be *stipulatio*. *Stipulatio* was a popular legal institution that established an obligation by way of questions and answers. When A asks B "Do you give me ten golds?" and B answers, "I give", then B is bound to give ten golds unilaterally. By concluding double *stipulatio*, one for the object and another for the price, parties could achieve the same goal as if they concluded a contract of sale.[15] An essential part of the *stipulatio* being "question" and "answer", it required both parties to be present at the same place with ability to speak and hear.[16] The introduction of consensual sales removed such requirement of presence. As long as the parties could communicate their will to sell and buy mutually, they did not need to be at the same location. People remotely situated from one another could now conclude a contract through messages and letters using their slaves.[17] The electronic medium today, which is often said to have changed "traditional" sales, is a kind of "slave", i. e., just a method of communication. A mere development of communication tools does not change the essential character of the consensual sale, which once was "new" in 2nd century BC in Rome.

---

14 Iulius Paulus was the second most quoted jurist from the late classical period.

15 Cf. in English language: *Francis De Zulueta*, Roman Law of Sale, Oxford 1945, 5.

16 Therefore, the deaf and mute were unable to conclude a *stipulatio*, while the blind could do so (D. 45,1,1 pr. Ulp. 48 Sab.).

17 Or friends by way of mandate (D. 17,1).

IV. Beyond Necessity? Consensual Contract plus *stipulatio*

When the procedure of entering into an obligation is too simple, however, it is quite natural that the obliged parties maintain indefinite feelings of anxiety towards the outcome of such procedure. The same concern that consumers have towards sales contracts online today, could perhaps be observed among Romans who were engaging in consensual contracts. Varro's book on agriculture teaches how a flock of sheep should be purchased.[18]

Varro, rust. 2,2,5–6[19]

In emptionibus iure utimur eo, quo lex praescripsit. In ea enim alii plura, alii pauciora excipiunt; quidam enim pretio facto in singulas oves, ut agni cordi duo pro una ove adnumerentur, et si quoi vetustate dentes absunt, item binae pro singulis ut procedant. De reliquo antiqua fere formula utuntur. Cum emptor dixit "tanti sunt mi emptae?" Et ille respondit "sunt" et expromisit nummos, emptor stipulatur prisca formula sic, "illasce oves, qua de re agitur, sanas recte esse, uti pecus ovillum, quod recte sanum est extra luscam surdam minam, id est ventre glabro, neque de pecore morboso esse habereque recte licere, haec sic recte fieri spondesne?" Cum id factum est, tamen grex dominum non mutavit, nisi si est adnumeratum; nec non emptor pote ex empto vendito illum damnare, si non tradet, quamvis non solverit nummos, ut ille emptorem simili iudicio, si non reddit pretium.

"In purchasing we take advantage of the variation which the law allows, some making more and others fewer exceptions; thus, some purchasers, when the price is fixed by the head, stipulate that two late-born lambs count as one sheep, and in the case of those which have lost their teeth from age, that they also be reckoned two for one. With this exception, the ancient formula is generally employed: when the purchaser has said, 'They are sold at such a price?' and the seller has passed, 'Yes', and the money has passed, the purchaser, using the old formula, says: 'You guarantee that the sheep in question are perfectly sound, up to the standard of a flock which is perfectly sound, expecting those blind of one eye, deaf, or *minae* (that is, with belly bare of wool), that they do not come from a diseased flock, and that title may legally pass – that all this may be properly done?' even after this has been agreed on, the flock does not change owners unless the money has been counted; and the purchaser still has the right to obtain a judgment against the vendor under the law of purchase and sale if he does not make delivery, even though no money has passed; just as the vendor may obtain a judgment against the purchaser under the same law if he does not make payment."

---

18 Varro was known as one of the most sophisticated members of *patricii* who wrote extensively, from which only several works have survived until today.

19 Text and translation from Loeb, Classical Library 283 (1935) 332 ff. On the text as "sales format" cf. *Eva Jakab*, Praedicere und Cavere beim Marktkauf, Munich 1997, 157 ff.

Although the consensual sale was already introduced in Rome in the 2nd Century BC, Varro suggests to employ "the ancient formula (*antiqua ... formula utuntur*)" from the 1st Century BC. The ancient form consisted of question and answer: the buyer asks "They are sold at such a price? (*tanti sunt mi emptae?*)" and the seller answers "They are (*sunt*)."[20] Applying this formula, the money would also be promised by the buyer to the seller. This is exactly the form used to conclude a *stipulatio*, using the same verb "*sunt-sunt*" which is required for its validity. Varro further explains the effect of such procedure saying that "even after this has been agreed on, the flock does not change owners, unless the money has been counted; and the purchaser still has the right to obtain a judgment against the vendor under the law of purchase and sale if he does not make delivery, even though no money has passed; just as the vendor may obtain a judgment against the purchaser under the same law if he does not make payment." (*Cum id factum est, tamen grex dominum non mutavit, nisi si est adnumeratum; nec non emptor pote ex empto vendito illum damnare, si non tradet, quamvis non solverit nummos, ut ille emptorem simili iudicio, si non reddit pretium.*) The first sentence seems to be referring to the effect of *stipulatio* and the latter to the consensual contract. The wording of *stipulatio* "whether it was sold" presumes the existence of a sales contract, which made the *stipulatio* causal. Therefore, "the flock does not change its owner" as long as the price is not yet paid. Here, the word "owner (*dominus*)", however, should not be understood technically, because neither *stipulatio* nor a sales contract has an effect to transfer ownership.[21]

On the other hand, "under the law of purchase and sale (*ex empto vendito*)" seems to be more technical. From a legal point of view, "*ex empto vendito*" should be understood as a reference to the *actio ex empto* and to the *actio ex vendito*, i. e. claims (*actiones*) arising from the sales contract (*emptio et venditio*). These actions to legally pursue their rights as buyers or sellers are given as the effects of consensual sale behind the transaction.

This practice of concluding a *stipulatio* together with consensual sale seems to have lasted until, at least, the late classical period. In some of the cases, *stipulatio* is used for the purpose of novation[22] while the others are concluded to add punitive clauses to the original contract of sale.[23]

---

20 The translation of the Loeb edition is "Yes". However, "*sunt*" literally means "they are" which corresponds to the question.

21 The ownership will only be transferred by a "real act" of transfer or other formal acts.

22 Cf. D. 18,5,3 Paul. 33 ed.

23 Cf. D. 18,7,7 Pap. 10 quaest.; D. 18,7,9 Paul. 5 quaest.; D. 19,1,28 Iul. 3 Urs. Fer.

D. 18,1,39,1 Iul.[24] 15 dig.

Verisimile est eum, qui fructum olivae pendentis vendidisset et stipulatus est decem pondo olei quod natum esset, pretium constituisse ex eo quod natum esset usque ad decem pondo olei: idcirco solis quinque collectis non amplius emptor petere potest quam quinque pondo olei, quae collecta essent, a plerisque responsum est.

"A man selling olives on the tree stipulated that the price should be ten pounds of oil to be produced from the crop. The probable interpretation is that he intended the price to depend upon the yield of the cram up to ten pounds. Hence, if the yield be only five pounds, the purchaser cannot claim more than that. This was the reply of many jurists."

This text shows an example of a *stipulatio* concluded for the sales price, which can already be claimed by the *actio* arising from the consensual sale. Although there seems to be no need for *stipulatio*, the parties who gave consensus to the sale of the olives on the trees, chose to conclude a *stipulatio* for the price of "ten pounds of oil to be produced from the crop". The parties might have concluded *stipulatio* to avoid the issue of confusion with a barter.[25] The other possible reason for the parties to conclude a *stipulatio* could be that the payment of the price was to be postponed until the production of oil. The payment of price can only be realised after all the process of acquiring oil out of the harvested olives. During this procedure, the seller has to bare a risk of non-payment. This might be the reason why the parties chose the "safer" option to conclude a *stipulatio*.[26]

The sale was not the only consensual contract that was combined with *stipulatio*.[27] The next text shows a case of partnership established by extremely cautious teachers of grammar and deals with the problem whether the *stipulatio* concluded by the parties should be interpreted as a novation or as an additional punitive clause.[28]

---

24 Aemilius Iulianus is one of the most prominent jurists of the 2nd century AD. He worked under Hadrian.

25 D. 18,1,1,1 Paul. 33 ed. It was especially important for the Romans to specify which contract they were concluding because the parties would not be legally bound if the transaction did not match the categories which were already set to create *actio*.

26 If they maintained the *actio venditi*, however, the problem of interpretation regarding the amount of the oil that has to be paid as a price, would not be an issue, since *actio venditi* is a *bonae fidei iudicium* and such circumstances would automatically be considered.

27 D. 17,2,41 Ulp. 20 ed.; D. 17,2,42 Ulp. 45 Sab.; D. 17,2,65 Paul. 32 ed.; D. 19,2,54,1 Paul. 5 resp.

28 An example of small business in Rome, cf. *Franz-Stefan Meissel*, Societas. Struktur und Typenvielfalt des römischen Gesellschaftsvertrages, Frankfurt 2004, 153 ff.; *Daniele Mattiangeli*, Societas und corpus, Vienna 2017, 530 ff.

D. 17,2,71 pr. Paul. 3 epit. Alf. dig.
Duo societatem coierunt, ut grammaticam docerent et quod ex eo artificio quaestus fecissent, commune eorum esset: de ea re quae voluerunt fieri in pacto convento societatis proscripserunt, deinde inter se his verbis stipulati sunt: "haec, quae supra scripta sunt, ea ita dari fieri neque adversus ea fieri? si ea ita data facta non erunt, tum viginti milia dari?" quaesitum est, an, si quid contra factum esset, societatis actione agi posset. respondit, si quidem pacto convento inter eos de societate facto ita stipulati essent 'haec ita dari fieri spondes?', futurum fuisse, ut, si novationis causa id fecissent, pro socio agi non possit, sed tota res in stipulationem translata videretur. sed quoniam non ita essent stipulati 'ea ita dari fieri spondes?' sed 'si ea ita facta non essent, decem dari?' non videri sibi rem in stipulationem pervenisse, sed dumtaxat poenam (non enim utriusque rei promissorem obligari, ut ea daret faceret et, si non fecisset, poenam sufferret) et ideo societatis iudicio agi posse.

"Two men formed a partnership to teach grammar, and agreed that they would share between them any profit they might make from that employment. They set down in a formal agreement of partnership the terms they wished to be observed, and then made a stipulation as follows: "Do you promise that the things written down above will be duly given and done, and that nothing will be done against the terms? Do you promise to give me twenty thousand if the things so stipulated are not given and done?" The question was asked whether it was possible to sue by an action on partnership if something was done against the agreed terms. This answer was given: "If, after making a formal agreement of partnership, they made a stipulation in these words, 'do you promise that these things that have been agreed will be given and done,' then it follows that, provided they did this as a novation, an action for partnership would not be possible, but the whole matter would be held to have the status of a stipulation." However, as they did not stipulate 'do you promise that these things that have been agreed will be given and done,' but 'do you promise to give ten if the things agreed are not done,' then the matter is not considered to have the status of a stipulation, but to be only a case of a penalty (as the promisor was not under an obligation in both directions, both to give and do, and to pay a penalty if he failed in this), and therefore proceedings can be undertaken by way of an action on partnership."

The teachers concluded a consensual contract of partnership, agreed on a *pactum*[29], and issued a document on the agreed term that they would share all the

29 *Pactum* is a mere agreement which does not give rise to *actio* but only provides *exceptio*. However, whenever *pactum* is agreed upon immediately after any consensual contracts, the *pactum* would be regarded as a part of the contract and could be claimed as arising from the contract. In this case, *pactum* was concluded immediately after the contract of partnership and therefore can be seen as a contractual condition added to the contract of partnership.

profits they would obtain from the business of teaching grammar. In addition, they concluded a *stipulatio* with the words "Do you promise that the things written down above will be duly given and done, and that nothing will be done against the terms? Do you promise to give me twenty thousand if the things so stipulated are not given and done?" The main issue in this text is whether the action of partnership could be admitted because, if this *stipulatio* was made for novation, the partnership would be terminated and there would be no action arising from the partnership, while the action should still be effective, if the *stipulatio* was concluded only to create punitive clause. Hence, the text deals mainly with the interpretation of the words used in the *stipulatio*. What interests us most, however, is that anxious laypeople trusted *stipulatio* even more than writing.

V. Warranty – Form for Security

As we have seen, one of the solutions to free Romans from their anxiety regarding a "new" consensual contract was to rely on the formality of *stipulatio*. *Stipulatio* was used, furthermore, as an express warranty against eviction as well as against any defects of the goods sold.[30] As the obligation of the seller was only to transfer the possession of the object at the current condition, basically, the seller was not obliged to transfer ownership to the purchaser, nor liable for the defect of the sales object.[31] Considering the general attitude of Romans towards *stipulatio*, it is rather natural that they simply added *stipulatio* to the consensual contract in order to provide security for such unexpected cases of misfortune.[32]

Warranty against eviction was given in a form of *stipulatio*, in which the seller promised to the purchaser that he would pay double the price, if the purchaser would be evicted.[33] By the time of late classical period, however, this practice of

30 Cf. D. 18,1,40,2 Paul. 4 epit. Alf. dig.; D. 18,1,43,1 Flor. 8 inst.; D. 18,7,6 pr. Pap. 27 quaest.; D. 19,1,4 pr. Paul. 5 Sab.; D. 19,1,11,12 Ulp. 32 ed.

31 Roman contract of sale obliges the seller only to transfer "empty (= sound) possession (*vacua possessio*)". In English language, cf. only: *Alan Watson*, Roman Law and Comparative Law, Athens, GA 1991, 63.

32 The words of warranty in *Varro*, rust. 2,2,5–6 appear as a part of the sequence of *stipulationes* and is recommended to use the form as a part of the transaction. Cf. also below: *Plaut.*, Bacch. 862–883. *Jakab* (fn. 19) 153 ff. introduces varieties of sources extensively. Cf. also in English: *Eva Jakab*, Sale and Community from the Roman World, in: Sale and Community Documents from the Ancient World. Individuals' Autonomy and State interference in the Ancient World. Proceedings of a Colloquium supported by the University of Szeged, ed. *idem*, Trieste 2015, 213–229, 215 ff.

33 In the early law, the evicted "purchaser" could not seek for remedy unless the ownership was trans-

stipulatio duplae was generally implied in the contracts of sale.[34] On the other hand, the general introduction of a warranty against defect was avoided, because some buyers might prefer to buy goods with defects for a lower price according to the purpose or usage of the goods to be acquired.[35] Therefore, it was left to the contracting parties, which defect should be listed to guarantee their non-existence.[36] As the market flourished,[37] however, *aediles curules*, a magistrate acting as a market police, intervened with the capacity to issue edicts for the sale of the most important goods in Roman society, i. e. slaves and cattle, in order to secure transaction in the public markets. Nevertheless, *aediles* did not follow the model of eviction to introduce a generic implication of the warranty but merely ordered sellers to notify certain defects to the buyers in order to avoid the deception of the vendors.[38] Consequently, the parties could now further negotiate on price, additional "service", or provide warranty against the defects, based on the *dictum*. In this manner, *stipulatio* against the latent defect of the goods sold, kept relying on individual negotiations and contracts.[39] *Stipulatio* was *per se* and without additional edicts, conceived by the Romans to be reliable.

ferred by way of *mancipatio*, in which case *actio auctoritatis* for double the price was allowed. Cf. *Max Kaser*, Das römische Privatrecht, Vol 1, Munich 1971², 132 f. In English: *Paul du Plessis*, Borkowski's Textbook on Roman Law, Oxford 2010⁴, 269.

34 D. 21,2,2 Paul. 5 Sab. *Stipulatio duplae* has no characteristic of novation. Therefore, *actio empti* would still be effective to claim the amount *quod interest*. Cf. *Rolf Knütel*, Stipulatio Poenae, Cologne 1976, 335 ff. However, the warranty against eviction could also be dropped according to individual needs of the contracting parties (Cf. *Plaut.*, Persa 525–526); *Dieter Nörr*, Probleme der Eviktionshaftung im klassischen römischen Recht, ZRG RA 121 (2004) 154 fn. 10.

35 *Jakab* (fn. 19) 152 gives a nice example of a slave being a sales object, who was a skilled painter but ill. There could be countless reasons for wanting a specific object including simple affection.

36 *Jakab* (fn. 32) 228. Cf. also *Varro*, rust. 2,2,6: "You guarantee that the sheep in question are perfectly sound, up to the standard of a flock which is perfectly sound, expecting those blind of one eye, deaf, or *minae* (that is, with belly bare of wool), that they do not come from a diseased flock, and that title may legally pass – that all this may be properly done?"

37 *Jakab* (fn. 32) 224, the markets were strongly controlled by the state.

38 D. 21,2,1,2 Ulp. 1 ed. aed. cur. Not for equivalence. *Berthold Kupisch*, Römische Sachmängelhaftung. Ein Beispiel für die "ökonomische Analyse des Rechts?", TR 70 (2002) 21–54.

39 The debate between *Jakab* and *Kupisch* went on further (*Eva Jakab*, Cavere und Haftung für Sachmängel. Zehn Argumente gegen Berthold Kupisch, in: Kaufen nach Römischem Recht, eds. *Eva Jakab* et al., Heidelberg 2008. One of the main issues they disagree on is what "ädilizische Stipulation" was, on which I will have to discuss on another occasion.

VI. *Stipulatio* – A Point of no Return

Verses from a comedy of Plautus in the 1st century BC, "Bacchides" may further show what *stipulatio* meant to the Romans. A young man, Mnesilochus, falling in love with one of the sisters Bacchis, prepares money to buy her off with the help of his slave, Chrysalis, because the courtesan was engaged in a contract of, probably, *locatio conductio* with a soldier named Cleomachus to provide "*opera* (work)" for the period of one year in exchange for money. However, Mnesilochus confesses the trick to his father Nicobulus, because he believed that his friend Pistoclerus was also in love with the same woman. Having found out that there were two women by the name of Bacchis, Mnesilochus asks his slave an even more difficult task, to deceive the father for the second time. Chrysalis successfully makes Nicobulus believe that his son was having an affair with a married woman, whose husband, he thought, was Cleomachus the soldier, using words with double meanings, *vir* and *mulier*. Frightened by the idea that his own son might be accused for committing adultery, Nicobulus asks Chrysalis to arrange a "*pactum*" with Cleomachus.

Plaut., Bacch. 862–883[40]
Nic.: … perii, pertimui miser.
Cleo.: tum illam, quae corpus publicat volgo suom, faxo se haud dicat nactam quem derideat.
Chry.: pacisci cum illo paulula pecunia potes.
Nic.: pacisce ergo, opsecro, quid tibi lubet, dum ne manifesto hominem opprimat neue enicet.
Cleo.: nunc nisi ducenti Philippi redduntur mihi, iam illorum ego animam amborum exsorbebo oppido.
Nic.: em illoc pacisce, si potest; perge, opsecro, pacisce quiduis.
Chry.: ibo et faciam sedulo. quid clamas?
Cleo.: ubi erus tuos est?
Chry.: nusquam. nescio. uis tibi ducentos nummos iam promittier, ut ne clamorem hic facias neu conuicium?
Cleo.: nihil est quod malim.
Chry.: atque ut tibi mala multa ingeram?
Cleom.: tuo arbitratu.
Nic.: ut subblanditur carnufex!
Chry.: pater hic Mnesilochi est; sequere, is promittet tibi. tu aurum rogato; ceterum uerbum sat est.

40 Text and translation from Loeb, Classical Library 60 (2011) 456 ff.

Nic.: quid fit?
Chry.: ducentis Phílippis rem pepigi.
Nic.: ah, salus mea, seruauisti me. quam mox dico 'dabo'?
Chry.: roga hunc tu, tu promitte huic.
Nic.: promitto, roga.
Cleo.: ducentos nummos aureos Philippós probos dabin?
Chry.: 'dabuntur' inque. responde.
Nic.: Dabo.

"Nic.: … I'm done for, I got such a shock, poor me.
Cleo.: Then I'll make sure that that woman who prostitutes her body to all and sundry won't say that she's found someone to laugh at.
Chry.: You can settle the issue with him for a small sum.
Nic.: Settle the issue, then, please, on any terms you like, so long as he doesn't surprise the chap in flagrante and kill him.
Cleo.: Now unless I'm given back two hundred Philippics, I'll swallow up their lives this instant.
Nic.: Well, settle it for that sum if possible. Go on, please, settle it for any price you wish.
Chry.: I'll go and do my best. What are you shouting for?
Cleo.: Where's your master?
Chry.: Nowhere. I don't know. Do you want to be promised two hundred Philippics now on condition that you won't shout around or pick an argument?
Cleo.: There's nothing I'd prefer.
Chry.: And on condition that I can heap many insults onto you?
Cleo.: At your discretion.
Nic.: How the rascal fawns on him!
Chry.: This is Mnesilochus's father. Follow me, he'll promise it to you. You should ask for the gold. As for the rest, we've had enough words.
Nic.: What's happening?
Chry.: I've made an agreement for two hundred Philippics.
Nic.: Ah, my salvation! you've saved me! How soon shall I say 'I'll give them to you'?
Chry.: You ask him. You promise him.
Nic.: I promise it, ask.
Cleo.: Will you give me two hundred good genuine gold Philippics?
Chry.: Say, 'they shall be given.' Answer him.
Nicobulus: I'll give them to you."

After much ado, the father and the soldier exchange the magic words, i. e. question and answer in the form of *stipulatio*: "Will you give me two hundred good genuine gold Philippics?" "I'll give them to you." This was the "point of no return" for Nicobulus that he would have to pay 200 golds no matter what happened. In fact, Nicobulus discovered the fact that Bacchis was not the soldier's wife but a courtesan.

> Plaut., Bacch. 1096–1098[41]
> Nic.: ... ita miles memorat meretricem esse eam quam ille uxorem esse aiebat, omnia ut quicque actum est memoravit, eam sibi <in> hunc annum conductam, relicuom id auri factum quod ego ei stultissumus homo promisissem: ...
> "Nic.: ... the soldier tells me that the woman whom that fellow said was his wife is a prostitute; he told me how everything was done, that he hired her for himself for this year, and that the money which I, like a complete idiot had promised him was the rest ..."

Without any ground, the father was obliged to pay the money, knowing that there was no threat to his son being sued for adultery. The audience of the play must have understood that Nicobulus cannot escape from the obligation, once he concluded *stipulatio*, or once he said the words "I'll give them to you". It must have been a common understanding amongst Romans that *stipulatio* must always be fulfilled. Thus, at the moment when *stipulatio* is concluded, parties cross the point of no return and the debtor cannot avoid being bound.

VII. Conclusion – A Future Contribution of Roman Law for the Electronic Sale of Goods?

Consumer protection has gradually become an important issue in law since the late 1980's, facing the fact that the balance of bargaining powers between buyers and sellers was completely lost.[42] Even in the modern world, where, unlike in Rome, every human being possesses legal capacity, it is unlikely that every individual is equally competent enough to assess and tackle all the issues arising from their transactions. After the Industrial Revolution, the objects of sale became mainly non-specific or generic goods due to the mass production, and the mass producers acquired increasingly powerful position for bargaining. In order to re-establish the balance, the law privileges consumers, which was alien to Roman law. Nevertheless, the similarity between the electronic sale of goods today and the consensual contract in Ancient Rome, might provide us with some suggestions to tackle with the current issues. In Rome, the transaction that people trusted was the formal act of *stipulatio*. It was used in many ways and played a

41 Text and translation from *Loeb*, Classical Library 60 (2011) 480 ff.

42 Cf. Product Liability Directive in 1985.

decisive role even after the consensual contract had been introduced. What we are still looking for in the context of electronic transaction could be something similar to this – an act that everyone trusts and can be confident that it would be followed. The other lesson, which could usefully be learned from Rome would be the provision of important information regarding the sales objects. *Aediles curules* in Rome obliged sellers to notify the buyers of certain defects and if this was not done, the transaction would be treated as if the non-existence of the defects were guaranteed.

Very recent phenomena triggered by the development of Internet technology might offer a chance for Roman law to be revitalised. Using applications, more and more private persons are engaging not only in buying products but also in selling them.[43] Domination of business in selling goods and the imperative to protect consumers can now be questioned. When the individuals with equal bargaining power are the players in the market place, consumer protection law would not be needed anymore. The role of companies providing platforms for such transactions between individuals should be rather similar to that of *aediles*. They are already issuing certain rules to provide order within their "market". If the contracting parties do not comply with those rules, they would be expelled from the platform.

Now might be the time that legal institutions created in Roman law and theories developed under its influences should be refocused[44].

---

43 *Ebay*, for example, writes: "We give sellers the platform, solutions, and support they need to grow their businesses and thrive." See <https://www.ebayinc.com/our-company/who-we-are/> (26. Apr. 2018). Their sellers are not necessarily business people but individuals who often have other occupations, see <https://www.ebayinc.com/our-company/partner-to-sellers/> (26. Apr. 2018). In terms of *locatio conductio*, the same would apply to *Airbnb* and *Uber*.

44 This article was inspired by a doctoral thesis written by a former student of the LL.D. program at Kyushu University, Ms Statip Yathayotin, "Consumer Protection in Electronic Commerce Under Thai Laws: Lessons from the European Union and the United States."

Yasunori Kasai, Tokyo*

"Information" in the Ancient and Modern

Hybris and Defamation in Ancient Greek and Roman Law

I. Introduction – Information and Rumour

1. What is "Information"?

The purpose of this essay is to find a way in which the notion of information can be explored by comparing it to the notion of rumour. What is "information"? What does it mean? We are surrounded by information and related words, such as information technology (IT), the information society, information law, information education and so on. But I failed in finding any kind of definition of information in both legal and philosophical Japanese dictionaries[1] as well as in textbooks of information law[2] though I was able to find definitions of related complex terms such as "The Law of Protection of the Individual Information" for example. English common law dictionaries[3] and textbooks of information technology law[4] also lack a specific definition for the term itself. If we attempt to

---

* This article is based on my paper read at a Roman law seminar entitled "Messages from the Antiquity" at Kyushu University in Fukuoka organised by Professor Toshiyuki Kono and Professor Mariko Igimi. I thank both professors for their kind invitation and responses of the audience. I also thank Professor Ulrike Babusiaux for her constructive criticism and her academic assistants for corrections and reformulation of my first draft. Lastly, not the least, my special thanks are, as always, due to Professor Emi Matsumoto for her help, both overall and in the chapter on modern Japanese legal history in particular.

1 Dictionary of Philosophy and Thought, eds. *Wataru Hiromatsu* et al., Tokyo 1998; Dictionary of Law, eds. *K. Takashi* et al., Tokyo 2016[5].

2 Information Law, An Introduction, eds. *Masahiro Sogabe* et al., Tokyo 2015.

3 Oxford Dictionary of Law, ed. *Jonathan Law*, Oxford 2018[9], s. v. information: "The written statement by which a prosecutor informs a magistrate of the offence for which a summons or warrant is required. A person who lays information before a magistrate is an informant. Information must contain a statement that describes the offences in ordinary language, identifies any legislation that creates it, and includes such particulars of the conduct constituting the commission of the offence as to make clear what the prosecutor alleges against the defendant (criminal procedure rules). The criminal justice Act 2003 also provides for a written charge and requisition for the accused to appear before the magistrates."

4 *Andrew Murray*, Information Technology Law, The Law and Society, Oxford 2016[3]. Murray discusses information in the contexts of digitisation (41–49) and of digital ownership (91–98). He seems to more or less identify information with something digitised. *Richard Susskind*, The Future

define a concept, one of the most important methods is the so called "dialectical" method which was first put forward by Plato. In the legal science, this method is exercised by way of "distinction" (*distinctio/divisio*). If we apply this method of distinction to the concept of information, it turns out that the concept of information defies such distinctions as "tangible" or "non-tangible", and "mobile" or "immobile".[5] If we turn our eyes away from the definition of information to some aspects in which information has been explored, the following common characteristics emerge: "omnipresent", "universal", "swift in diffusion", "society-related", "value/interest-related".[6] In that sense "money" or "god (if any)" which has a similar nature as that of information may come to mind.[7] Information is, indeed, not to be understood just as "(big) data". It spreads instantly and everywhere in society because it is assumed that it contains some value or interest. In order to investigate the unique nature of information, we shall look for an analogy in the ancient world.

2. Rumour in Ancient Greece and Rome

In the *Aeneid* 4,173–197, Vergil says as follows:

> Extemplo Libyae magnas it Fama per urbes,
> Fama, malum qua non aliud velocius ullum:
> mobilitate viget virisque adquirit eundo,
> parva metu primo, mox sese attollit in auras
> ingrediturque solo et caput inter nubila condit.
> illam Terra parens ira inritata deorum
> extremam, ut perhibent, Coeo Enceladoque sororem
> progenuit pedibus celerem et pernicibus alis,
> monstrum horrendum, ingens, cui quot sunt corpore plumae,

---

of Law, Facing the Challenges of Information Technology, Oxford, revised paperback edition, 1998. There Susskind had already discussed law as information, but not the legal aspect of information (71–101).

5 *Fritz Schulz*, History of Roman Legal Science, Oxford 1946, 62–69.

6 Cf. *Kotaro Nawa/Hitoshi Yoshioka*, Myth and Truth of the Information System, From Nuclear Power Station to Information Technology, Tokyo 2015. Nawa compares information with things and services and points out "the strangeness of information".

7 The best legal account of money can be found in *Charles Proctor*, Mann on the Legal Aspect of Money, Oxford 2012[7]; see also 'Money' in Western Legal Tradition, Middle Ages to Bretton Woods, eds. *David Fox* et al., Oxford 2016 and *Louis Gernet*, 'Value' in Greek Myth, in: Myth, Religion and Society, Structuralist Essays by Marcel Detienne, Louis Gernet, Jean-Pierre Vernant and Pierre Vidal-Naquet, ed. *Richard L. Gordon*, Paris/Cambridge 1981, 111–146.

tot vigiles oculi subter (mirabile dictu),
tot linguae, totidem ora sonant, tot subrigit auris.
nocte volat caeli medio terraeque per umbram
stridens, nec dulci declinat lumina somno;
luce sedet custos aut summi culmine tecti
turribus aut altis, et magnas territat urbes,
tam ficti pravique tenax quam nuntia veri.
haec tum multiplici populos sermone replebat
gaudens, et pariter facta atque infecta canebat:
venisse Aenean Troiano sanguine cretum,
cui se pulchra viro dignetur iungere Dido;
nunc hiemem inter se luxu, quam longa, fovere
regnorum immemores turpique cupidine captos.
haec passim dea foeda virum diffundit in ora.
protinus ad regem cursus detorquet Iarban
incenditque animum dictis atque aggerat iras.

"At once Fama went through the great cities of Africa, Fama, swifter than any other evil; she thrives through motion and gains strength as she goes. She is small and timorous to begin with, but soon she lifts herself into the air, striding on the ground and her head hidden in the clouds. The story is that Earth, incited by her anger at the gods, bore her as her last daughter, a sister for Coeus and Enceladus, swift-footed and speedy-winged, a terrifying, huge monster. She has as many eyes underneath (wondrous to tell) as she has feathers on her body, and as many tongues and sounding mouths, and as many are the ears that she pricks up. At night she flies shrieking through the shadows between earth and sky, and does not let her eyes droop in sweet sleep. By day she sits watching on rooftops or high towers, and terrifies great cities. She clings to fictions and distortions as much as she brings news of the truth. This was the creature that then delighted in fillings that had not indiscriminately: that Aeneas, born of Trojan blood, had come, and that fair Dido saw fit to unite herself to him as her husband; now they were spending the whole winter long snug in their wantonness, oblivious of their royal duties, the slaves of base lust. Such were the things that the loathsome goddess spread all around through men's mouths. Straightaway she turned her steps to king Irabas, inflaming his mind with what she said and heaping up his anger."[8]

Ovid gives us a full description of the house of Fama in the *Metamorphoses* 12,39–66:

8 *Verg.*, Aen. 4,173–197, translation from *Philip Hardie*, Rumour and Renown, Representations of Fama in Western Literature, Cambridge 2012, 79.

Orbe locus medio est inter terrasque fretumque
caelestesque plagas, triplicis confinia mundi;
unde quod est usquam, quamvis regionibus absit,
inspicitur, penetratque cavas vox omnis ad aures:
Fama tenet summaque domum sibi legit in arce,
innumerosque aditus ac mille foramina tectis
addidit et nullis inclusit limina portis;
nocte dieque patet: tota est ex aere sonanti,
tota fremit vocesque refert iteratque quod audit;
nulla quies intus nullaque silentia parte,
nec tamen est clamor, sed parvae murmura vocis,
qualia de pelagi, siquis procul audiat, undis
esse solent, qualemve sonum, cum Iuppiter atras
increpuit nubes, extrema tonitrua reddunt.
atria turba tenet: veniunt, leve vulgus, euntque
mixtaque cum veris passim commenta vagantur
milia rumorum confusaque verba volutant;
e quibus hi vacuas inplent sermonibus aures,
hi narrata ferunt alio, mensuraque ficti
crescit, et auditis aliquid novus adicit auctor.
illic Credulitas, illic temerarius Error
vanaque Laetitia est consternatique Timores
Seditioque repens dubioque auctore Susurri:
ipsa, quid in caelo rerum pelagoque geratur
et tellure, videt totumque inquirit in orbem.
Fecerat haec notum, Graias cum milite forti
adventare rates, neque inexspectatus in armis
hostis adest. […]

"There is a place in the middle of the world between earth, sea and the regions of the sky, at the borders of the threefold universe. From here can be seen everything everywhere, however distant in space it is, and every sound reaches these hollow ears. This is the domain of Fama, and she has chosen a dwelling at the top of the citadel, and made numberless entrances and a thousand openings in the building, with no doors shut off the entries; it lies open day and night. The house is made all of echoing bronze, the whole thing sounds out, and repeats voices and doubles what it hears. There is no peace inside, nowhere silence, but there is no shouting aloud, rather the murmuring of a low voice, like the noise of waves of the sea if heard from afar, or like the sound returned by the last rolls of thunder when Jupiter has made the dark clouds crash out. Crowds fill the hall; the fickle mob comes and goes, and thousands of made-up rumours mingling with true wander about, sending a babble of words rolling around. Some of these fill empty ears with talk, others bear tales to other places, and the fiction grows in scale, and each new authority adds something to what has been heard. There are to be found Credulity and reckless Error, empty Joy and anxious Fear, sudden Sedition and Whispers of doubtful author. The mistress herself sees what is done in the sky, at sea, and on earth, and searches through the whole world. She had made it known that the Greek ships were arriving with a stormy army, and the armed enemy's presence was not unexpected."[9]

It becomes clear that all the attributes of information mentioned above such as "omnipresent", "universal", "swift in diffusion", "society-related", "value/interest-related" appear in both passages above. Sharing the same features as the information, *fama* can, I think, be compared to information.

Fama (information) about the Greeks' attack against the Trojans had been already spread before they reached Troy. Then, how about the information about the result of the war and the return of the Greeks? In Agamemnon, the chorus reports the following:

Aeschylos, Agamemnon 475–487:
πυρὸς δ᾽ ὑπ᾽ εὐαγγέλου
πόλιν διήκει θοὰ
βάξις·εἰ δ᾽ ἐτήτυμος,
τίς οἶδεν, ἤ τι θεῖον †ἐστιν μὴ† ψύθος;
τίς ὧδε παιδνὸς ἢ φρενῶν κεκομμένος,
φλογὸς παραγγέλμασιν
νέοις πυρωθέντα καρδίαν ἔπειτ᾽
ἀλλαγᾷ λόγου καμεῖν;
γυναικὸς αἰχμᾷ πρέπει
πρὸ τοῦ φανέντος χάριν ξυναινέσαι.
πιθανὸς ἄγαν ὁ θῆλυς ὅρος ἐπινέμεται
ταχύπορος ἀλλὰ ταχύμορον
γυναικογήρυτον ὄλλυται κλέος.

"Prompted by the fire that brought good news, word has passed swiftly through the city; but who knows whether it is true, or is some divine deception? Who is so childish or so stricken out of his senses as to have his heart fired up by the message of the flame when it was fresh, and then to wilt when the talk changes? It is just like a woman in command to authorise thanksgivings before the situation is clear. A woman's ordinance

9 *Ov.*, Met. 12,39–66, translation from *Hardie* (fn. 8) 151.

is too persuasive, gaining much ground and quickly flourishing; but quickly perishing, a rumour proclaimed by a woman vanishes."[10]

In the passage above, the rumour (*kleos*) is described as swift-spreading, with an ambiguity between true and deceptive, strongly influential, as well as (interestingly) associated with women. The rumour is spoken by another agent that is the citizens' voice and murmur. The chorus sings as follows:

Aeschylus, Agamemnon 456–474:
βαρεῖα δ' ἀστῶν φάτις σὺν κότῳ·
δημοκράντου δ' ἀρᾶς τίνει χρέος·
μένει δ' ἀκοῦσαί τί μοι
μέριμνα νυκτηρεφές.
τῶν πολυκτόνων γὰρ οὐκ
ἄσκοποι θεοί, κελαι-
ναὶ δ' Ἐρινύες χρόνῳ
τυχηρὸν ὄντ' ἄνευ δίκας
παλιντυχεῖ τριβᾷ βίου
τιθεῖσ' ἀμαυρόν, ἐν δ' ἀΐσ-
τοις τελέθοντος οὔτις ἀλ-
κά. τὸ δ' ὑπερκόπως κλύειν
εὖ βαρύ· βάλλεται γὰρ ὄσ-
σοις Διόθεν κεραυνός.
κρίνω δ' ἄφθονον ὄλβον·
μήτ' εἴην πτολιπόρθης,
μήτ' οὖν αὐτὸς ἁλόνθ' ὑπ' ἄλ-
λῳ βίον κατίδοιμι.

"The talk of the citizens, mixed with anger, is a dangerous thing: It is the equivalent of a publicly ordained curse. I have an anxiety that waits to hear of something happening under cover of night. For the gods do not fail to take aim against those who have killed many, and in time the black Furies enfeeble him who has been fortunate against justice, reversing his fortune and corroding his life, and when he comes to the land of the unseen, he has no protection. And to be excessively praised is dangerous: a thunderbolt is launched from the eyes of Zeus. I prefer a prosperity that attracts no envy: May I neither be a sacker of cities, nor myself be captured and see my life subjected to another."[11]

---

10 Text and translation from Aeschylus, Oresteia: Agamemnon, Libation-Bearers, Eumenides, *Alan H. Sommerstein*, Loeb Classical Library 146, Cambridge, Mass. 2008, 55–57.

11 Text and translation by *Sommerstein* (fn. 10) 52–55.

The voice (*phatis* = *fama*, rumour) is the one which Agamemnon is most afraid of, because he would be envied by the citizens. The discussion scene between Agamemnon and Klytaimnestra is worth being cited:

> *Aeschylus*, Agamemnon 933–939:
> {Κλ.} ηὔξω θεοῖς δείσας ἂν ὧδ᾽ ἔρδειν τάδε;
> {Αγ.} εἴπερ τις εἰδώς γ᾽ εὖ τόδ᾽ ἐξεῖπεν τέλος.
> [935] {Κλ.} τί δ᾽ ἂν δοκεῖ σοι Πρίαμος, εἰ τάδ᾽ ἤνυσεν;
> {Αγ.} ἐν ποικίλοις ἂν κάρτα μοι βῆναι δοκεῖ.
> {Κλ.} μή νυν τὸν ἀνθρώπειον αἰδεσθῇς ψόγον.
> {Αγ.} φήμη γε μέντοι δημόθρους μέγα σθένει.
> {Κλ.} ὁ δ᾽ ἀφθόνητός γ᾽ οὐκ ἐπίζηλος πέλει.
> "K(lytaimestra): Might you have vowed to the gods, in a moment of danger, that you would do this thing?
> A(gamemnon): Yes, if somebody with proper knowledge had prescribed this ritual.
> K: And what do you think Priam would have done, if he had had a success like this?
> A: I definitely think he would have walked on embroideries.
> K: Then do not feel shame at the criticisms of mortals.
> A: All the same, the buzz of popular talk is something very powerful.
> K: But he who is not envied is not enviable."[12]

Agamemnon is very afraid of the criticism of the citizens because their rumour (*pheme* = buzz) is very powerful. Nonetheless, he complies with the challenge of Klytaimnestra (943 *pithou*) and steps on the embroideries. There is no need to mention the result. He does not comply with the rumour and pays for it.

Odysseus' case is quite the opposite to Agamemnon's case. The rumour about Odysseus whether he is still alive or not, cannot reach the people of Ithaca. This is partly because he has been held on the isolated island of Kalypso for many years where the message cannot reach anybody. Also there are quite few misleading pieces of rumour. Odysseus himself keeps his identity secret and even gives out false information to the people whom he encounters until the very end which coincides with the start of his revenge. Penelope on the other hand also does not trust anyone until the very end. When she says that he defies (*peitheis*) her stubborn mind,[13] they come to share the same information.

From these observations, it seems to become clear that the rumour in the ancient world is a parallel to the information in the modern world, in terms of space and speed. And both are notions which are related to "interest" or "value".

---

12 Text and translation by *Sommerstein* (fn. 10) 106–109.

13 *Hom.*, Od. 23,230.

The neutral information is no information that is of value or interest. Information is regarded as information as long as it remains related to some interest or value of either a third party or the society. Odysseus' and Agamemnon's information always remains a rumour because the other parties including the gods are interested in whether they are alive or not.

Depending on the parties concerned, the interest or the value of information varies; to one party it may be high and positive but to the other low and negative. In conflicts and disputes it is contradicting. And also to the third party it may change, depending on the situation and on which side of the parties concerned the third stands on. The rumour embodies this very changeable feature of information.

In law and litigation, it is always the negative side of the rumour that matters. The legal issue which arises from the negative side of the rumour seems to be the defamation both in civil and criminal law. I shall examine how the Greeks and the Romans face and treat defamation. I shall also quickly look at the common law's handling of defamation, and lastly at the attitude of early modern Japanese law in this context. Through these analyses, it is hoped that a suggestion of the dealings with information both in legal and social contexts will be offered.

II. *Hybris* in Greek Law

Sir Frederick Pollock, the third Baronet (1845–1937), grouped in his book "The Law of Torts"[14] all the torts into the following three categories with reference to the effect of the wrongful acts or omission:

Group A: Personal Wrongs
Group B: Wrongs to Property
Group C: Wrongs to Person, Estate, and Property Generally
The Group A is further divided into the four sub-groups:
1 Wrongs affecting safety and freedom of the person:
Assault, battery, false imprisonment.
2 Wrongs affecting personal relations in the family:
Seduction, enticing away of servants.
3 Wrongs affecting reputation:
Slander and libel.
4 Wrongs affecting estate generally:

14 *Sir Frederick Pollock,* The Law of Torts, A Treatise on the Principles of Obligations Arising from Civil Wrongs in the Common Law, London, 1901^{6}, 7–9. (The first edition was published in 1887, the 15th ed. in 1951).

Deceit, slander of title, fraudulent competition by colourable imitation, etc.
Malicious prosecution.
Extortion or injury by intimidation of third persons, procurement of wrongful acts, conspiracy, etc.

Then he argued in the cited section that each of them has its own distinctive characteristics with reference to the nature of the act or omission itself:

> In Group A, generally speaking, the wrong is willful or wanton. Either the act is intended to do harm, or, being an act evidently likely to cause harm, it is done with reckless indifference to what may befall by reason of it. Either there is deliberate injury, or there is something like the self-seeking indulgence of passion, in contempt of other men's rights and dignity, which the Greeks called *hybris*. Thus the legal wrongs are such as to be also the object of strong moral condemnation. It is needless to show by instances that violence, evil-speaking, and deceit, have been denounced, apart from any secular legal prohibition, by righteous men in all ages. If anyone desires to be satisfied of this, he may open Homer or the Psalter at random. What is more, we have here to do with acts of the sort that are next to crimes. Many of them, in fact, are criminal offences as well as civil wrongs. It is a common borderland of criminal and civil, public and private law.[15]

It should be remarked here that the Greek word, *hybris*, is used to denote various kinds of the behaviour in group A such as assault, battery, seduction, enticing, slander and libel, all of which are, indeed, discussed in Greek and Roman law.

Aristotle, in the discussion of "anger" (*orge*) put forward the notion of *hybris* as follows:

> *Aristoteles*, Rhetorica 1378 b 13–34:
> [...] τρία δ' ἐστὶν εἴδη ὀλιγωρίας, καταφρόνησίς τε καὶ ἐπηρεασμὸς καὶ [1378 b 15] ὕβρις· ὅ τε γὰρ καταφρονῶν ὀλιγωρεῖ ὅσα γὰρ οἴονται μηδενὸς ἄξια, τούτων καταφρονοῦσιν, τῶν δὲ μηδενὸς ἀξίων ὀλιγωροῦσιν· καὶ ὁ ἐπηρεάζων φαίνεται ὀλιγωρεῖν. ἔστι γὰρ ὁ ἐπηρεασμὸς ἐμποδισμὸς ταῖς βουλήσεσιν οὐχ ἵνα τι αὐτῷ ἀλλ' ἵνα μὴ ἐκείνῳ· ἐπεὶ οὖν οὐχ ἵνα αὐτῷ τι, ὀλι- [1378 b 20] γωρεῖ· δῆλον γὰρ ὅτι οὔτε βλάψειν ὑπολαμβάνει, ἐφοβεῖτο γὰρ ἂν καὶ οὐκ ὠλιγώρει, οὔτ' ὠφελῆσαι ἂν οὐδὲν ἄξιον λόγου, ἐφρόντιζε γὰρ ἂν ὥστε φίλος εἶναι. καὶ ὁ ὑβρίζων δὲ ὀλιγωρεῖ· ἔστι γὰρ ὕβρις τὸ πράττειν καὶ λέγειν ἐφ' οἷς αἰσχύνη ἔστι τῷ πάσχοντι, μὴ ἵνα τι γίγνηται [1378 b 25] αὐτῷ ἄλλο ἢ ὅ τι ἐγένετο, ἀλλ' ὅπως ἡσθῇ· οἱ γὰρ ἀντιποιοῦντες οὐχ ὑβρίζουσιν ἀλλὰ τιμωροῦνται. αἴτιον δὲ τῆς ἡδονῆς τοῖς ὑβρίζουσιν, ὅτι οἴονται κακῶς δρῶντες αὐτοὶ ὑπερέχειν μᾶλ-

15 *Pollock* (fn. 14) 8–9.

λον διὸ οἱ νέοι καὶ οἱ πλούσιοι ὑβρισταί· ὑπερέχειν γὰρ οἴονται ὑβρίζοντες· ὕβρεως δὲ ἀτιμία, ὁ δ' ἀτιμά- [1378 b 30] ζων ὀλιγωρεῖ· τὸ γὰρ μηδενὸς ἄξιον οὐδεμίαν ἔχει τιμήν, οὔτε ἀγαθοῦ οὔτε κακοῦ· διὸ λέγει ὀργιζόμενος ὁ Ἀχιλλεὺς "ἠτίμησεν· ἑλὼν γὰρ ἔχει γέρας αὐτὸς" καὶ "ὡς εἴ τιν' ἀτίμητον μετανάστην", ὡς διὰ ταῦτα ὀργιζόμενος. [...]

"There are three species of belittling: contempt, spite, and insult [hybris]; for one who shows contempt belittles (people have contempt for those things that they think are of no account, and they belittle things of no account); so, too, the spiteful person; for the spiteful person is an impediment to [another's] wishes, not to get anything himself but so that the other does not. Since, then, there is no gain for himself, he belittles; for clearly he does not suppose [the other] will harm him (or he would be afraid and would not belittle) nor that [the other] might benefit [him] in any way worth mentioning; for then he would be taking thought so as to become a friend.

The person who gives insult (*hybris*) also belittles; for insult is doing and speaking in which there is shame to suffer, not that some advantage may accrue to the doer or because something has happened but for the pleasure of it; for those reacting to something do not give insult but are retaliating. The cause of pleasure to those who give insult is that they think they themselves become more superior by ill-treating others. That is why the young and the rich are given to insults; for by insulting they think they are superior. Dishonor is a feature of insult, and one who dishonors belittles; for what is worthless has no repute, neither for good not evil. Thus, Achilles, when angered, says: '{Agamemnon} dishonored me; for taking my prize, he keeps it himself.' (*Hom.*, Il. 1,356) and, as a reason for his anger: "{He treats me} like a dishonored vagrant."[16]

In Aristotle's definition of *hybris* two points are noteworthy. Firstly, if someone is reacting to his opponent, he is merely getting his own back (taking revenge), not committing any kind of *hybris*. If he is responding with the aim of getting some kind of pleasure (*hedone*) he is committing a *hybris*. This becomes apparent if we read the following passage.

Aristoteles, Rhetorica 1379 a 28–33:

Αὐτοὶ μὲν οὖν οὕτως ἔχοντες εὐκίνητοι πρὸς ὀργήν, ὀρ- [1379 a 30] γίζονται δὲ τοῖς τε καταγελῶσι καὶ χλευάζουσιν καὶ σκώπτουσιν· ὑβρίζουσι γάρ. Καὶ τοῖς τὰ τοιαῦτα βλάπτουσιν ὅσα ὕβρεως σημεῖα· ἀνάγκη δὲ τοιαῦτα εἶναι ἃ μήτε ἀντί τινος μήτ' ὠφέλιμα τοῖς ποιοῦσιν· ἤδη γὰρ δοκεῖ δι' ὕβριν.

"People so disposed then are easily moved to anger, and they become angry at those who laugh at them and scoff and mock; for these wantonly insult them. And those doing such harmful actions as are signs of wanton insult [*hybris*]. Necessarily, these

16 Translation by *George A. Kennedy*, Aristotle, On Rhetoric, A Theory of Civic Discourse, New York/Oxford 2007², 116 f.

actions are of the sort that are not in response to something [done earlier by the sufferer] and not beneficial to those who do them; for only then does it seem they are done through *hybris*."[17]

This makes it obvious that the behaviour of *hybris* is not that of taking a revenge, namely it is not reciprocal. The goal and result of the hybristic behaviour is exclusively to feel oneself better or comfortable, it is a kind of inner and psychological matter. Therefore it is not easy to ascertain whether or not the *hybris* actually occurs in a specific case. Secondly, it is the notion of the shame (*aischyne*) that can establish the fact that someone suffers the *hybris*. The feeling of the shame does not occur between the two parties, but in front of the third party, or more broadly in society. This becomes again visible in Aristotle's *Rhetorica*:

Aristoteles, Rhetorica 1379 b 24–30:
[...] ἔτι τοῖς ὀλιγωροῦσι πρὸς πέντε, πρὸς οὓς φιλοτι- [1379 b 25] μοῦνται, [πρὸς] οὓς θαυμάζουσιν, ὑφ᾽ ὧν βούλονται θαυμάζεσθαι, ἢ οὓς αἰσχύνονται, ἢ ἐν τοῖς αἰσχυνομένοις αὐτούς· ἄν τις ἐν τούτοις ὀλιγωρῇ, ὀργίζονται μᾶλλον. καὶ τοῖς εἰς τὰ τοιαῦτα ὀλιγωροῦσιν ὑπὲρ ὧν αὐτοῖς αἰσχρὸν μὴ βοηθεῖν, οἷον γονεῖς, τέκνα, γυναῖκας, ἀρχομένους. καὶ τοῖς [1379 b 30] χάριν μὴ ἀποδιδοῦσιν· παρὰ τὸ προσῆκον γὰρ ἡ ὀλιγωρία.
"[...] Further, {they become angry} at those belittling them before five classes of people: those with whom they are rivals, those they admire, those by whom they wish to be admired, or {those} before whom they are embarrassed or {those} who are embarrassed before them. If someone belittles them among these they become all the more angry. And {they become angry} at those belittling others whom it would be shameful for them not to defend, for example, parents, children, wives, dependents. And {they become angry} at those not returning a favor; for the belittlement is contrary to what is fitting."[18]

From the passages cited above it becomes clear that, firstly, someone's behaviour, which includes various types of activity such as speaking, writing as well as physical assault, can be regarded as *hybris*, when his aim is exclusively to work out his emotion (anger) and to make himself comfortable, and when the suffered person feels ashamed in the presence of the third party. The first requirement is thereby subjective and the second is objective. And we should not forget that the reciprocal behaviour such as taking revenge is not a *hybris*. Let us look at the *hybris* and hybristic behaviour from a legal point of view. Douglas

17 Translation by *Kennedy* (fn. 16) 119.
18 Translation by *Kennedy* (fn. 16) 120.

MacDowell, the eminent classical scholar specialised in Greek law and comedy summarises the *hybris* as follows:

> A fundamental element of it is having energy or power and misusing it self-indulgently. Characteristically its driving force is the energy of a young man who has had plenty to eat and drink and behaves like a frisky horse, and it is often found in men who have wealth and political power; but it is not necessarily confined to the young or the wealthy. Its characteristic manifestations are further eating and drinking, sexual activity, larking about, hitting and killing, taking over people's property and privileges, jeering at people and disobeying authority both human and divine. A person shows *hybris* by indulging in conduct which is bad, or at best useless, because it is what he wants to do, having no regard for the wishes or rights of other people.[19]

The *hybris* appears in a wide range of Greek activities and in the context of the symposion, which is one of the most important features of Greek culture; it is fully envisaged by the work of Oswyn Murray.[20] Here I shall concentrate on the legal texts. First of all, Demosthenes cited the law of *hybris* in his speech "Against Meidias" as follows:

> *Demosthenes*, Against Meidias 21,47:
> ΝΟΜΟΣ.
> Ἐάν τις ὑβρίζῃ εἴς τινα, ἢ παῖδα ἢ γυναῖκα ἢ ἄνδρα, τῶν ἐλευθέρων ἢ τῶν δούλων, ἢ παράνομόν τι ποιήσῃ εἰς τούτων τινά, γραφέσθω πρὸς τοὺς θεσμοθέτας ὁ βουλόμενος Ἀθηναίων οἷς ἔξεστιν, οἱ δὲ θεσμοθέται εἰσαγόντων εἰς τὴν ἡλιαίαν τριάκοντα ἡμερῶν ἀφ᾽ ἧς ἂν γραφῇ, ἐὰν μή τι δημόσιον κωλύῃ, εἰ δὲ μή, ὅταν ᾖ πρῶτον οἷόν τε. ὅτου δ᾽ ἂν καταγνῷ ἡ ἡλιαία, τιμάτω περὶ αὐτοῦ παραχρῆμα, ὅτου ἂν δοκῇ ἄξιος εἶναι παθεῖν ἢ ἀποτεῖσαι. ὅσοι δ᾽ ἂν γράφωνται γραφὰς ἰδίας κατὰ τὸν νόμον, ἐάν τις μὴ ἐπεξέλθῃ ἢ ἐπεξιὼν μὴ μεταλάβῃ τὸ πέμπτον μέρος τῶν ψήφων, ἀποτεισάτω χιλίας δραχμὰς τῷ δημοσίῳ. ἐὰν δὲ ἀργυρίου τιμηθῇ τῆς ὕβρεως, δεδέσθω, ἐὰν ἐλεύθερον ὑβρίσῃ, μέχρι ἂν ἐκτείσῃ.
>
> "The law.
> If anyone treats with *hybris* any person, either child or woman or man, free or slave, or does anything illegal against any of these, let anyone who wishes, of those Athenians who are entitled, submit a *graphe* to the *thesmothetai*. Let the *thesmothetai* bring the case to the *Eliaia* within thirty days of the submission of the *graphe*, if no public busi-

19 *Douglas M. MacDowell*, The Law in Classical Athens, London 1978, 129.
20 *Oswyn Murray*, The Symposion, Drinking Greek Style, Essays on Greek Pleasure 1983–2017, ed. *Vanessa Cazzato*, Oxford 2018, 183–195.

ness prevents it, or otherwise as soon as possible. Whoever the *Eliaia* finds guilty, let it immediately assess whatever penalty seems right for him to suffer or pay. Of those who submit private *graphai* according to the law, if anyone does not proceed, or when proceeding does not get one-fifth of the votes, let him pay 1000 drachmas to the public treasury. If a money penalty is assessed for the *hybris*, let the person be imprisoned, if the *hybris* is against a free person, until he pays it."[21]

Additionally, Demosthenes speaks of *hybris* in his speech "Against Macartatus":

Demosthenes, Against Macartatus 43,75:
ΝΟΜΟΣ.
Ὁ ἄρχων ἐπιμελείσθω τῶν ὀρφανῶν καὶ τῶν ἐπικλήρων καὶ τῶν οἴκων τῶν ἐξερημουμένων καὶ τῶν γυναικῶν, ὅσαι μένουσιν ἐν τοῖς οἴκοις τῶν ἀνδρῶν τῶν τεθνηκότων φάσκουσαι κυεῖν. τούτων ἐπιμελείσθω καὶ μὴ ἐάτω ὑβρίζειν μηδένα περὶ τούτους. ἐὰν δέ τις ὑβρίζῃ ἢ ποιῇ τι παράνομον, κύριος ἔστω ἐπιβάλλειν κατὰ τὸ τέλος. ἐὰν δὲ μείζονος ζημίας δοκῇ ἄξιος εἶναι, προσκαλεσάμενος πρόπεμπτα καὶ τίμημα ἐπιγραψάμενος, ὅ τι ἂν δοκῇ αὐτῷ, εἰσαγέτω εἰς τὴν ἡλιαίαν. ἐὰν δ' ἁλῷ, τιμάτω ἡ ἡλιαία περὶ τοῦ ἁλόντος, ὅ τι χρὴ αὐτὸν παθεῖν ἢ ἀποτεῖσαι.

"The law.
The Archon is to take care of orphans, *epikleroi*, houses that are destitute of heirs, and all women who remain in the houses of their deceased husbands on the claim they are pregnant. The Archon is to take care of these and he is not to allow anyone to mistreat (*hybrizein*) them. And if anyone does mistreat (*hybrizei*) them or does contrary to law or custom (*paranomon*), he is authorised to penalise him according to the rating. And if he thinks the offender deserves a greater penalty (*meizonos zemias*) he is to summon him within five days, and, having written down whatever penalty seems right to him, he is to bring him before the *Heliaia*. And if he is convicted, the *Heliaia* is to assess whatever penalty the convicted offender is to suffer or pay."[22]

Looking at both passages cited from Demosthenes' speeches, it does not seem to be fitting that the *hybris* has been commonly translated as an outrage or an excess to adequate behaviour. The situation and relationship between the two parties is complex. In the first case, the plaintiff (Demosthenes) and the defendant (Meidias) are relatives and the latter is the tutor/guardian of the former. Indeed, litigations between family members are not rare in classical Athens. In

21 Translation by *Douglas Macdowell*, Demosthenes, Against Meidias, Oration 21, Oxford 1990, 117.
22 Translation by *Adele C. Scafuro*, Demosthenes, Speeches 39–49, in: The Oratory of Classical Greece, ed. *Michael Gagarin*, Vol 13, Austin 2011, 173–174.

the speeches 27–31 Demosthenes himself sued his guardians (and vice versa) over his properties during the guardianship. He tried to get back his allegedly own property and succeeded. This is not the matter of *hybris*, because getting one's own back is a kind of reciprocal behaviour and not the matter of *hybris* as Aristotle argues. But Meidias' case is the matter of *hybris*. Why did Demosthenes sue his guardian because of *hybris*? Meidias punched Demosthenes while he was leading the training of the chorus. It thereby definitely happened in the presence of the other citizens. Meidias' behaviour is typical among the *hybris* behaviour. Why did he commit the *hybris*? Did he punch Demosthenes out of anger? If so, why did he get angry to such a degree? Is it because he lost his case against Demosthenes? Strangely, no reason is offered to us in the speech.

However, even more strangely, the two parties somehow reconciled with each other. The speech 21 was delivered (or prepared) for a *probole*, which is a kind of preliminary meeting for the assembly, not a trial in the strict sense. The result of this meeting, if there was any, is not known. It is however clear that Demosthenes went on to a trial procedure at the assembly. Why? Many things remain unanswered and indeed are impossible to answer. The only thing I can say here is that in even such a seemingly simple and typical case as Meidias', the action of *hybris* is not directly employed, it is merely referred to.[23] Indeed, the plaintiff of the *hybris* who cannot obtain one fifth of the total of votes will be fined for 1000 drachmae because the *hybris* procedure is one of the *graphe* (public suit).[24] This is another reason why the number of *hybris* cases is so small. From these observations mentioned above it becomes clear that the *hybris* is a very delicate matter involving the behaviour and emotion of the parties and relationships between them as well as their relationships with the third party (citizens in this case). Also, in both cases it is said that the victim of the *hybris* includes not only free men but also their slaves, children and wives. Who are the valid parties in the *hybris* procedure? The direct victim of the *hybris* can be a slave or a woman. But the victims in legal terms are never slaves and women, but their masters. As Aristotle says above, the emotion of the anger can emerge if someone whom the master is expected to protect is undervalued.[25] As we see below, this point will be also intensively discussed in Roman law.

23 Cf. *Robin Osborne*, Law in Action in Classical Athens, in: *idem*, Athens and Athenian Democracy, Cambridge 2010, 171–204, especially 197 (first published in: The Journal of Hellenic Studies, Vol 105, 1985, 40–58): Osborne offers a full list of the *graphai* and *dikai* cases in classical Attic orators and shows that those of *hybris* are extremely few, almost none.

24 *Alick R. W. Harrison*, The Law of Athens, Vol 2, London 1998^2, 74–82.

25 *Arist.*, Rh. 1379 b 24–30.

It is also noted here that in both passages the notion of the *hybris* and the behaviour against the law (*paranomon*) are used in almost the same sense and are thereby convertible. And the notion of *nomos* here seems to have a very wide range of meaning, between a particular statute and a (unwritten) custom. Therefore the notion of the *hybris* has also a wide-ranging meaning and it is very difficult to judge whether a particular behaviour can be regarded as a *hybris* or not.[26] The judgment depends on the aim of the offender, the emotions of anger and shame of the victim, their social relationship, and how third parties (officials, jurors, and citizens) evaluate the case. However, the Greek law did not develop the discussion of the *hybris*. Nor did it elaborate the notion of the *hybris*. It did not establish the criteria of under what conditions we can confirm that the relevant behaviour is a *hybris*. For this we need to look at Roman law.

III. *Iniuria* in Roman Law

The notion of *hybris* is translated into Latin as *contumelia* which is one of the types of *iniuria* in the Institutes of Justinian. It was explored in great detail by Roman jurists. First of all, I shall cite the passages concerning *iniuria* in both the Institutes of Gaius and Justinian.

> *Justinian*, Institutes 4,4:
> Generaliter iniuria dicitur omne quod non iure fit: specialiter alias contumelia, quas a contemnendo dicta est, quam Graeci *hybrin* appellant, alias culpa, quam Graeci *adikema* dicunt, sicut in lege Aquilia damnum iniuria accipitur, alias iniquitas et iniustitia, quam Graeci *adikian* vocant. cum enim praetor vel iudex non iure contra quem pronuntiat, iniuriam accepisse dicitur.
> 1. Iniuria autem committitur non solum cum quis pugno puta aut fustibus caesus vel etiam verberatus erit, sed etiam si cui convicium factum fuerit, sive cuius bona quasi debitoris possessa fuerint ab eo, qui intellegebat nihil eum sibi debere, vel si quis ad infamiam alicuius libellum aut carmen scripserit composuerit ediderit dolove malo fecerit, quo quid eorum fieret, sive quis matrem familias aut praetextatum praetextatamve adsectatus fuerit, sive cuius pudicitia attemptata esse dicetur: et denique aliis pluribus modis admitti iniuriarum manifestum est.
> 2. Patitur autem quis iniuriarum non solum per semet ipsum, sed etiam per liberos suos quos in potestate habet: item per uxorem suam, id enim magis praevaluit. Itaque si filiae alicuius, quae Titio nupta est, iniuriarum feceris, non solum filiae nomine te-

26 *Yasunori Kasai,* In Search of the Notion of *aequitas* (*epieikeia*) in Greek and Roman Law, Hiroshima Law Journal 37 (2013) 543–564; *Murray* (fn. 20) 183–195.

cum iniuriarum agi potest, sed etiam patris quoque et mariti nomine. Contra autem, si viro iniuria facta sit, uxor iniuriarum agere non potest: defendi enim uxores a viris, non viros ab uxoribus aequum est. Sed et socer nurus nomine, cuius vir in potestate est, iniuriarum agere potest.
3. Servis autem ipsis quidem nulla iniuria fieri intellegitur, sed domino per eos fieri videtur: non tamen isdem modis, quibus etiam per liberos et uxores, sed ita cum quid atrocius commissum fuerit et quod aperte ad contumeliam domini respicit. Veluti si quis alienum servum verberavit, et in hunc casum actio proponitur: at si quis servo convicium fecerit vel pugno eum percusserit, nulla in eum actio domino competit.

"*Iniuria*, the Latin name of this delict, in its general sense, denotes all wrong conduct. Its specialised senses are first, contempt, in Latin *contumelia*, from the verb *contemnere*, which the Greeks call *hybris*; second, fault (*culpa*), which the Greeks call *adikema* and which is the sense the word has in the Aquilian delict; third, unfairness and injustice, which the Greek call *adikia*, such as you suffer when a praetor or a judge gives a wrong judgment against you.
1. Contempt is committed not only when someone is struck with a fist or with clubs, or even flogged; but also when a vocal attack is made on him; when his goods are seized like a debtor's by someone who knows he owes him nothing; when someone writes, makes up, or publishes a defamatory book or poem, or intentionally procures its writing, composition or publication; or when someone follows about a lady or a youth or a girl, or indulges in sexual harassment; also of course in many other ways.
2. Someone can be the victim of contempt not only in his own person but also through his children if they are still within family authority, also through his wife – that being the view which has prevailed. If you commit a contempt against someone's daughter, who is married to Titius, an action can be brought against you not only for the daughter herself but also for the father and the husband. By contrast when a husband is subjected to a contempt, his wife has no action. It is reasonable that wives should be defended by husbands, not vice versa. A father-in-law can have an action for a contempt to his daughter-in-law when the husband is within family authority.
3. The law holds that no contempt can be committed against a slave, but that the delict can be committed against an owner through a slave. This does not happen as with wives and children but only where something more gross occurs, manifestly in contempt of an owner. For example, where one person flogs another's slave. There is an edictal action for that. No action lies to the owner where someone abuses a slave vocally or strikes him with a fist."[27]

27 Translation by *Peter Birks / Grant McLeod,* Justinian's Institutes, London 1987, 46, 127.

Gaius, Institutes 3,220–225:

220. Iniuria autem committitur non solum, cum quis pugno puta aut fuste percussus vel etiam verberatus erit, sed etiam si cui convicium factum fuerit, sive quis bona alicuius quasi debitoris sciens eum nihil sibi debere proscripserit sive quis ad infamiam alicuius libellum aut carmen scripserit sive quis matrem familias aut praetextatum adsectatus fuerit et denique aliis pluribus modis.

221. Pati autem iniuriam videtur non solum per nosmet ipsos, sed etiam per liberos nostros, quos in potestate habemus, item per uxores nostras, quamvis in manu nostra non sint; itaque si veluti filiae meae, quae Titio nupta est, iniuriam feceris, non solum filiae nomine tecum agi iniuriarum potest, verum etiam meo quoque et Titii nomine.

222. Servo autem ipsi quidem nulla iniuria intellegitur fieri, sed domino per eum fieri videtur; non tamen iisdem modis, quibus etiam per liberos nostros vel uxores iniuriam pati videmur, sed ita, cum quid atrocius commissum fuerit, quod aperte in contumeliam domini fieri videtur, veluti si quis alienum servum verberaverit, et in hunc casum formula proponitur; at si quis servo convicium fecerit vel pugno eum percusserit, non proponitur ulla formula nec temere petenti datur.

223. (omissum)

224. Sed nunc alio iure utimur. Permittitur enim nobis a praetore ipsis iniuriam aestimare, et iudex vel tanti condemnat, quanti nos aestimaverimus, vel minoris, prout illi visum fuerit; sed cum atrocem iniuriam praetor aestimare soleat, si simul constituerit, quantae pecuniae eo nomine fieri debeat vadimonium, hac ipsa quantitate taxamus formulam, et iudex, qui possit vel minoris damnare, plerumque tamen propter ipsius praetoris auctoritatem non audet minuere condemnationem.

225. Atrox autem iniuria aestimatur vel ex facto, velut si quis ab aliquo vulneratus aut verberatus fustibusve caesus fuerit; vel ex loco, velut si cui in theatro aut in foro iniuria facta sit; vel ex persona, velut si magistratus iniuriam passus fuerit, vel senatori ab humili persona facta sit iniuria.

220. "Now, contempt is committed not only when someone is struck with a fist or with clubs, or even flogged, but also when a vocal attack is made on him, when his goods are advertised for sale as a debtor's by someone who knows he owes him nothing, when someone writes a defamatory book or poem about someone, or when someone harasses a lady or a youth; and finally in many other ways.

221. Now, we can be the victim of contempt not only in our own person but also through our children, if they are still within paternal power, and also through our wives, even if they are not in marital subordination to us. And so, for instance, if you commit a contempt against my daughter, who is married to Titius, an action can be brought against you not only for my daughter herself but also for both myself and Titius.

222. The law holds that no contempt can be committed against a slave, but that the delict is committed against the owner through the slave. But we do not suffer contempt in

quite the same way as through our wives and children but only where something more gross occurs, manifestly done in contempt of the owner, for example, where one person flogs another's slave. There is a pattern formula in the Edict for that. There is a pattern formula for the case where someone abuses a slave vocally or strikes him with a fist, nor is one readily given on application to the praetor.
223. (omitted)
224. But now the law is different. The praetor allows us to put our own value on the contempt and the judge condemns either for our valuation or for such lesser sum as seems right to him. But as the practice is for the praetor to set the value of an aggravated contempt himself, if he at the same time settles the amount of the defender's special undertaking for his appearance in court, we put that same sum as the upper limit in our formula. Although the judge can go lower, out of respect for the praetor's authority he will generally not be so bold as to reduce the judgment below that figure.
225. Contempt, however, can be aggravated: in conduct, as where someone is wounded by another or flogged or struck with clubs; in place, as where he is subjected to a contempt in the theatre or a city square; in person, as where a magistrate suffers a contempt, or a senator at the hands of a common person."[28]

According to Peter Birks, the main Roman delicts are divided in the following way: *furtum* and *damnum iniuria datum* have to do with wealth; *furtum* is concerned with wrongful redistribution of wealth and *damnum* with wrongful waste; *iniuria* by contrast protects the human personality. That is a generic and abstract way of encompassing the many different aspects of life in which people need respect and consideration from others. Such include their bodily integrity, their personal freedom, their sexuality, their privacy, their good name. Different cultures have different approaches and emphases. The Roman way was to bring the various interests together in a single right, to an equality of respect: one free man ought not to belittle the individuality of another. The idea is too rarefied for a court to apply directly to the facts of everyday life. It is also too modern. The jurists themselves did not much theorise about what their law was doing, or how. They just accepted it.[29]

The claim of *iniuria* (*actio iniuriarum*) has a formula in which the plaintiff must clarify what kind of compensation it is and how much the defendant must pay. It should be noted that the judges are not single *iudex*, but plural called *recuperatores*. Also more importantly, it is still under discussion among scholars whether both the availability of this procedure and the amount of the compen-

---

28 Translation by *William M. Gordon/Olivia F. Robinson*, The Institutes of Gaius, London 1988, 190–192, 397–401.

29 *Peter Birks*, The Roman Law of Obligations, ed. *Eric Descheemaeker*, Oxford 2014, 221.

sation should be considered and estimated according to *bonum aequum* (good and fair), or if the amount was estimated freely. Otto Lenel and Peter Birks think that both the availability and the amount should be considered and estimated according to *bonum et aequum*.

In Julian's commentary to the edicts, there are eight types of *iniuria*, such as *convicium* (shouted invective), *ademptata pudicitia* (sexual seduction), *iniuria* against the slave, etc. One of them is discussed by David Daube in his famous article with the title "*Ne quid infamandi causa fiat*" ("let nothing be done to cause infamy").[30] Based on his reconstruction of the text, Daube argues that the original text should be read as "whereas *Numerius Negidius* wore sack cloth and ashes *Aulus Agerius* for the sake of infaming him". Only sack cloth and ashes is the Biblical, and not the Roman, manifestation of grief and mourning. Daube also argues that the sanction against this behaviour is disfranchisement. However, Daube's reconstruction and interpretation was not able to obtain enough support from other scholars. Birks explains the formula for the action of *iniuria* as follows: The *actio iniuriarum* had a formula which directed the trial court to assess the defendant's conduct according to a standard of decency and fairness. The crucial words were *bonum aequum*. The plaintiff had to say what *iniuria* he had suffered. He did that in a "whereas"-clause. It was called the "*demonstratio*" of the formula. Later on, in the part called the condemnation, he had to put in his own valuation of the damages which he ought to be awarded. That would operate as a maximum. The programme for the trial would emerge from the proceedings *in iure* looking like this:

> Whereas [here would follow a factual description of the wrong alleged to have been suffered by *Aulus Agerius*], which matter is the subject of the action, in whatever sum of money it shall on that account seem decent and fair (*bonum aequum*) to the judge for *Numerius Negidius* to be condemned to *Aulus Agerius*, for so much money, to a maximum of –, let the judge condemn *Numerius Negidius* to *Aulus Agerius*; if it does not appear, let him absolve.[31]

Birks sums the content up as follows. The gist is damage to reputation even if not in the aggravated way which Daube maintains. It is useful to recall how defamation and affront relate. Defamation is narrower. One who defames me affronts me, but one who affronts me does not necessarily defame me. If he calls me a liar and a cheat I shall be upset, outraged and so on, even if he does not tell anyone

---

30 *David Daube*, 'Ne quid infamandi causa fiat', The Roman Law of Defamation, in: *David Daube*, Collected Studies in Roman Law, eds. *David Cohen* et al., Frankfurt a. Main 1991, 465–500, first published in: Atti del Congresso, Verona 1948, Vol 3, Milan 1951, 413–450.

31 *Birks* (fn. 29) 222–223.

else or let them hear. The reason for recalling this relationship is to make it plain that a figure which deals in defamation is not necessarily out of place in a group concerned with affront or contempt.[32]

Giving a modern example, he explains the meaning of *hybris* (*contumelia*) in the following way: we have already seen that *contumelia* was the specialised sense which *iniuria* acquired as the name of this delict. "Contumely" is not a good translation. For us it tends to mean no more than "abuse", though the adjective "contumelious" is wider. I have been using "contempt". Whatever the word, the underlying idea is of attaching so much importance to oneself, blowing oneself up to such a size, that one can belittle others. Queue-jumping is a good example. You have been waiting at the bus-stop for half an hour. I sweep in at the front of the line. If you do no more, you think: "Who does he imagine he is?" Or take talking during a play. "Don't they think there is anyone else here?" The reaction "How dare you" is not about braving retaliation. It is about arrogance. The Greek word was "*hybris*".[33]

As Birks argues that what matters in *hybris* is not the emotion of someone who suffers but the emotion of the third party (or society) in a particular situation. This creates a kind of triangle relationship among the offender, the victim and the third party (society). This structure of the *hybris* is exactly what Tony Weir says about English tort of defamation:

> The basic rules of the common law of defamation can be stated quite simply. A is liable for saying anything to C about B which would be apt to make an average citizen think worse of the latter. Certain qualifications will have to be made later, and it will be seen that one or two defences are available, but in principle B can sue A without having to show that what A said was false, that it caused him any harm, or that A was at any way at fault in saying it.[34]

Just consider how remarkable this is in a tort book! Also Weir says about "publication" as follows:

> The fact that no action lies unless the communication has been made to a third party (a single third party will suffice) shows that the tort is concerned with reputation rather than self-esteem: you can be as rude as you like to a person (provided you don't cause a damaging physical reaction), or keep doing it (harassment), but you cannot be rude

32 *Birks* (fn. 29) 229.

33 *Birks* (fn. 29) 231–232. Concerning *iniuria* (*contumelia*) see *Joe Sampson*, The Historical Foundations of Grotius' Analysis of Delict, Leiden 2018, 239–241.

34 *Tony Weir*, An Introduction to Tort Law, Clarendon Law Series, Oxford ^{2}2006, 162.

> about him, unless he is dead (the proposal that speaking ill of the dead should be actionable has fortunately not been accepted, or writing history would be impossible).[35]

Now we shall look at a parallel to the *iniuria* in Common law which is the defamation. David Ibbetson compares the *iniuria* between Roman law and common law as follows:

> The development of the *iniuria* from Twelve Tables to the Institutes and the Digest of Justinian in Roman law looks similar to that of the defamation of Common law which develops from action of trespass. But the structural difference between the two systems is reflected in the approach to formal rules. For example, as regards the liability for making statements about a person, in English Law, the relevance of the truth of the statement depends on the tort in issue. In defamation it is a complete defence,[36] in breach of confidence it is no defence at all. Roman law was more complex. Sometimes it would be relevant, sometimes not.[37]

Also a difference lies in technique. Roman law was jurists' law, so that unclear cases were discussed in terms of the specific sub-delicts and the general principles. English law, by contrast, has its focus on the courtroom and the decision in the lawsuit. We do need to know whether certain fact-situations fall within one tort or the other, of course, but it is equally important in practice to know whether they can be manipulated so as to appear to fall within an established tort. We shall look at the *iniuria* more precisely, firstly, about *contumelia*, secondly about *adversus bonos mores*. English writers tend to translate *contumelia* as insult and thereby drawing the parallel with the tort of defamation. But the temptation to do this has to be resisted. The Romans themselves saw it as the equivalent to the Greek *hybris*, which focusses on a lack of appropriate respect towards another person. Ibbetson suggests "disrespect" as a better English translation. He argues that disrespect necessarily exists in the context of a relationship, the relative status of the parties is important. However, although the relationship between the parties is of importance, the clear focus of the idea of *contumelia* is on the wrongdoer. Therefore the offender needs to be intentional, but the victim needs no subjective element and even a child can be a victim. The

---

35 *Weir* (fn. 34) 180.

36 Cf. *Harold J. Laski*, Laski v. Newark Advertiser Co., Ltd. & Cyril E. Parlby, before Lord Goddard, Lord chief justice of England and a special jury, The Laski Libel Action, Verbatim Report, Daily Express, London 1947.

37 *David Ibbetson*, *Iniuria*, Roman and English, in: *Iniuria* and the Common Law, eds. *Eric Descheemaeker* et al., Oxford 2013, 34–36.

core of the *contumelia* lies in the deliberate behaviour of the offender to harm the victim regardless of the interest of the victim.[38] This is exactly what Aristotle says about the motive of the offender's act, exclusively act out of anger in his rhetoric which I mentioned earlier.

The second element is *adversus bonos mores*. There appear to be different opinions between Roman jurists (between Ulpian and Paul for example). But as Ibbetson argues that only by reference to the social interpretation of the relationship between the parties concerned the question of whether disrespect has occurred or not can be addressed.[39] Here I should like to argue that the social interpretation does depend on how the third party evaluates their relationship and behaviour in a particular case.

Ibbetson compares Roman *iniuria* with English counterparts: "Historically, the structure of English law of torts has been very different from that of the Roman law of delicts. Within the latter the principal division was between *iniuria*, which covered wrongs to free men, and *damnum iniuria* based on the *lex Aquilia*, which covered damage to property." By contrast, by the 14th century, English common law had provided a remedy for the blameworthy causation of loss, whether through damage to property or injury to the person, in the form of the action of trespass. From the middle of the 18th century, the law was starting to focus on negligence as a basic condition of legal liability. As a result in English law little formal distinction could be drawn between deliberately and negligently caused injury. By the middle of the 20th century, English tort law did not normally distinguish in substance between cases of deliberate wrongdoing and those of negligence; all was seen through the lens of negligence. Nonetheless, although there was no difference in substance, the distinction between deliberate and negligent misconduct was being made through the award of damages.[40]

Ibbetson concludes:

> English law does not have, and has never had, a tort equivalent to the Roman's *iniuria*. But if we disaggregate the elements of *iniuria* it is possible to see its component parts at work within English law: a special treatment of wrongs committed deliberately and with contempt for others' dignity, resulting in an injury to feelings. However, as things stand the claimant's action has to be fitted within some established tort, with the result that there is a palpable twisting of legal rules when attempts are made to squeeze some *iniuria*-like claim within the boundaries of that other tort. The restructuring of trespass as a deliberate tort, together with the development of other torts based on the abuse of

38 *Ibbetson* (fn. 37) 40–42.

39 *Ibbetson* (fn. 37) 43.

40 *Ibbetson* (fn. 37) 43–47.

> power – a classical aspect of *hybris* and *contumelia* – makes it easier to see the *iniuria* typology within the framework of substantive Common law, though as yet there are no signs of the linkages between different torts being made explicit as a step towards the creation of a specific tort.[41]

Comparing *iniuria* in Roman law with defamation in English law, Ibbetson seems to succeed in making the features of (what he calls) the deliberate wrong-doing behaviour in each law by far more visible than the other previous studies on this subject. Lastly we shall look at the *iniuria* (defamation) cases in modern Japanese law.

IV. Defamation in Modern Japanese Law

The case of defamation, i.e. claim against the degradation of one's social reputation, was one of the most popular types of tort claims before the modern civil code was enacted in Japan in 1896–98.

One of the first researches using the Civil Judgment Files[42] tells us several important aspects of our early defamation cases.[43] Tort cases were relatively small in number in the Early Meiji period,[44] until around 1890. First tort cases appeared in the late 1870s, most of which were about unpaid debts.[45] Interestingly

41 *Ibbetson* (fn. 37) 47–48.

42 In 1992, the Supreme Court of Japan announced that all Civil Judgements files (Minji-Hanketsu-Genpon), which had been kept longer than 50 years since the judgment was given, should be destroyed. Soon after this announcement, lawyers both academic and practising, both of legal history and positive law such as civil law and civil procedure, decided to make an appeal to the Supreme Court and in the end it was decided that all the files should be kept in the National Archives and are now in the process of data-basing. The documents hitherto hardly accessible are now open for the research into the law and legal practice in the early Meiji period, when Japan underwent modernisation. It is very ironical that if the Supreme Court had not declared the abolition of the files, the lawyers would not have paid enough attention to them and the research would not have started. We must thank the Supreme Court for its initial wrong decision. Cf. <http://db.nichibun.ac.jp/ja/category/minji.html>.

43 *Nobuhisa Segawa,* Litigation on Honour in the Early Meiji Period, An Aspect to the Formation and Evolution of Law of Torts, in: Law and Justice in the Early Meiji period, eds. *Yoshimitsu Aoyama* et al., Tokyo 2003, 155–194.

44 It seems that tort cases were rare in the very beginning: this kind of disputes between individuals may have been handled, in principle, outside the court.

45 The civil cases were brought in a criminal procedure, because the plaintiff was not able to distinguish civil cases from criminal ones. It is generally said that the civil liability had not been conceived nor pursued separately from the criminal responsibility in the traditional Japanese society.

enough, among the tort cases in the early period of modernization, defamation cases were relatively frequent. They show some peculiarity. If we search through the data base of the early judgments by the key words "reputation" or "honour" and "apology", claims concerning defamation appear only from around 1883. The cases are roughly divided into two groups: 1) the cases in which the restoration is sought for the reputation lowered by a wrong accusation, 2) the cases of defamation caused by media, i. e. by newspapers and political journals.

The appearance and increase of cases on defamation can be explained firstly by the increase of tort claims in general. The latter increase itself can be explained by a new legislation: the Criminal Code and the Code of Criminal Instruction both of which came into force in 1882. Thanks to the article 46 of the former and the article 2 of the latter code, it became clear that the civil liability was distinct from the penal responsibility. The article 59 of the supplementary provision of Criminal Code, even if it provided only for the civil claim caused by a crime, was interpreted as showing the principle of civil liability of torts in general. It was quite often that people, accustomed to the *Ritsu-ryo* system (adapting the imported Chinese codes' system) which had been established with criminal matters at its core, made criminal complaints to pursue civil matters: they initiated a criminal procedure against the "wrongdoer" who did not perform his obligation. Based on the distinction between the civil and the criminal, the court dismissed such prosecution. Then, the former accused now claims defamation for the wrong accusation. We can find many defamation cases of this type in the Civil Judgment Files of the late 19th century. The reason why these cases extinguished after around 1905, can be found not only in the change of people's behaviour, but also in the change of the criminal policy, which abandoned the encouragement of such complaints. Under the Code of Criminal Instruction, the public prosecutor was not allowed much discretion of whether or not to pursue. This meant that more or less the criminal complaints led directly to the prosecution under this code. After 1905, the need for private complaints decreased.

The increase in number of the second group of defamation claims, i. e. the defamation of media can be related to the change in journalism. In the 1880s big newspaper companies declined due to the political oppression by the government and were taken over by many local newspapers. These focused on articles appealing to the mass public, such as scandals, risking the reputation of the people. While the first group of defamation claims decreased in number later, the latter occur constantly until nowadays. The two groups of defamation, mentioned above, differ whether it requires malice or grave fault to constitute defamation. For the defamation caused by a wrong accusation, we find an article in the Code of Criminal Instruction. The article 16 requires explicitly maliciousness or grave fault of the author to constitute defamation. If the accused (defendant) is dismissed or discharged, he can ask for damages from the accuser or the claimant if the case was maliciously prosecuted or caused by a grave fault. Even if the accused was guilty, he can ask for the same against false statements done maliciously or by a grave fault. This article was drafted by Gustave E. Boissonade, French professor who also drafted the Criminal Code and the Civil Code for Japan. The requirements of maliciousness or grave fault reflect his belief that the criminal complaint is useful to the society, although there is a high chance of making mistakes by the claimant. As for the defamation by journalism, there was no such provision and, therefore, much discussion in the court whether or not one of these elements was necessary. As some cases show,[46] some lawyers and judges required maliciousness according to English law, but the others did not, according to "the theory of natural law". Boissonade did not require "the intention to injure the reputation" for the civil responsibility. Thus we can here observe the opposition of the English school and the French school among the Japanese lawyers.

46 As an example we look at the judgments by the Supreme Court on 25 December 1885 and on 9 March 1889. In the judgment by Supreme Court (then Supreme Tribunal) on 25 December 1885 we see a lawyer justify himself by referring to the English law and the Court accepting his opinion. A journal wrote: "Patent medicine brings no effect and no harm to you. It does not matter whether or not you take it. It is the same thing as drinking water or tea...Though it is named medicine, in truth it has nothing to do with disease..." 40 pharmacists in Tokyo claimed that "the journal should publish for five days the clause of retraction dictated by claimants in its own paper and in its own expense". The first instance admitted that the defendant could not assert ineffectiveness of the medicine controlled and authorised by the ministry, and that it injured the credit of claimants, "going beyond the scope of the liberty of speech", and ordered the required retraction (for 7 days!). The appeal court acknowledged that the medicine, 80 to 90 percent of which are without effect according to the official report, cannot be considered as equal to water or tea, and, that the reputation is worth a special protection, ordered the retraction and its publishing for five days. The case went to the Supreme Court. The lawyer of the defendant then argued referring explicitly to the English law. "If we observe it according to the pure logic as well as consulting the English tort law", defamation needs 1) the designation of the claimant, 2) maliciousness of the defendant, 3) falsity of the statement. This case lacks all of the three elements. He proposed as means of defense the fair comment. In the end, the claimant should establish the result of the degradation. The Court judged that the statement is on the patent medicine in general and does not designate nor imply any particular pharmacy... The maliciousness is not acknowledged. Thus it lacks the element constituting the defamation. The Court can admit no responsibility, either civil or criminal, concerning this article." Here, the defendant and the Court followed the example of the English law, to require maliciousness as one element of the defamation. In the other case (Supreme Court, 9 March 1889), the defendant appealed the decision of the Appeal Court of Tokyo, which admitted a defamation whose author was not malicious but "careless". The defendant referred to the Anglo-American tort law which requires maliciousness. The Court turned down the appeal in saying that "it is natural that the person whose carelessness caused injury to the reputation of another cannot get rid of the liability to compensate the damage".

In 1922, a new Code of Criminal Procedure was introduced, establishing that the defamation through wrong accusation should require a fault, following the principle of civil liability declared in the article 709 of the Civil Code. The reason for this change can be found in the expansion of the power of investigation by the public prosecutor as well as in the enhanced efficiency of the public investigation, not so much by the need for the complaints as before. The latter is less decisive on whether to start the criminal procedure now that the public prosecutor is authorised more discretion. As for the effect of defamation, besides the damages in money, other remedies have been admitted. A certain type of remedy, i.e. the publication of apology,[47] has been favoured in modern Japan, which is not unrelated to a pre-modern custom. There have been many ways of the publication of an apology admitted by the courts, but it seems restricted to two manners: "declaration by name of the Court" of the apology (the article 401 of the draft (of 1877) of the Criminal Code of Japan)[48] and "retraction and apology by the Court by the name of the author of defamation, and its publication", which inherited the tradition since the Edo period of "*Wabi-shomon*" (evidence of apology).

The article 723 of the Civil Code (1896) reads as follows: "If a person has injured the reputation of another, the Court may on the application of the latter make an order requiring the former to take suitable measures for the restoration of the latter's reputation either in lieu of or together with damages."

The compilers of the Civil Code seem to have consulted the examples of other countries as well as the national judiciary practice, and decided to provide for the "suitable measures". Then the practice developed into forming the two types of remedies mentioned earlier. In this way the defamation is finally taken into the category of tort, being homogenised with other torts.[49] Until recently, the practice of defamation cases worked for a long period by way of combining the publication of apology and the consolation money, which was not too costly. To the contrary, we witness a recent trend to make the consolation more expensive, in the cases, *inter alia*, of the defamation by commercial mass-media. If, in practice, the inexpensive pecuniary damages have been complimentary with the publication of apology, it is now time to re-examine the way of thinking, which has limited the non-pecuniary loss only to the mental suffering. Moreover, we

---

47 Other non-pecuniary remedies were widely admitted in the judgments of the early period of Meiji such as the retraction of the discourse or the direct expression of apology.

48 *Boissonade* prescribed the publication of the judgment acknowledging a criminal defamation in the newspaper, and handing out the copies of the judgment to the victim, inspired by the German Criminal Code (Art. 165 and 200). This provision was not adopted in the definitive text of the Criminal Code of 1880.

49 *Segawa* (fn. 43) 179.

notice that this direction may possibly suggest the lesser importance of the publication of apology in present and future times. If so, it might predict some other social relations emerging than those which used to need the apology in public and a relatively small amount of money for consolation. Those (new) relationships seem to be the social relations with no apology in public or in private. The analysis of the civil judgments cases of the defamation before the codification of the Japanese civil code illuminates the complexities and interactions of the traditional and modern, civil and criminal, in the Japanese attitudes towards law. But is it just a historical phenomenon? I do not think so.

In the modern Japanese law, modelled upon the western law, civil and common, the law of defamation is divided in civil and criminal. But the issues, legal, social, and political, which the defamation case raises, cannot be properly solved if the case is treated as a civil case separately from a criminal, or vice versa. In other words the defamation case does cover both civil law and criminal law. If I look at the Japanese law textbooks both of civil law and criminal law, it seems that the defamation is treated in more details in the textbooks of criminal law rather than in those of civil law.[50] In Japanese civil law the defamation is not much explored mainly because its scholars have been almost always discussing the cases of non-deliberate wrongdoing (negligence), not of the deliberate. Also in Japan there is no punitive compensation system. Scholars have long believed that the apology in public will, as a kind of social sanction, compensate for the low amount of compensation. But as Segawa suggests, this system will not work well as the Japanese society is changing.[51] In criminal law the offender can be not guilty if he can establish that his behaviour is oriented to "public-interest" and that he has a reasonable ground for his believing that the fact is "true" (cf. Criminal Code 230–2). But the point is not the matter of truth or falsehood, but the matter of "likeliness". If the rumour has spread, the victim can no longer recover his face (value) and can suffer a huge amount of economic loss such as recent cases of Fukushima Daiichi power plant. Indeed, food, such as vegetable and fish, produced in the Fukushima area is avoided by consumers because of the "rumour" of the contamination. And again the civil law cannot rehabilitate the victim enough, economically and socially, because of the low amount of compensation and the ritualised apology in public.

50 Cf. *Takashi Uchida*, Civil Law, Tokyo 2013; *Atsushi Yamaguchi*, Criminal Law, Tokyo 2015.
51 *Segawa* (fn. 43) 194.

V. Conclusion

If we compare the *hybris* and *iniuria* with the Japanese law of defamation, some remarkable similarities emerge.

Firstly, the rarity: in Greek law the offender is very rarely (or almost never) liable for the *hybris* although there are quite many references in orators' speeches. It seems uncertain whether Roman law of defamation found many cases where the offender found liable/guilty, although there are quite many sources referring to *iniuria* in the Institutes (Gaius and Justinian) and the Digest 47.10. Also, in Japan cases of defamation are rather few, both civil and criminal and in civil litigation the cases often result in agreement (compromise). Why only a few cases?

Secondly, from the point of law and procedure, *hybris*, *iniuria* and defamation cover both civil and criminal law. Of course, we cannot naively apply the modern distinction between civil and criminal to Greek and Roman law. However, as Japanese law of defamation before the codification shows, the inter-relationship between civil and criminal played a very interesting role in the development of the law of defamation.

Indeed, the notion of civil liability was only developed through the criminal procedure. At the beginning of westernisation of Japanese law, Japanese people did not have a notion of civil responsibility (obligation and torts are also not really divided). This seems rather similar with the *hybris* procedure by *graphe* in which in theory anyone can bring the *hybris* case, although the plaintiff is not the professional prosecutor, and although in practice persons who bring the case have usually some interests in relevant cases. But it should be remarked that the defendant calls his opponent's behaviour of bringing his case as sycophancy, malicious prosecution, and its action as *hybrizein* (contempt).

Thirdly, the issue discussed in each case is not the matter of truth or falsehood, but the matter of "likeliness" which the Greeks called *eikos*. In English law, uniquely enough, the establishment of the truth or falsehood is the plaintiff's responsibility. If he cannot establish, the defendant is not liable.

The Greeks and the Romans always discussed the rumour (*fama*). In Japanese law, if the defendant can establish that he/she believed the rumour, which is not based on the truth, is based on the reasonable grounds, by which I mean the ordinary person, namely the society, regards the fact as true reasonably, he/she is not liable. But the victim suffers a lot from the rumour, as is shown by Fukushima Daiichi power plant cases mentioned above.

The Greeks and the Romans never discussed rumour (*fama*) from the point of view of truth or falsehood. It is, they well believe, always something between true and false. They evaluated the rumour from the point of view of the social relationship between the parties, namely from the point of the third party.

Information in kind cannot be identified. But the social aspect of information can be clarified from the point of view of the value and interest of the parties concerned and the third party. The Greeks and the Romans called it the rumour (*fama*). From this point of view, the legal aspect of information can be analysed, which they called *hybris* and *iniuria*, and defamation in common law, in terms of its violation.

Although the remaining ancient sources, legal and non-legal, will not be able to solve the issues of *hybris* and *iniuria*, they certainly illustrate the complexities and difficulties in solving these issues.

List of Contributors

Prof. Dr. Carlos Felipe Amunátegui Perelló
Pontifica Universidad Católica de Chile
Alameda 340
Facultad de Derecho, piso 4
CL-8320000 Santiago de Chile
CHILE
E-Mail: camunate@uc.cl

Prof. Dr. Ulrike Babusiaux
University of Zurich
Rämistrasse 74 / 41
CH-8001 Zürich
SWITZERLAND
E-Mail: ulrike.babusiaux@uzh.ch

Prof. Dr. Frits Brandsma
Faculty of Law
PO Box 72
NL-9700 AB Groningen
THE NETHERLANDS
E-Mail: f.brandsma@rug.nl

Prof. Dr. Mariko Igimi
Kyushu University
Faculty of Law
744 Motooka, Nishi-Ku
Fukuoka
JP-819-0395
JAPAN
E-Mail: igimi@law.kyushu-u.ac.jp

Prof. Dr. Yasunori Kasai
University of Tokyo
7-3-1 Hongo Bunkyo

Tokyo
JP-113-0033
JAPAN
E-Mail: kasai@l.u-tokyo.ac.jp

Prof. Dr. Wataru MIYASAKA
Himmelbla 207
Komagi 354
Nagareyama
Chiba
JP-270-0132
JAPAN
E-Mail: miyasaka.wataru.gn@u.tsukuba.ac.jp

Prof. Dr. Johannes PLATSCHEK
Ludwig-Maximilians-University
Professor-Huber-Platz 2
DE-80539 München
GERMANY
E-Mail: johannes.platschek@jura.uni-muenchen.de

Dr. Pompeo POLITO
Sapienza Università di Roma
P.le Aldo Moro, N. 5
IT-00185 Roma
ITALY
E-Mail: pompeo.polito@gmail.com

Prof. Dr. Sasaki TAKESHI
Kyoto University
Yoshida-honmachi
Sakyo
Kyoto
JP-606-8501
JAPAN
E-Mail: sasaki.takeshi.6n@kyoto-u.ac.jp

Prof. Dr. Cornelius G. VAN DER MERWE
University of Stellenbosch
Department of Private Law

Faculty of Law
ZA-7600 Stellenbosch
SOUTH AFRICA
E-Mail: cgvdm@abdn.ac.uk

Index of Sources

I. Ancient and medieval sources

1. Legal sources

2. Literary sources

3. Documentary sources

II. Modern legal sources

1. Statutes and provisions

2. Court decisions

European Union

Germany

Japan

Index of Terms